HEALTH CARE AND POLITICS

An Insider's View on Managing and Sustaining Health Care in Canada

David Levine

Véhicule Press

Published with the generous assistance of the Canada Council for the Arts, the Canada Book Fund of the Department of Canadian Heritage, and the Société de développement des entreprises culturelles du Québec (SODEC).

Cover design: David Drummond
Typeset in Minion by Simon Garamond
Printed by Marquis Printing Inc.

LIBRARY AND ARCHIVES CANADA CATALOGUING IN PUBLICATION

Levine, David, 1948-, author
Health care and politics : an insider's view on managing and
sustaining health care in canada / David Levine.

Includes bibliographical references and index.
Issued in print and electronic formats.
ISBN 978-1-55065-401-1 (pbk.). – ISBN 978-1-55065-410-3 (epub)

1. Medical care – Political aspects – Canada. 2. Medical care –
Canada. 3. Medical care – Québec (Province). I. Title.

RA395.C3L477 2015   362.10971   C2014-908342-4
C2014-908343-2

Published by Véhicule Press, Montréal, Québec, Canada
www.vehiculepress.com

Distribution in Canada by LitDistCo
www.litdistco.ca

Distributed in the U.S. by Independent Publishers Group
www.ipgbook.com

Printed in Canada on FSC certified paper.

Contents

Acknowledgements

I would like to thank the many people who through their teaching, mentoring, support and criticism have helped me thoughout my career and thus helped write this book. Special thanks also go to: Anne-Marie Tardif, a colleague and friend for over 30 years, who began writing this book with me and set the tone; Dr. Georges Bélanger, head of the Department of Surgery at the Verdun General Hospital who taught me how to work with physicians; Georges Bossé, André Bisson, Nick Mulder and Victor Goldbloom, my Board chairs who supported my ideas and accepted my management style. I would very much like to thank my publishers Véhicule Press, especially Nancy Marrelli, who worked over each page with me to to focus my ideas and produce the final version. I would also like to thank Éditions du Boréal for the French translation and their initial acceptance of this project many years ago.

Preface

My grandparents came to Quebec from Russia and Poland as young adults with their parents in 1905. They settled in Montreal and my father was born in 1910, my mother in 1919. At home the families spoke Yiddish, the language they spoke in their country of origin, and also English. Like most Jewish immigrant families, mine integrated into the Anglophone rather than the Francophone community of Quebec.

A great deal has changed in Quebec since my childhood. In September of 2012, while my partner and I were travelling in the Alsace-Lorraine Valley on the border between France and Switzerland, we came to a small town surrounded by vineyards. Standing at the counter of one of the local vineyard stores waiting to be served, I heard a very familiar Québécois accent and I turned to see two couples in their early 60s. I said hello in French and commented that it was nice to hear French from home. One of the women said, "Who are you? I recognize your voice." Her husband asked, "Are you David Levine, the health care administrator?" I said yes and was surprised that I had been recognized through my voice. I thought about this for a while, as it was not the first time it had happened. I speak French well enough, though certainly not like a Francophone Quebecker. I learned to speak French from Francophone friends and colleagues but my Anglophone accent remains. As a result, when I speak in public in Quebec, and especially on radio and television, my voice is recognized.

The more I thought about this episode, the more I believed that my being recognized went deeper than just voice recognition. The language issue in Quebec is at the foundation of Québécois identity and in a community of only seven million in the sea of English North America, language has been an issue for hundreds of years. Language has so marked Quebec's development that an Anglophone who has learned to speak French from the street, university, work, or friends, and who has a unique accent, can be recognized by his voice alone.

I have managed some of Quebec and Ontario's more complex health care organizations. I had the opportunity to be a junior minister of health and Quebec's delegate general in New York City. These positions have allowed me to look at policy development and political decisions from the inside and I believe all these experiences have provided me with a perspective that gives me a better understanding of Quebec and of our health care system.

I have written this book because I believe other health care managers can benefit from my experience and use some of the tools and strategies I have developed to better their own skills as managers. I have gained an understanding of leadership and the ways to build it in this very complex and unique managerial environment. My involvement in government has allowed me to see first-hand what influences political decisions and how political decision-making affects all aspects of health care. I hope that once managers, policy-makers, and the population have a better understanding of the problems in the health care system, the barriers to change, and how to overcome these barriers, they will then also better understand why the state of health care is what it is today and see a path to a better future. My experiences over an interesting and varied career have given me special insight into the problems in the health care system, the barriers to change, and what is needed to remove those barriers. I think it is important to share these reflections and analysis.

The existing health care model is becoming less and less sustainable, and I believe passionately that we must change the model to a more robust and sustainable one that better meets the needs of our population. I hope this book opens up that discussion on how we move into the future.

Introduction

THE STORY I WOULD LIKE to tell is a simple one about Quebec, about health care, and about my experiences with both. In the context of Quebec's social and political changes through the 1960s and the years following, the story, however, becomes more complex. This book covers the period from 1975 to the present, 2015, a period when I was fortunate to be involved in the introduction of Quebec's new universal health care system, and I also had the opportunity to manage many health care institutions and to reflect upon these experiences. During this time, Quebec went through major social and political changes that included the emergence of a very strong independence movement.

In *Health Care and Politics* I wish to share with the reader a wide variety of career experiences and the lessons I have learned. I discuss how to effectively manage the offering of acute-care services in our hospitals, and how to coordinate care from a regional authority. Based on thoughtful reflection of my long career in health care, I bring forward the issues affecting public policy and health care, with particular attention to the issues of most concern to Canadians. I analyze the reasons for the present state of affairs and examine the barriers to implementation. Finally, I introduce my proposed solutions for a more sustainable and effective organization of health care.

Health care is a major concern for Canadians and Quebeckers, one that persistently shows up on all polls as a problem that needs a solution. But we have many concerns and questions:

▸ Why is it so hard to find a family physician?

▸ Is our health care system financially sustainable?

▸ Why is there so little health care coverage evenings, nights and weekends?

▸ Why do we wait so long for care in Emergency?

- Why do we wait so long to see a specialist our general practitioner (GP) says we need to see?

- Why do we wait so long for surgery in a universal public health care system?

- Why is it so difficult to find home care for the elderly and the chronically ill?

- Why are there so many errors in medicine, especially in the use of medication?

- Why is it so difficult to get the vulnerable and the chronically ill to comply with their care plans and participate in their own health care?

- Why is the prevention of illness and the promotion of health of so little interest?

These and many more questions are asked regularly, and after working in health care in Canada for 40 years, I realize that the answers to these problems and their solutions are well known. The question then is: If we know the solutions to these problems, why have we not been able to put them into practice?

In this book I hope to answer the questions I have just posed—questions that are on the minds of so many Canadians—and to propose solutions I believe are both practical and realistic. We are entering a new world of medical discovery, often referred to as personalized medicine, in which we use the decoding of the human genome to predict individual prevalence for certain illnesses and also to help determine which medications will work in a patient's body. As we enter this new era of medical discovery, our challenge is to develop our willingness and ability to overcome the barriers to the changes that are needed to implement the solutions for a sustainable, universal health care system that is responsive to the needs of our communities.

CHAPTER ONE

Growing Up and Getting into Health Care

Childhood and Education

I WAS BORN IN 1948 in Montreal and spent my first three years living with my parents and grandparents over my grandfather's second-hand store on Notre-Dame Street at the corner of Atwater in the Francophone neighbourhood of St-Henri. Even after we moved to an apartment in NDG (the Notre-Dame-de-Grâce district of Montreal), a predominately Anglophone enclave, my sister and I spent almost every weekend with our grandparents. I spent hours in the store with my grandfather and, as I grew a little older, he let me wrap the customers' various purchases in old newspapers from a large pile on a table. My grandfather spoke Yiddish, a bit of English and a bit of French—enough to bargain with his customers. This bargaining was my first contact with what I realized later was a form of negotiation that happens all over the world. It is both a social as well as a business exchange and it seemed to me that each of these elements was as important as the other.

My grandfather would buy and sell anything and everything, and there were always people coming and going. He repaired toasters and telephones, sharpened axes and polished pots. To some the shop was a junk store, but to me it was a museum and a continual source of wonder. The store was frigid in winter as there was no insulation in the wooden walls and the only heat was a wood stove towards the back. I can remember sitting around the stove with my grandfather to keep warm, drinking tea that my grandmother regularly brought downstairs. If we were lucky, the hot tea would come with her very special mandelbrot cookies.

My grandfather died when I was 13, the store was sold and my grandmother came to live a block away from us in NDG. My mother was a bookkeeper and my father a men's clothing salesman. Mother

13

stopped working when we moved out of my grandparents' home after my sister was born. My father seemed to me to be working all the time. Growing up in a Jewish family, no matter what the degree of religious observance, there is one value that is constant: education. For my parents' generation, a Jewish education was important even if you were not religiously observant, so for 10 years, from grade one to grade 10, I left my public school at three in the afternoon and walked for about a half-hour to my Hebrew school. After two hours of classes, I would arrive home at 6:00, eat supper, and spend the rest of the evening doing homework—lots of homework. My father followed everything I did in school. He studied every one of my report cards and when my friends came over he asked, to my great embarrassment, what marks they received in specific subjects. He kept a little black book to keep track not only of my marks, but those of my friends. One might think this behaviour a bit strange, but there was something about his approach and presence that kept me focused and gave me the desire to succeed.

I joined the acting club and the debating team in high school and really enjoyed acting and speaking in public. I was quite short and it wasn't until I entered university that I grew to my current six feet. My mother had insisted that I take acting classes as a child, despite my great resistance; it was not until later that I understood the advantages of this training. She also skied and arranged skiing lessons for me so we could ski together; very quickly I moved far beyond her ability to follow me. I loved skiing and couldn't wait for the weekend to arrive. I joined the Canadian ski patrol as soon as I could as a way to ski on a regular basis throughout university.

I did well in my final year of high school and, as the CEGEP system (the two-year pre-university college program equivalent to what was then Ontario's grades 12 and 13) did not yet exist, went directly to university after grade 11. I was admitted to McGill University and, since I enjoyed math and science, I had the choice of entering medicine or engineering. At that time it was the biggest decision in my life and I really did not know what to do. Jewish families push their kids to be professionals. "My son the doctor" or "My son the lawyer" was often heard in the Jewish community then. There is a story I have told many times about that decision and my uncle Seymour. I was 16 in 1965, and I asked for advice from my uncle who was an engineer with his own small business, specializing in heating, cooling, plumbing and electricity. There was no shortage of work at the time and his business was continually growing. Expo 67 was two years away, the James Bay hydroelectric project was beginning, and he recommended that I take up engineering as a career.

I did go into engineering, even though his three boys all became physicians. I eventually realized that medicine would have been a better choice for me and it seemed to me that my uncle's advice had been less about my choice than it was about his children and his preferred choices for his own family. In later years at family gatherings, there were no fewer than seven or eight physicians around the table, since many of my cousins became doctors, and they often all ganged up on me, the hospital CEO trying to manage the system. It seemed to me that they were always complaining about some aspect of health care. I was proud to defend the system and often wondered whether or not my values would have been different if I had become a physician.

McGill from 1965 to 1970 was undergoing a period of dramatic change. Students around the world were making their voices heard and the protests against the Vietnam War and the killings at Kent State made this a very real time of change. I was elected as the engineering representative on the McGill student council in my third year and became much more politicized and aware of social issues, particularly the issues of Quebec. McGill Français was a growing movement and I participated in the 1968 demonstration that clearly recognized the need for changes in the status quo in Quebec. These first experiences with the need for social change and with politics were to shape much of what I did in the future. I graduated from McGill in 1970 with an engineering degree and a new chapter of my life began.

Getting into Health Care

It was in England, in 1970, that I felt the first symptoms of what was to become my professional passion. I was 21 and had just finished my training as a civil engineer. As a result of receiving the Athlone Fellowhip from the British Board of Trade, I had the opportunity to do postgraduate studies in biomedical engineering at the Imperial College of Science and Technology in London. Despite not having chosen medicine as a career, I now found myself doing research in two of England's major academic health-science centres. I enjoyed working in the hospital alongside the physicians, researchers and administrators, and the complexity of the organizations fascinated me.

My interest in health care remained with me when I returned to Montreal in 1972 and, as an Anglophone, looked for work in an anglophone hospital. I found myself at the Royal Victoria Hospital at the Meakins Christie Animal Research Lab. I quickly realized that this was not the type of work or environment that would excite and stimulate me. I was also ashamed of not being able to speak French to the Francophone physicians and staff. It was clear to me that I had to learn French and re-orient my career.

Wanting to kill two birds with one stone, and without realizing how this decision would change the course of my life, I enrolled at the Université de Montréal in the master's program in health administration. In the first semester, in my first class in economics with Professor Jacques Parizeau (future premier of Quebec), I realized that even with my best effort I would not be able to follow his lecture in French and I was going to fail. With all the courage I could muster, I asked to meet Mr. Parizeau who agreed to help me and asked me to meet him once every two weeks for an hour of discussion. We began in English and then moved on to French, speaking on a multitude of subjects, mainly in economics, but also on issues concerning the future of Quebec. I was becoming less and less unilingual…and more and more Québécois.

At that time, the health care system in Quebec was experiencing a major change. In Canada, a new federal law was forcing the provinces to adjust their health care system to the requirements of a universal health care model. This major change did not occur without heated discussions between Ottawa and the provinces. In Quebec, the Castonguay-Nepveu Commission (1966-1970) had just submitted the last part of its report to the government, describing the Quebec model of universal health care. The Quebec Health Insurance Board, created in 1969, was responsible for managing fee-for-service payment to physicians, who initially resisted this model. The government developed the local community health centres (Centres local de services communautaires or CLSCs), as recommended in the commission's report, and gave them the mandate to provide all community health and social services (family medicine) throughout Quebec. The government's intention was for CLSCs to become the entrance point to the health care system and the cornerstone of front-line services distributed geographically throughout Quebec, responding to the health and social needs of the local population.

This new model was well before its time and, though well sup-ported by some, it created mistrust within the medical sector and in many community organizations that believed their roles would no longer be necessary. The medical community saw the CLSC front-line model as a move to introduce a salary model of remuneration that would place physicians under the jurisdiction of a state employer. The drive to maintain physician autonomy in the face of the new universal health care model strengthened the resolve of family physicians to not participate in the CLSC project. Community groups, on the other hand, were afraid of losing their funding as money for social and community services would move into the public CLSC sector.

I strongly supported the reform, having done my master's thesis on the development of the CLSC model of care. The changes being announced were enormous, but the values being proposed reflected my own values. I believed that health care is a right and not a privilege of the more wealthy in our society, and that the state has the responsibility to ensure the health and well-being of the population. For me, universal health care represents a powerful tool for collective development based on the values of solidarity, equity and compassion.

I completed my master's degree in health administration in 1975 and was fortunate to land the position of Chief Executive Officer (CEO) of CLSC Saint-Louis-du-Parc, one of the first 10 CLSCs that were being introduced in Quebec.

From Theory to Practice

I was 26 years old when I started as director of CLSC Saint-Louis-du-Parc. I knew the principles of modern health care management and was familiar with the CLSC concept. I had a great deal of enthusi-asm, but very little practical experience.

CLSC Saint-Louis-du-Parc is situated in the heart of Montreal. Close to 70,000 people live in the territory bounded by Van Horne

Street to the north, Sherbrooke Street to the south, Saint-Denis Street on the east and Avenue du Parc on the west. This is a densely populated urban area where more than 40 different cultural communities live and work. In 1976, a large portion of the population spoke neither English nor French. Certain communities—Greek, Portuguese and Italian—were older, more established communities, while others—for example, the Vietnamese—were recent arrivals and less well-established. Education levels were low and problems of poverty, poor housing, unemployment, delinquency and adaptation were important social issues.

When I arrived at the CLSC, there was a provisional governing Board, a team of three temporary people, and a small office on Jeanne-Mance Street. The members of the Board, as well as the three employees, came from the community. The main cultural communities in the territory were represented on the Board and it became clear that the dynamic among Board members was fragile. Everyone was concerned with the particular issues of their community and whether their community would receive their share of the new services to be offered.

There was, however, a common theme that rallied all members of the Board, the staff and the community: mistrust of the future CLSC that was being implanted. The many very active community organizations in the area felt threatened by the arrival of the CLSC, which was perceived as an extension of government and its civil service. They were afraid of coming under the control of, or being absorbed by, the CLSC, which had greater financial resources and the ability to pay higher salaries. The CLSC could hire dozens of professionals and had an annual budget from government far greater than the community organizations that were constantly struggling to survive.

My First Lessons in Management

Reflecting on my first months at the CLSC, I realize how much this period influenced my style of management and helped me in managing more complex institutions. At that time, I was functioning by instinct and it would have been very difficult to explain the decisions I made and the reasons why I responded one way or another.

Experience had already shown me that the first months at the head of a new organization often determine the dynamic for years to come. In practice, a new leader has only a short time to gain the confidence of the board, management team and staff, and establish his or her credibility. It is also during the first months of a new mandate that the executive director must succeed in creating a common vision, building the team, and earning recognition as the principal leader of the organization. This challenge is even greater in health care institutions since the physicians, the professionals, the unions and staff all have their own visions and objectives. It is not a simple matter to conciliate these different visions, especially as the new leader must take into consideration the vision of the Ministry of Health and the regional authority, which provide the financial resources for the organization.

Gaining Confidence, Establishing Credibility

How to gain the confidence of the Board and the staff? How to establish my credibility? I didn't know the recipe at the time, but my reflex was to listen. Most members of the Board were well-connected and respected in their community. It was clear to me that their expertise and knowledge constituted a wealth of information for the CLSC and I quickly realized how important it would be to have them share that knowledge. Through the Board members, I was able to open doors to the many diverse parts of the community and gain respect through my interest and concern for their issues. I also gained credibility with the Board members, who were pleased to show me what they knew about their community and their role in the community. They came to understand that I needed them and that they would have a real influence in the development of the CLSC.

During those first months, I spent a lot of time listening to, and individually meeting Board members. I wanted to learn their concerns, their fears and their vision of what the CLSC should become and should offer the community. I learned a great deal about the people themselves, their sensibilities, their values and their expectations, along with the needs and concerns of the community. I realized later how important this was in building relationships with the Board and staff, and how important this step is to good leadership.

as to what these new institutions should be offering in the health care system. On the other hand, the vision being put forward by community organizations and social workers was more preoccupied with social change and the determinants of health, rather than curative-care services. It was clear up to what point the vision and its implementation were inseparable from the values and aspirations of those charged with implementing that vision. This is true in all organizations, but more so in health care because physicians and other health care professionals have their own values and vision as to what is good for their patients, and they are the only ones with legal authority to treat those patients.

After defining the vision, we began to plan our first offering of services. To whom, what, by whom and where, were questions that needed to be answered. These questions generated others. Who was the final arbiter in choosing the path to be taken? There were divergent opinions from staff and someone needed to decide. It became clear that we were reaching a point where the management of the CLSC was put into question and, in my role as director, I was directly implicated. Like many other young managers in social and community organizations, I was part of the era of "classical left-wing management" theory. Co-management appeared to me to be the ideal model and one that I believed would be well accepted by staff. In this model, each director is fully responsible for his or her sector of activities, decisions are made by consensus and there is no single supreme authority. In the beginning, all members of the team endorsed this model and everyone was in agreement with the experiment. No one had any experience within community organizations and we wanted a model that was different from a traditional organization.

Six months after our retreat, I felt that there were increasing tensions among members of the team and that staff were becoming less satisfied with the work environment. Two of my directors asked to see me. Their demand was simple: They wanted me to do my job! They didn't ask me to become a traditional "boss" but to assume my role as leader. For them, co-management was difficult and posed a variety of problems. They were very competent professionals— one was a nurse and the other a social worker with many years of experience—but they felt the need for a leader who supported their work, encouraged them, and with whom they could discuss their projects and concerns. You can imagine how surprised I was by their request. I believed that each partner in the co-management model was comfortable and I had not been aware of the malaise that was developing. These two directors were very well-respected, determined and autonomous, yet they indicated a need to be reassured and supported. They needed to know that there was someone with whom they could share the weight of the responsibilities they had undertaken.

My thoughts on the nature and the importance of leadership really began at the time of this encounter. My understanding of leadership has continued to evolve, but there is one aspect that became very clear at that very early stage of my career: In accepting the role of leadership, an executive director accepts the responsibility for the whole organization and all its components. He or she makes a commitment to the organization, the staff and the clients, which must always be respected, no matter what the circumstances.

Working with the Union

My first experience with a union began in a singular way. When I arrived at the CLSC, there were three employees. Over the following months, as the organization developed, new employees were hired and a request for union accreditation was imminent. I was not aware of the dynamics of the union movement, even less so with that of the CSN (Centrale des syndicats nationaux), a union that strongly supported the social and political evolution of Quebec.

My first contact with the union was to influence the way I would work over my career with this very important component of all health care organizations. This contact came about through my secretary and later close friend at the CLSC, Micheline Poulin, who was 21 years old at the time and didn't lack self-confidence. She entered my office on that fateful day saying, "David, we need to talk. The CLSC now needs a 'real boss'." I was not sure I understood clearly what was being asked. She explained that since it was now a Government of Quebec certified member union of the CSN, the CLSC now needed someone who would be in charge. At the time, this first "union demand" seemed strange: I did not see myself as a "real boss" and I did not have the intention of becoming one. Over the following weeks, I saw the union executive gradually being transformed into a select club. Slowly but surely, union life became the principal interest of its members. I finally began to understand the need for a figurehead was really the need for an adversary. In the absence of a boss, it was more difficult to conduct or maintain an ongoing confrontation. Without a visible enemy, it was more difficult to mobilize the troops.

During the 1970s, the union movement in Quebec, especially the CSN, had a large social vision as part of their mission and their role in society. They were there to protect their members but also to fight against injustice, exploitation and poverty. There were strong concerns around social change and equitable distribution of wealth.

During my three years at the CLSC, there was never a real conflict, mainly because I refused to become a "real boss," but also because there was a common set of values and objectives among the union executive, the Board of the CLSC, and myself. Everybody was working towards a vision of community development in which the health and well-being of the population was influenced by the improvement of the social and economic well-being of the community.

In later years, I was called upon to manage various conflicts with the unions, and with physicians and other professional groups in my organization. I was able to confirm, except on rare occasions, that an attitude of confrontation inevitably generates a similar attitude in one's opponent, whereas a less rigid, more open attitude generates a healthier dialogue.

The image of a brick wall comes to mind. When you hit a brick wall, you risk hurting yourself and, in addition to the pain, you will certainly feel frustration and often anger. If the wall is made of rubber, the risk of injury is much less; you will be disappointed at not breaking through but there will be less chance of being carried away by anger and frustration.

Experience has taught me that a constructive dialogue requires well-disposed participants. As such, it is important to invest the time and effort necessary to create a positive climate with a union. It is important to build trust, respect and credibility and gain a reputation for honesty and fairness. One is more likely to be respected if one shows respect.

Working with the Doctors

In all of the health care institutions I have worked at, the medical group is probably the most influential. I understood this theoretically when I arrived at the CLSC, and during my 37 years of practice it has been confirmed many times. My understanding of the relationship with physicians began during my internship at the Montreal General Hospital while earning my master's degree. Dr. Harvey Barkin, CEO of the Hospital, was my tutor. I had the opportunity to follow this imposing physician—imposing not only for his physical stature, but also for the respect he inspired among fellow workers. I saw leadership in action and was very lucky to do so.

I remember the day Dr. Barkin gave me the best advice of my career—on how to live with physicians in a hospital. We were in his office, which was more like a doctor's office than that of a CEO, and he was putting on his white lab coat when he said to me, "To succeed in this business [managing a hospital], you must learn to know and understand your docs." If your doctors appreciate you, you can work miracles; if not, they will break you and you can say goodbye to the objectives you are trying to achieve, and most likely to your job. You cannot do anything in a hospital without the approval of the majority of the physicians. If you must make a decision that will disappoint your medical staff be sure to find a way that will allow them to live with the decision. The message was clear: to manage a hospital you need to know your physicians and understand their needs and objectives. This advice is as true today as it was in 1974.

In the CLSC, however, living with your physicians was not an issue for the simple reason that there weren't any. It was thus in the CLSC that I began a long career in recruiting physicians. The difficulty of recruiting and keeping physicians became a constant concern in whatever organization I was managing, whether at the Verdun Hospital, Notre-Dame Hospital or the Ottawa Hospital.

At the CLSC, physician recruitment was a particular problem. On the one hand, staff at the time were against the presence of physicians because they wanted a more social, less health curative role for the CLSC, and on the other hand, a large majority of family physicians/general practitioners in Quebec were boycotting the CLSC movement because they did not want to be on salary under the jurisdiction of a government agency. I was convinced that family physicians needed to be the gatekeepers of the health care system, as described in the Castonguay-Nepveu Commission, and that they played a key role in a multidisciplinary team. However, the Board and the staff did not share this conviction. There was, in fact, outright opposition to a strong presence of physicians in the CLSC because of the lack of trust in the medical model. A movement rejecting the medical curative model and describing the dangers of over-medicalization was receiving considerable support at this time of social change in Quebec. There was a move to avoid using CLSC resources for health services since considerable resources were already devoted to curative care in the hospitals and physicians' offices.

On their part, family physicians refused to leave their offices to practice in a CLSC. Their reasons were many: fear of finding themselves under government supervision, opposition to the idea of being a salaried employee, the difficulty of working with other professionals, loss of authority, and even a worry of losing exclusive jurisdiction concerning patient care. No matter what the reasons, the result was the same: a lack of physicians in the CLSC.

Throughout Quebec the same phenomenon was repeating itself. The only doctors agreeing to participate in the CLSC adventure were considered marginal, that is to say, physicians who were socially committed, young for the most part, and interested in a particular aspect of health care, such as women's health, public health, prevention. Those CLSCs able to attract physicians were able to provide greater access to their population and more complete services to their community. As there were few physicians in Montreal willing to work in the CLSCs, it became clear that we would not be able to fulfill the basic needs of our community for medical services. This was my first real defeat and I was quite discouraged. I was convinced that the lack of physicians would not allow the CLSCs to achieve their objectives as a doorway to the health care system that could provide appropriate services to the community. Realizing the importance of a medical presence, if the ideal solution was not possible, I had to find an alternative.

My reflex was to turn towards the Montreal General Hospital where I maintained good relations with the physicians and managers I had met during my internship. After discussions with Dr. Barkin, who was still CEO of the Hospital, and Dr. Walter Spitzer, epidemiologist and head of the family-practice unit, it was accepted that the family-medicine residents would hold their clinics in the community at our CLSC. The presence of physicians dramatically changed the CLSC's dynamic with the community and within only a few months there was a significant increase in clientele. Staff who were initially against physician involvement came to appreciate the stimulating presence of young doctors in training.

The agreement, however, had some major pitfalls. The physicians' presence was not stable and as students moved on there was less continuity of care. The clinic became more of a walk-in centre than a true family-practice environment. When the Montreal General Hospital closed their family-medicine program, the CLSC lost their physicians.

The CLSCs never managed to overcome the lack of physicians, and government policy never created the conditions that would provide the incentive for physicians to work in the CLSCs. It was only after the recommendation of many commissions across Canada that the importance of family practice was later recognized as the cornerstone of an efficient health care system. And it is only in the last decade that there has been a concerted effort to develop this model.

As a result, the CLSCs never developed their full potential and have been highly criticized as an expensive model not fulfilling the needs of the community. This attempt to develop a strong primary-care presence in the community could have profoundly changed the way health care is practiced today. If the objective is to combine health and social services in a single organization, a strong medical presence working hand-in-hand with other professionals is essential to gain the confidence of the population, and this in turn opens the door to prevention, promotion, public-health education and social change.

Negotiating with the Ministry of Health
Among the responsibilities of the CEO in health care, there is one that is essential and at the same time very vague. Few CEOs are well prepared for it and it is very difficult to formally teach this responsibility in school. I am referring to the ability to negotiate with the Ministry of Health and their regional counterparts. Each

new project must be presented for approval and this means a continual back and forth with civil servants in Quebec. Cultivating these relationships is essential for a CEO, and in those early days of the CLSCs, some were better able to do this than others. Health care in the 1970s was very centralized; it slowly became decentralized as it was understood that innovation and creativity require a degree of autonomy. Unfortunately, the last decade has seen centralization of authority to the detriment of the efficiency and productivity of our health care system.

The ability to negotiate in these circumstances is a fine art that requires a good understanding of the relationship between politics and health care. I have discovered that it is an art that must be learned over time, and negotiating relies on the same abilities, no matter what the situation. You must know and understand with whom you are negotiating, what their needs and ultimate objectives are, the pressure they are under from their superiors, but, most especially, you must be able to develop good relations. (I will discuss this further in chapter 10.)

Lessons I Learned

When I left the CLSC in 1977 after three years, there were 150 employees working at three sites. Multiple services were being offered to the population and a program of care for the elderly was introduced through the integration of the University Settlement community group and the Greek community clinic. The CLSC's relations with the community were continually improving and it was no longer seen as the enemy, but rather as an important partner in achieving community objectives.

It was during this time that I began to understand the role and importance of a board of directors. Our health care boards are composed of volunteers who give their time and energy for what they consider a noble cause. There are times, however, when members support personal interests or those of the group they represent rather than the target population as a whole. It is important for a CEO to gain the confidence and support of his or her board because that provides the credibility he or she needs to function efficiently in the organization. Creating a healthy relationship between the board and the CEO is mandatory to the success of the organization. The board's governance role makes it responsible for strategic planning, developing a common vision, evaluation of performance and self-evaluation, and these are essential to any healthy organization. The relationship with the board requires both time and effort on the part of the CEO and must remain a priority at all times. Board conflict is the single most important factor that can destabilize an organization, and it is the responsibility of the CEO and the board chairs to manage this dynamic well.

The role and importance of physicians as individuals or as a group are key factors to the success of any health care organization and of the health care system itself. This lesson, which began at the CLSC, has repeated itself over and over and I have learned that it can be one of the greatest barriers to a successful health care system. The existing difficulties that prevent an effective partnership between the government and the federations of specialists and general practitioners does not allow for the most appropriate offering of services to the population.

My first experience in team-building at the CLSC demonstrated to me how important a good team could be to the success of an organization. It is important to choose candidates whose personalities, values, beliefs, and competence will coalesce to form a coherent whole. The objective is achieved when the team benefits from the strength of each of its members while supporting, nourishing and providing energy to each member. At the CLSC, I had the chance to build a young team whose strength was more its enthusiasm than its experience. The team was small and I was able to directly follow their growth and evolution. As the years went by, I found myself at the head of much larger organizations and I was no longer able to follow the team's evolution as closely as I would have liked. More than ever before, I had to rely on the ability of my senior management team to ensure that the vision we had agreed upon was being implemented in a way that rallied all staff and created a healthy working environment. Choosing team members became the most important and, at the same time, the most stressful of responsibilities.

It was this first experience that taught me the importance of respect. The ability to listen, to encourage, to support and to ask for help when needed are all important aspects of gaining this respect. I learned that a healthy work environment leads to a productive work environment and that mutual respect is a key factor. The CEO is responsible for setting the tone: To be respected, one must respect others at all times and in all circumstances. Above all, with the help of my team, the CLSC gave me the confidence to become a better manager. The CLSC became a reality: People were hired, offices were set up, mail was answered, paycheques were delivered, records were kept, and there were more and more services offered to the population. I had the unique opportunity to create a new organization and I had proved to myself that, with help, it could be done. Not only was I able to do the work and manage the organization, I realized I really enjoyed doing it.

The CLSC movement never achieved its original objectives. The vision presented in the Castonguay-Nepveu Commission Report (1970) was well ahead of its time and reflected the desire for change and social engagement in Quebec. The premise of the report is that a system led by strong primary-care family physicians is what is required to better manage population health and well-being, and this premise still holds true today. I will demonstrate in the following chapters how this vision can be implemented and what changes are required in the way we manage health care to find the solutions to the problems posed at the beginning of this voyage.

CHAPTER TWO

My Introduction to Politics

IN FEBRUARY 1977, Bernard Landry, who later became premier of Quebec, asked me to join his team in his new portfolio as minister of state for economic development. Mr. Landry had been asked by René Lévesque to be the minister after the Parti Québécois won the election in November 1976. Mr. Landry asked if I was interested in contributing to the growth and development of a new Quebec.

You might be wondering how this request came about and the story is a simple one. While repairing my motorcycle in front of my house on Lajoie Avenue in the Montreal neighbourhood of Outremont in 1974, a man stopped by and started to talk to me in French. I was still not feeling as comfortable speaking French as I would have liked, but I answered as best I could. He introduced himself as my next-door neighbour and said he was interested in my bike, a BSA 650 that I had acquired while in London and had brought back to Quebec. We started talking and I described my time in London doing graduate work, and he told me about his time in Paris as a student. He had three young children and he and his wife, Lorraine, were lawyers. I excused my French and explained that I was just completing my degree at the Université de Montréal in administration and that learning French had been a crash course but that it had allowed me to be hired recently as CEO of a local CLSC. We became friends and, over many meals together and much discussion about Quebec and Québécois history, I became more and more interested in Quebec politics.

When I had arrived back in Montreal from England and was looking for work, I took a part-time job teaching science and math in adult education. I met a young Francophone woman who was teaching French to immigrants and we became friends. She was politically very active and through her I met a number of young people very much involved in politics in Quebec and the Parti Québécois. One was Pierre Simard, then secretary to a very young

M.N.A., Claude Charron, who had been elected in 1970 and 1973 for the Parti Québécois from the Montreal riding of Saint-Jacques. I and my girlfriend at the time, later my wife Arlene, an Anglophone sociologist who spoke French very well, started to spend weekends with these new friends, and I was beginning to be immersed not only in French but in Quebec politics and the passion young Quebecers were feeling for the independence movement that was growing in popularity. When I told my friends that I had met Bernard Landry, they quickly explained to me how important both he and Mr. Parizeau, whom I had met at the university, were in the Parti Québécois.

My wife and I became closer to the Landry family, and my understanding of and sympathy for the values and beliefs of the Parti Québécois kept growing. When Bernard asked me in 1976 if I would help him in his campaign for a seat in the National Assembly in the riding of Fabre in Laval, it was easy for me to say yes. I was asked to work with the Anglophone population of the riding and I gained experience in how an election campaign is run. I learned about planning strategy, preparing campaign material, distributing the material, hanging up posters, calling door to door and getting out the vote on Election Day. What I remember most clearly is how committed everyone was to a belief in the potential for Quebec to become a nation which would bring in the social changes I valued. The energy involved was limitless but nobody expected the PQ to win. You can imagine everyone's surprise when the PQ was elected with a majority on November 15, 1976.

When Bernard offered me a chance to join the Quebec civil service to work with the team on the economic development of Quebec, I decided to take him up on it. I never knew how this offer came to be, whether it was that Mr. Parizeau, at the time Quebec's minister of finance, had brought forward my interest in economics, my friendship with Bernard, my growing interest in Quebec, or perhaps all of the above. I left the CLSC, my first experience of leadership and responsibility, for a new experience that would lead to a set of consequences that could never have been predicted at the time.

Entering Politics

I spent three and a half years learning the dynamics of govern-ment. I had the chance to participate every second Thursday morn-ing at the meeting of the eight ministers involved in economic development. They would present their projects and then a discussion would ensue as to how each project could help develop the economy of Quebec. I saw men and women passionate about what they were doing and realized how being passionate is essential to getting things done. By watching Bernard Landry, I learned how to manage a meeting of very strong people and how not to lose focus of one's objectives. And I learned how to deal. The art of dealing is essential in government but it is also true in all management situations. I found out how laws get passed, budgets determined and projects approved. I also learned a great deal more about Quebec.

The Civil Service

This was a period of social change and an opportunity to put into practice the democratic values in which I believed. There was a sense of being able to change the world and it was exhilarating. No-fault automobile insurance, agricultural zoning, and land and forestry management were only a few of the interesting files that were discussed. One of our files was raising the minimum wage and the importance of minimum revenue.

What was most exciting about what I was doing was the chance to watch Jacques Parizeau, Lise Payette, Jean Garron, Yves Bérubé, Rodrigue Tremblay and others argue and discuss different dossiers. The academic level of the arguments for or against a project and its benefit for the people of Quebec was at a very high level because many of the ministers were academics with Ph.Ds. This was a group of highly intelligent people committed to the cause of growing and developing Quebec, and with the desire and belief that Quebec should be a nation fully in charge of all the means necessary for its own development. I also got to know a civil service that was very professional and highly committed. Everybody was young and the possibilities were endless.

The civil service in Quebec had been expanding since the arrival of the Liberal government of Jean Lesage, and the Quiet Revolution in Quebec was expressed most vividly in its civil service. The place to be for bright, young graduates in the 1960s and '70s was in the new civil service. Building a new, modern society, developing the economy of Quebec, expressing one's cultural identity, building a new educational system, and introducing universal health care were part of the many changes during this period. There was pride, there was status, there was respect from the media and the population, and there was much opportunity. Civil servants were the leaders of the time, and innovation and creativity were sought after. Senior civil servants became mandarins of the state and often found positions as heads of industry when they left. That is not the case today. With time, the civil service grew exponentially and then entered a period of self-protection and self-preservation. When the government created the agencies of Health and Social Services there was supposed to be a major reduction in the staff at the Ministry of Health in Quebec City, with a transfer of resources. This never occurred and, in fact, the level of staff at the Ministry increased, creating a duplication of services and waste of resources.

Getting the Call

One day in the fall of 1979, I was told that Mr. René Lévesque wanted to see me. I was surprised and quite nervous. I had never been alone with Mr. Lévesque before and had no idea what he wanted. Imagine my astonishment when he asked me if I would stand as the PQ candidate in the upcoming by-election in D'Arcy-McGee in west-end Montreal. This is an almost exclusively English-Jewish riding and had been held for many years by Dr. Victor Goldbloom, a man I greatly admired and who, in later years, would be my Board chair at the Montreal Health and Social Services Agency for ten years.

I was very honest with Lévesque and said that I was not interested in making politics my career and would be going back to health care administration after the referendum. He looked at me very seriously and said, "Mr. Levine, don't worry about going into politics, you have absolutely no chance of winning the election in D'Arcy-McGee." He said there would be very good media coverage and that this would provide me with an opportunity to talk to a community that was very anxious about the PQ's project for an independent Quebec and the proposed referendum on Quebec sovereignty. The Jewish community was very afraid of nationalism in any form; many had lost relatives in the Holocaust. I had done some public speaking and had been invited by the Jewish community to speak at a number of gatherings to explain the PQ's position. Lévesque said that I had a good understanding of the issues and the reasons why Quebec's independence was so important to so many Francophone Quebecers. I had been working with, and come to know, many ministers in Lévesque's cabinet, and saw a group of very bright, highly educated people committed to the development of Quebec and to social values that I knew were similar to those of the Jewish community. I had already spoken about Quebec at a number of Sunday-morning breakfast clubs at local synagogues and was being asked to take this opportunity to try to alleviate some of the fears that were being expressed by the Jewish community of Montreal. These fears were justified by Jewish history but not by the reality of Quebec or by the men and women who were leading the province.

I was taken quite aback by Lévesque's request as I had never even thought of going into politics and, for an English-speaking Jewish boy, Quebec's independence was not an easy cause to defend in a predominately English-Jewish riding, an area where my parents and relatives lived. Sentiment in Quebec was very strong at this time, both for and against independence, as the June referendum was only six months away and it was on everyone's mind. I spoke to many of my friends and they were all willing to help over the next four weeks, so I told Lévesque that I would accept his request. I had no idea that this gesture would follow me throughout my life or that it would cause the public outcry that it did much later when I was chosen for the position of CEO of the Ottawa Hospital.

I think the hardest thing for me was telling my parents that I had become the PQ candidate in their riding. They did not understand my support for Quebec's independence or the PQ. I tried to explain that I shared the values and beliefs of Mr. Lévesque and the PQ regarding social change and that I believed Quebec independence was a way to achieve these goals. They could not accept my decision. My parents were very proud of me, my academic achievements, my community and synagogue work, and my appointment as the head of a new CLSC in Montreal. They were embarrassed by my association with the PQ. My father was a regular user of the YMHA, a Jewish community and sports centre where he attended the gym class every morning, and where he got many negative comments from his gym partners. I remember my parents commenting at the time that they loved their son but would not recommend anyone vote for him!

Putting together a campaign is always a challenge and a great deal of non-stop work during the election period. In this case, it was even more difficult as every group I met was a hostile one and most of my presentations ended up in arguments that were not rational but emotional. I kept explaining as best I could the issues at stake for Quebec and I was able to gain sympathy as a good speaker who was able to explain the issues well. Even the media said I was a good, bright, dynamic candidate and it was too bad I was running for the PQ. Needless to say, I lost soundly but I believe I was able to help the community and others in Quebec better understand the issues at stake.

Back to Health Care

For the next two years I was the assistant vice-president and director of coordination for the Commission of Occupational Health and Safety (CSST) in Quebec. Bill 17 had just been approved by which workers' compensation was moved to the new commission. I was responsible for the implementation of the regional programs of prevention and spent two years developing these programs. My passion, however, remained in the direct delivery of health care services and I kept looking for opportunities to return. A position was advertised for the CEO of the Verdun General Hospital in Verdun, a municipality in the southwest region of the Island of Montreal, and I decided to apply.

CHAPTER THREE

The Verdun General Hospital

Returning to Managing a Health Care Institution

LEAVING THE SECURITY of a job in government for a position with a fixed-term contract is not easy. In applying for the position of CEO at the Verdun General Hospital, I knew I was doing just that. After five years as an administrator in the public sector, with full job security for the rest of my life, I nevertheless wanted to return to the field I loved most: managing health care institutions. This time it was a hospital that attracted me and, although I had no previous experience as a hospital CEO, I knew that the only way I would get a job like this was to apply and let my passion for the role do the rest.

Verdun General Hospital was located in a provincial Liberal riding with a strong, well-known member of the National Assembly (M.N.A). Although I was pretty sure my chances of success were slim, I wanted to better understand the selection process. "Never go to a job interview unprepared," I said to myself, so I studied the Hospital's previous annual reports, enquired about the outgoing CEO, who was leaving to run a large teaching hospital, and learned about the community the Hospital served. It was also useful to visit the Hospital and walk the corridors to get a feel for the environment and the physical layout of the organization. Despite having not yet run a hospital, I had to convince the selection committee that I was the best person for the job. I had to know the issues currently affecting the Hospital and have a clear idea how I would do the job. I knew from previous experience that the selection committee would be looking for someone who could show commitment and enthusiasm, someone with a good understanding of the challenges, as well as a vision of how he or she would lead the organization. With this approach, there is always a good chance of being chosen if there aren't better candidates or political issues that interfere with the selection committee's evaluation. I believed then, as I do now, that you must be passionate about what you want to do, and your skill and passion should be seen and heard during the interview.

I was offered the position and, in 1982 at 33, I was given the opportunity to run a hospital with over 1,400 employees and 150 physicians. I was to get my first lessons before I actually began the job. It had to do with the very powerful role physicians play in the management of a hospital. I remembered Dr. Harvey Barkin's remarks during my internship at the Montreal General Hospital in 1974 about the role of physicians in a professional bureaucracy: "The key to success in managing a hospital is your medical staff: Listen to them," he had said. One day, I received a phone call from the secretary of Dr. Georges Bélanger, neurosurgeon and head of the Department of Surgery at the hospital. He asked me to attend a little supper he had arranged at Les Halles, one of the fanciest and most expensive restaurants in Montreal. I readily agreed but was more than a little nervous when the day arrived, wondering what the purpose of the evening would be.

After arriving at the restaurant, I was led into a private room and introduced to Dr. Bélanger, as well as the heads of all the departments at the hospital. I could see immediately that they were here to size me up, and also, as I learned later, to judge whether I would in some way be a threat to them and their own particular vested interests. I was asked question after question and, though I was not quite sure what the right or wrong answer was, I made sure that no matter what approach I chose, I said that I would always consult the physicians and ensure that their issues and concerns were taken into consideration.

The purpose of the meeting, I felt, was clearly to tell me who the key players were in the Hospital and what they would be watching for as I assumed my new role. Dr. Bélanger was the most important medical leader there at that time, and remained so for many years, though the other physicians did not always support him. We eventually became very good friends and I remained in contact with him for many years after he retired. He taught me a great deal about hospitals and the role that physicians play, but more importantly, he taught me what doctors are most concerned about. Their concerns vary depending on their specialty and it is important to understand the differences among the groups.

At the end of the evening, it was evident that a very important contact had been made, and I learned later from Dr. Bélanger that

I had not disappointed the physicians and had set the groundwork for building good relations with the medical staff.

My First Months

In my first few months at Verdun General Hospital in 1982, I had to get to know the organization as quickly as possible in order to understand the key issues we were facing. Everybody in an organization is watching the new CEO at the beginning, and I have found that the more one is present during those first few months—the more one is visible and available—the more one has a positive impact on the hospital staff and the perception of the CEO. "I saw the CEO today, he came to the department. He asked many very good questions and seems quite interested in what I had to say." Comments like these establish the CEO as belonging to the organization as a real and tangible presence—and as someone who listens.

As I moved around the organization visiting departments and talking with staff, I was already well aware that there was a $2 million deficit, but I did not mention it in my conversations. The concerns of staff are not always the same as management and in the beginning it is important to listen to the concerns of staff. I had to develop my credibility and respect in the hospital, with my staff and the people I was to work with. It was a critical time to develop strong, personable relationships with the medical staff, the Board, and the senior management team. The knowledge I gained from listening during those first few months also allowed me to evaluate the organization and better understand its weaknesses and strengths. I knew that once I had done this, I would then be able to better plan my own leadership strategy around the key issues and concerns of the Hospital. As we all know, the honeymoon for any new appointee or newly elected person does not last long and must be used well. The investment of time and energy at this early stage would reap many dividends in the months and years to come.

Getting to Know the Organization | Finding a Mentor

Because this was my first job as the CEO of a hospital, I recognized that there was much I didn't know and that I would need the help of someone who did. Most importantly, I needed to know about the Hospital, as I was moving into an organization with its own personality and culture, and it was my responsibility to become as familiar with it as possible. The person I sought out to help me was the previous CEO of the Verdun General Hospital, Claude Desjardins, who had just been appointed head of the Maisonneuve-Rosemont Hospital in Montreal. I wanted to learn as much as possible about my Hospital and its staff through his experience. At the time of his departure, he was well known and liked by the management team, the physicians, the Board and the staff of the Hospital. Everyone had been very satisfied with his work.

Although Claude is seven years older than me, the similarity in our lives is striking. When I met Claude in 1982, my wife was pregnant and we were expecting twin girls that June. I had arrived at the Hospital in March knowing that things in my life were going to change very quickly. Claude and his wife, Louise, invited us to dinner and, upon arriving at their home, we were introduced to their twin five-year-old girls who were born only months after Claude's arrival at Verdun. You can imagine the bond that was created between us! We have been close since that time.

From Claude, I learned a great deal about the Hospital. He helped me to quickly grasp who the key players were and of whom to be wary. He also helped me to fully understand where the strengths and weaknesses were in the organization. But most important of all, I had found a colleague who enjoyed discussing health care management and we have never stopped talking. When I had a problem, Claude was always there to give advice, and when I needed a partner in a project, I could always count on his support. Our careers continued to unfold in tandem; later, over a period of 10 years, Claude headed the Laval regional health agency while I headed the Montreal agency.

As long as I have known Claude, I have been impressed by the way he always collects information about what is going on. He taught me the importance of being plugged in and of staying plugged in to all of the formal and informal networks of communications that surround a CEO in a hospital. He taught me to be open with the media and to get to know the key health journalists, since they tend to be well informed with very well-developed networks. He also stressed the importance of getting to know the minister of health and his cabinet, the deputy minister, the assistant deputy ministers, and the many other key players in the health field. Claude made many introductions for me, and if there is a lesson to be learned, not only by managers in health care but in all fields, it is that you should try to find a mentor who has credibility and knowledge and is willing to share his or her experiences. Your mentor should also be well-connected and willing to make as many introductions for you as possible. I have discovered that most CEOs are happy to share their knowledge with others, but that most CEOs seldom seek out a mentor or ask for this kind of help.

Getting to Know the Key Players

The structure of authority in a hospital is complex and unique. The main lines of division are among the board, the medical staff and the CEO. The board and the CEO represent the corporate interests of the hospital. Through legislation and the bylaws of the organization, the board and the CEO manage the hospital on behalf of the provincial government and the community at large. The medical staff, however, is self-governed and not necessarily managed by the CEO or the board. The medical staff is licensed to practice medicine from the various professional bodies governing the many medical specialties and sub-specialties. Hospital boards grant physicians privileges to practice medicine in the hospital and, once awarded, these privileges are almost impossible to remove unless there is a very serious offence by the doctor. Physicians are responsible for admitting patients and determining their course of treatment. In this way, they have a major influence on how a hospital runs and how its resources are spent. Physicians are paid with a fee-for-service based on a negotiated agreement between the doctors' union and the government. These are, then, the major zones of power in a hospital, and though there are many other internal zones of influence—the unions, the nurses, senior management, the foundation, and the volunteers, for example—the real power lies with the board, CEO and the physicians. How a CEO functions across these zones determines how effective he or she will be.

The Physicians

When I first arrived at Verdun, Claude suggested I meet with each of the heads of the medical departments individually so I could develop personal rapport with each one. I have used this advice in each hospital I have had the privilege to run. It has been very important in setting the groundwork for my management style in hospitals.

It is essential to find common areas of interest with each medical leader. As a biomedical and civil engineer, I was knowledgeable about medical equipment, research and construction, and through these areas was able to tap into the specific interests of each group of physicians. I was able to develop a personal relationship with each of the heads of departments and divisions, and was able to focus on their concerns, their worries and where they saw themselves and their departments in the future. I asked if they would like me to meet the other members of their department and I made sure I was always available for this.

I discovered that Radiology and Laboratory Services were concerned about access to equipment and the number of exams they would be doing, as this determined their revenue. Surgery was concerned with their operating-room time and available beds. Medicine was concerned about their beds not being taken over by Surgery, and that there be some control over the emergency room, as most of their cases came directly from there. Obstetrics and Gynacology were concerned about the closing down of the birthing unit, which was being proposed by the regional council. Family Medicine was worried whether or not they had a place in a community hospital run by specialists and whether they would have beds of their own. What I realized was that, in each case, the main concerns were around the volume of activity at the Hospital. This is a prime factor in determining the income of physicians, who are paid per episode of care.

I also learned that it is paramount to understand the dynamics inside each group of physicians, as well as the dynamic between groups, since many of the positions taken by each group are based on these dynamics.

Working with the Board

I was aware how important it was to gain the confidence of the Board in the first few months, but my strategy needed adjusting. Boards that are new and do not have a history of working together, as was the case with the CLSC, need a different approach from a well-established board with a strong president. In all cases, a CEO must pay attention to each member and develop a relationship that is specific to each. With a well-established board, the role of the president is very important to good board dynamics.

This is what I found at Verdun and my strategy was to work closely with the chair of the Board and continually reinforce the role of the chair. I would go out to lunch with my chair before each Board meeting to establish the agenda, review issues, prepare the resolutions, and discuss how the Board would respond to the different issues and who was likely to oppose what was being proposed. I then discussed my key concerns for the Hospital and what I felt was coming up.

Finances were always an issue since we were always struggling between the Hospital deficit and the pressure from our physicians to respond more rapidly to the needs of their patients, as well as to upgrade outdated equipment. In times of crisis or in dealing with controversial issues, I might have spoken to my chair daily, but this was a rare occurrence.

The role of the board and the CEO must be clearly established from the beginning. The board approves the vision, goals and mission of the organization. Through its board committees, it ensures that the financial situation of the hospital is healthy, that the volume and quality of services are according to the approved operational plan, and that new programs and capital investment are approved in accordance with the hospital's policies and government directives. The board must not manage the day-to-day operations of the hospital. Most problems happen when the board of the hospital, often through the personality of its chair or some of the members, does not distinguish between the role of the board and the day-to-day management of the hospital by the CEO. When the board chair starts to meet with physicians, management or the unions, there is a major problem of leadership and confidence in the hospital. This is a delicate issue at times, and I have always helped my board chairs deal with these contradictions to ensure that the roles are clear for the organization. When this clarity can no longer be maintained, it is time for the CEO to leave.

The Team

In addition to the physicians and the boards, the third authority in any hospital is the office of the CEO, and this includes the senior management team. The team is the extension of the CEO, and success or failure is often based on the quality of the team. In Quebec, the options for a CEO to choose the team he or she wants are much more limited than elsewhere. Quebec considers the CEO and senior management as civil servants, part of the civil service. Salaries are determined by a salary scale based on the size category of the institution and the number of years of experience. Management salaries are negotiated between the management associations and the government. The situation in Ontario is very different and is more of a business model: Hospitals are private, non-profit corporations and the board determines the salary of the CEO; the CEO decides the salaries of the staff; each board decides in its bylaws how board members will be chosen (in Quebec this is determined by legislation); each VP has a contract with a buyout clause and the CEO does not need to justify to anyone his or her decisions to change the members of the senior management team. In Quebec, there are no buyout clauses and there is a form of job guarantee. It is necessary to show incompetence in Quebec to be able to remove someone from his or her position and this has to be demonstrated over a period of time.

The management team at Verdun was already in place when I arrived and I had to spend the first few months evaluating everyone's strengths and weaknesses before changing the team. I realized that there were weak elements in the team but it was very hard to address this given the job security managers have in Quebec. As a result, I had to keep weaker people on the team and compensate with an extra effort on my part, or by counting on the other members of the team to fill in the gaps.

Everybody Loves a Winner

When I took over the leadership of the Verdun General, I knew that first impressions counted. The tone of one's leadership is established very early on and I have found that a very important image to promote is the image of a winner. The expression "everybody loves a winner" is true and we all want to be on the winning team, led by someone we consider a winner. I did not clearly realize this at the time and, as in most cases, learned it by accident. As a father of a young son and expectant father of twins, I was very sensitive to all issues dealing with babies. The majority of the workforce in a hospital consists of women and, throughout their careers, childcare responsibilities are a major concern. I realized that if the Hospital could offer a daycare environment, the impact would be positive for mothers, who could bring their children, especially babies and young infants, to work with them. Ultimately, it would also be a great help for staffing the Hospital. I was positive there would be less absenteeism and that mothers could come back to work earlier after pregnancy, and with greater peace of mind knowing that their child was just downstairs in the same building. Visiting at lunchtime would be possible and breastfeeding mothers could attend to their babies when required.

I began to look into this and discovered that projects had already been presented to the past administration, but that they had never been seriously considered, mainly for lack of space. I studied the issue and was confronted with my first challenge. The best space for a daycare centre was the physicians' staff lounge: the perfect size and located at the side entrance of the hospital. A lounge for the medical staff is an important issue. It is not only a comfortable place to relax for a minute or two between patients, it is also a place to meet and discuss the issues in the Hospital. As I was soon to learn, for physicians, having a space of their own is an important symbol, as well as a practical requirement. It did not occur to me, in my enthusiasm to create a daycare centre, that taking away the physicians' lounge might not be the safest move for a young CEO trying to win medical staff support in the early days of his tenure. I was proposing to use the operating room lounge as the lounge for all the physicians.

Inevitably, this became a real challenge. The women employees of the Hospital had formed a parents committee and were very active. I wanted to establish the daycare centre and I looked for ways to convince the physicians that this was of value to the Hospital and that, though I was planning to take away their lounge, I was very focused on their issues and would work hard to see them implemented. The four key physicians at the time were Drs. Georges Bélanger, head of Surgery; Michel Simard, head of Lab Services and president of the Council of Physicians, Dentists and Pharmacists Léo Norbert, head of Radiology; and Dr. Claude Boudreau, head of Medicine. I made sure to speak to each of them personally and I took my proposal to the Medical Advisory Committee.

I took a look at the projects already proposed by these physicians and asked them for their priorities. Dr. Bélanger was looking for a surgical day unit to increase the volume of day surgery. This was interesting to me because it was an innovative move at a time when there was the beginning of a shift from hospital beds to ambulatory services, an approach where patients are sent home after four to six hours following minor surgeries, thus avoiding an overnight stay in hospital. Dr. Simard wanted his lab construction project to be given top priority, while Dr. Boudreau felt that Medicine needed a new dialysis unit, as they were not able to cope with the number of new patients needing dialysis. Dr. Norbert had the dream of installing a CT scanner at the Hospital, the first in Quebec outside a major teaching hospital, to allow his team to remain at the forefront of radiological services.

I believed the projects being put forward were good for our patients and good for the Hospital. By showing concern for the issues the physicians were raising, I was able to focus attention on the positive initiatives and not on the loss of the medical staff lounge. The daycare centre was opened 10 months later. This was seen as a win for the staff and had a real impact on the attitude towards management in the Hospital. Within a year, there was a new day surgery unit, a new dialysis unit, and phase one of lab construction was underway. By 1985, a CT scanner was up and running at the Hospital, purchased by the newly formed foundation. There were many winners here and this set the tone for my administration of the Hospital.

I cannot stress enough the importance of the first months in a new organization. It is a time for the CEO to know what is going on and to be known, and a time to begin building respect and credibility as a good leader. It is during this period that it is also critical to begin the strategy the CEO will use to move the enterprise forward. After this initial period of getting to know the organization, it is then most important to follow through, get some concrete results, and show that you are a winner.

My Strategy

After the first three months developing my understanding of the key issues, I tried to lay out for myself a strategy for managing the organization. There was a $2 million deficit that had to be addressed and this was weighing heavily on the Board, and the staff, who were worried about job loss. Management tools and systems were weak, and new management tools had to be introduced to allow for greater efficiency. There was almost no internal communication in the Hospital to let the staff know what was happening and I saw this as an essential tool for pursuing all other objectives. Most importantly, there was no common vision for the direction the Hospital was to take in the future.

As I look back 30 years, I know that my approach was in no way as systematic as it might appear in my writing and that things did not happen in such a clear, linear fashion. My strategy was to develop a common vision that would allow the Hospital to position itself for the future, and clearly define a set of goals and objectives that everybody could strive to achieve.

I chose a strategy that included the key players in the Hospital and involved them as much as they wanted in the running of the Hospital. This meant learning how to manage with the physicians and how to change the culture of confrontation between management and the unions that I had witnessed over my first few months.

In cutting costs and making the Hospital more efficient, I adopted a strategy of "development" as much as possible, while still cutting back. The idea was to find resources, no matter how small, to stimulate development in different sectors of the Hospital. I developed a strategy of innovation and I tried to instill a culture of innovation in the Hospital and encourage new ideas from the staff.

Developing a Common Vision

The Board had not developed a clearly defined vision or direction for the Hospital so I introduced a visioning exercise to allow the Hospital and the Board to arrive at a consensus. I looked for a process that would involve as many people as possible and came across strategic planning, a new exercise that industry had been using for a while but that was new to the public sector. This is a process whereby an environmental study is conducted to determine the population being served by the hospital, the health needs of that population, and which other services are being offered by other institutions. The strengths and weaknesses of the hospital are then defined. Using this information, the hospital elaborates its mission and the services that it should be offering. Priorities are defined and a plan is developed to achieve the objectives put forward. Physicians, other professional staff, management and the board are very involved in this process and this involvement helps to ensure a strong buy-in to the results.

The Verdun General Hospital had been serving the community since 1932, and through the 1950s was one of the major specialty teaching hospitals in Montreal. As new hospitals were built during the 1950s and 1960s, the Université de Montréal relied more on the downtown teaching hospitals, and there was a shift of specialty residents to the newer hospitals. Verdun took on the role of training family-medicine residents. The battle for residents in our hospitals is important to understand because it is a driving force influencing what hospitals do and how they do it. Specialists need the hospital and its resources to practice their profession. They hospitalize patients and then keep them in hospital for a course of treatment. While in the hospital, the patient must have 24-hour-a-day medical coverage until discharge. Specialists agree to teach and spend time with students for which they are rarely paid, but in return the residents and interns, who are completing their required training in a hospital (two years for a family physician, four years in a specialty program, and five years in a sub-specialty program, such as cardiac surgery), are available on call to cover the patients on nights and weekends so that the specialist does not have to be present. Fourth- and fifth-year residents are often very skilled physicians and they are right up to date with latest innovative medical practice, and the value of a teaching hospital is the learning dynamic and synergy that develops between the staff physician and the resident, which helps the physicians of the hospital keep up to date.

In Quebec, the number of residency placements in a medical field is set by the government, which uses these limits as a way to control the number of new physicians entering the profession. In the 1980s, with the cost of health care rising, governments in Quebec and throughout Canada made two major decisions. The first was to cut the total number of residents as a way to control cost in the system. The second was to change the ratio of specialists to family physicians from 60 percent/40 percent to 50 percent/50 percent. While the first decision is now almost universally held to have been a mistake from which we are continuing to recover (the analysis failed to take into account a number of changes in the way physicians now practice medicine, and feminization of the medical profession, with women working fewer hours than their male counterparts), the second decision was a very important one in beginning to recognize the importance of primary care. While the move to training more family physicians did not achieve its cost-cutting potential, since a full primary-care system was not put into place and there was no reduction in the use of high-cost hospital services, it nevertheless set a new direction for the organization of physician services by putting greater emphasis on primary care and patient management.

Both of these decisions caused havoc, however, in the teaching hospitals and the battle for residents began. Verdun lost its specialty residents but was able to develop a family-medicine program. At the same time, the medical schools were expanding their family-medicine programs and their research programs in primary care, population health, public health and clinical epidemiology. More and more places were being opened for the residents in family medicine in all teaching hospitals as the number of places in specialty programs was being reduced. The major teaching hospitals wanted more residents in family medicine to fill the gaps in their call schedule left by the reduction in specialist placements. As a result, the major teaching hospitals were calling for the closure of the family-medicine programs in the community hospitals like Verdun and Cité-de-la-Santé in Laval, Quebec.

I realized that an academic vision to support and build up the quality of the family-medicine teaching program was essential to the survival of the Hospital as a teaching institution. I was able to develop a strong consensus around this vision. There was agreement that family medicine was essential to the Hospital and that a strong program was a way to recruit residents. But, initially, the specialists at the Hospital were not ready to give up beds to the Department of Family Medicine so that GPs could hospitalize their patients and manage them as they would in many of the non-teaching hospitals in which they worked. Eventually, the specialists had no choice but to give in and move a portion of their beds to the Department of Family Medicine.

To support this vision of a progressive, dynamic community teaching hospital remaining at the forefront of specialty medicine, it was essential to modernize the medical equipment at the Hospital and develop new and innovative medical programs. This was the driving approach through most of the years I was there.

I wanted the Hospital to take on the challenge of being best in its category, and I believe now that this was also my own personal mission and vision for the organization. This meant not only being the most efficient in the delivery of services at the lowest cost, but also being the most innovative, with a reputation for trying new programs and new ways of doing things. I believed that this would be the way to excite the staff and develop the sense of commitment and belonging that is so important to a hospital.

Including Physicians in the Management of the Hospital

As CEO of a hospital, you have no choice but to pursue a collaborative management approach with the physicians. Both division heads and department heads are important; division heads, working hierarchically under heads of departments, are sometimes stronger and more influential than their department heads. The medical hierarchy also includes the elected leaders of the medical advisory council, the representatives of the medical staff on the board, and also the natural leaders who have influence through the quality of their clinical work, their research, or their teaching skills. All these physicians must have direct access to the CEO of their organization and know that their concerns, problems and projects will be heard.

Already in 1982 at Verdun (as in most hospitals today), financial issues were a daily concern, if not a daily headache, for the CEO. Costs were rising and I especially followed the cost of medical supplies and drugs on a weekly basis. I noticed that the overall supplies in Radiology were rising more quickly than the number of exams. I made enquiries and was told that a new contrast medium was being used in Radiology. This is a substance injected into a patient, like a dye, to enhance the quality of the X-ray image. I called Léo Norbert, the head of Radiology, and he explained that until recently an ionic substance was used as contrast medium and that there was an allergic reaction to the product in a very few cases, often in the elderly, and some patients would go into anaphylactic shock and die. A new non-ionic contrast medium had just come out that reduced to almost zero the chance of an allergic reaction. The problem was that the new product was 10 times the cost of the old product. The physicians felt they had no choice but to use the safer product. I asked him if he realized that we were talking of a multi-million-dollar increase in cost and if he had heard any rumours as to whether the minister of health was prepared to pick up the cost. The answer was no. I discovered that other colleagues were in the same situation. The Department of Radiology and the physicians worked out a protocol of risk and where the risk was below a given level the old substance was administered, while for higher risk cases the new medium was authorized. Using the protocol we were able to keep the cost down to a 20 percent increase.

This is one example of a trend that is a regular occurrence in health care. There is constant introduction of new medication, new technology, and new and better ways of treating patients. There is also usually a rising cost related to these developments. This issue is very relevant today as the cost of new technology is skyrocketing. What should be the process for accepting and paying for new technology, who should be making these decisions, and what role does the population play in deciding how much of their tax dollars they want to spend on health care, and for what services?

The following example once again demonstrates how the cost of new medication poses a dilemma for health care administrators, physicians and government. Jean Proulx, the head of Nephrology (with whom I had developed a very good relationship and who was trying hard to control his budget), came into my office one day looking very troubled. "I know we just replaced all our dialysis machines and we are trying to contain costs with better purchasing of supplies, but we have a dilemma and I can't do this alone," he said. He went on to explain that a new medication had just been approved for dialysis and that it was regarded as a major breakthrough. It was a drug that would change people's lives for the better, and in some cases it would give them back their lives. The medication was called erythropoietin and it increases the red blood cell count of patients on dialysis to such an extent that those who previously could not work, got tired just moving around, and needed blood transfusions on a regular basis, were now returning to work and feeling what it was like to be alive once again. The cost per patient per year was huge and we were already spending, at the time, over $20,000 per patient per year for dialysis. (Today the cost is closer to $35,000.) I started to take the same approach as I had done in Radiology and asked if we could somehow target the use of this new drug to those patients who needed it and could benefit the most. The answer I got back from Dr. Proulx only intensified the dilemma.

Dr. Proulx made clear to me that those patients who could benefit from the drug would truly benefit—their lives would be changed. In such circumstances, how could we ethically not provide the medication? As is often the case, the ministry does not hear about the impact of these new medications until the system has to start paying. The drug companies had been giving the new drug to the Hospital for free on a trial basis and the results were unbelievable. Every patient wanted to be put on the protocol when they saw the improvement the drug provided. The Hospital could not afford to pay for the added cost but, on the other hand, could not morally withhold the drug. We agreed to monitor the situation and to design a protocol that would indicate use of the drug only for those patients whose improvement due to medication would make a difference to their lives. I was clear that the decision about who should receive the drug should always be a medical one and that my job was to lobby the regional council and government for the new funds required.

It has always been my view that this process of lobbying for new funds after a drug is introduced is a very inefficient way to manage the introduction of new drugs and technologies. There must be a body that can evaluate the technology and then decide whether or not the technology should be authorized for distribution, and to whom it should be made available. The appropriate funds should also then be made available. There are already technology-assessment organizations in many provinces, yet they have no authority to set policy, they can only make recommendations to the ministries of health. It usually takes a long time before funds to pay for the new drugs and technologies are made available and, in many cases, this is long after the new drug or technology is in use.

These are examples of managing with the physicians. The number of times this occurs is increasing because each new drug, each new surgical technique, each new improvement in medical material has a cost and a benefit and we are continually struggling with the dilemma. What is essential, what is an improvement, what would be nice to have? As long as there is an open dialogue with the physicians and the issues are debated freely, it is possible to have a common position and support each other.

I have also found that managing conflict with and between physicians, mainly over resource distribution, is a delicate matter. There is a lot of ego involved and each doctor sees himself or herself as a one-person business. I have found that the more complex the organization, the more difficult it is to manage in this zone of influence, and as mergers have occurred with large teaching hospitals it has become almost impossible. It is the conflict among physicians in mergers that can be a major stumbling block to the hospital's success.

The philosophy of "divide and conquer" does not work in a hospital. I have found that strong medical leadership is far better than weak or divided leadership. I need medical approval, or at least a willingness to wait and see the results of a new proposal. With strong leadership, which includes the heads of departments and the medical advisory staff, it is sufficient to ensure medical involvement from the beginning and that the interests and concerns of the physicians are taken into consideration. I have never brought a proposition to the board of a hospital that did not have the support of the medical council. Once the leadership is convinced that it is their role to manage the other physicians in the hospital (and not the CEO's role), the relationship that develops between the medical staff leadership and the CEO can be very powerful.

At Verdun, Dr. Bélanger was very influential and played a prominent leadership role. At one point, members of the Department of Medicine were unhappy at what they perceived to be the stronger influence of Surgery throughout the Hospital and they mounted a campaign to replace the head of the medical advisory council with a physician who would be more supportive of the Department of Medicine and their requests for resources. Unfortunately, in proposing and electing a puppet president they chose an individual whose need for recognition was so strong that he intervened in every issue to the ultimate frustration of the Board, myself and many physicians. During this period, it was much harder to move things forward and arrive at a consensus on issues.

At Notre-Dame Hospital, where I later became CEO, there was a strong medical staff but once the Hospital was forced to merge with two other smaller teaching hospitals, the conflicts which had always existed between the medical staff of rival hospitals was now brought inside the newly merged hospital and they are still tearing the Hospital apart. The merger of the Ottawa Hospital led to a different series of challenges, stemming not only from rival hospitals but from the French/English dynamic of Ottawa as well. I have found that managing with physicians in conflict situations is sometimes almost impossible. Even so, without physician collaboration, or at least a majority consensus, it would not be possible to manage a hospital.

A Strategy of Openness and Negotiation with the Union

In my previous dealing with unions, I had never yet met a really militant one where the battle lines were drawn and all that was important was winning the war. A war takes two sides willing to fight, otherwise there is no war. At Verdun, the sides were clearly marked. Previous to my arrival, the dominant and most militant union was the CSN, which represented the maintenance, cleaning, laundry, food services, clerical staff and auxiliary nurses. There had been a lockout at the Hospital in response to union activity and this set the stage for an ongoing dynamic of confrontation.

I was convinced at the time, and still am today, that a strategy of negotiation is always preferable to confrontation. This might seem obvious, but when one is on the front line it is often difficult to turn the other cheek. There is an attitude in hospital human resources (HR) departments that to compromise is to show weakness, and that means defeat and humiliation. So HR frequently sees itself as the brick wall holding back the forces of evil, while the unions find the resistance they expected to be there.

My biggest challenge was to change the attitude of the labour-relations team at Verdun, and this was very much linked to the personality of the people involved and the overall attitude of management. I remember arguing with my VP human relations about the need to change our approach, and his resistance to showing any weakness. He said, "David, before I worked in HR, I was president of the union at the hospital. I know how they think, I know what they want and the games they play." I told him we had to change the rules of the game and he'd better rewrite the rules if we were going to continue working together.

Telling the director of HR or the director of labour relations to change his or her approach does not alter the fundamental attitude throughout the organization. A change of this magnitude always implies a change in attitude for all of management and for the culture of the hospital. The change in attitude towards the unions is not divorced from an overall approach to management in a hospital. Treating colleagues with respect, asking for and offering help and support, rewarding and encouraging excellence all affect labour relations.

I repeat over and over again that the job of a hospital is to treat people. This is a one-on-one, person-to-person business and if staff is not happy, or if there is an atmosphere of confrontation, it is almost always felt by the patients we are treating. I have become more and more sensitive to this reality over the past 35 years and now know that the well-being of the spirit and the soul of a hospital is an important factor in the quality of care. This can literally be a matter of life and death. The number of medical accidents, employee health and safety issues, and errors in medication increase with increasing stress and conflict in the organization. The cost of this is never calculated and that is a serious mistake.

The choice of director of HR is crucial to the climate of an organization; most candidates come from previous roles in HR departments in hospitals or elsewhere. There are many technical issues that must be dealt with in HR. Other than labour relations, there is payroll, recruitment, benefit management, training and education, and occupational health and safety. I always wanted someone who focused on human-resource development and could come up with new ideas to stimulate and excite staff and to instill a sense of belonging and of commitment to the patients and the hospital. It is not easy to find someone like this and I have always had to support this role myself.

My strategy of negotiation and dialogue has led me into numerous traps along the way. For example, unions have sometimes wanted to negotiate with me directly and this should not happen. Used as a last resort to put the final touches on a difficult negotiation, this is appropriate, but it must not be seen as a move to bypass the existing structures or labour relations will be undermined. I learned this the hard way after agreeing to meet with the union leadership when

I arrived at Verdun, following my strategy of getting to know the organization. As they brought up issues and as I wanted to be seen as a leader who could get things done and who was sensitive to union issues, I proceeded to get more involved than I should have.

Eventually, I was being asked by the union to get involved in almost every issue, which meant I had taken away a part of the legitimacy of the labour relations department. My approach was also resented by several front-line managers who saw this as giving in to the unions and making them more demanding and more difficult to deal with. As I began to understand all the subtleties of managing with the unions in the Hospital, I was able to put my involvement into perspective and the word spread that I was a fair but very hard negotiator.

After the first five years at Verdun, this strategy began to pay off. One of the more difficult issues in a hospital is the number of part-time positions. Because a hospital needs to run seven days a week, 24 hours a day, there are many part-time positions. Hospitals try to keep staffing tight, with a large number of occasional staff on call to fill in during vacations and sick leave. This creates many part-time positions and not a lot of job security, but has been used in the past to avoid the possibility that there might be an extra person every now and then. To create more stability in the workforce, a program was developed to convert part-time hours on the on-call list into permanent full-time positions. This meant that the union had to accept workers covering different jobs in different places during their work week, which had never existed before, and management had to take the risk of a surplus employee on a given unit every now and then. With some goodwill, the program was a success and both union and management have gained. This could not have been done if the model of confrontation had not been altered.

There were two strikes I remember while at Verdun and both indicated that the strategy I had chosen was paying off. Nurses in Quebec went on strike and I remember being in front of the picket line talking to the nursing executive when an ambulance drove up. Emergency services were covered during the strike but there was cancellation of all surgery. Ten minutes later, someone said that nurses were needed in the operating room and, without hesitation, three nurses stepped forward to cover and were let through the picket line by their colleagues. The atmosphere was one of respect and I was proud of the changes that were happening in labour relations.

I am more convinced than ever of the value of a non-confrontational strategy in managing with our unions, but to achieve this in the hospital requires a major change in the managerial culture of the organization. This change must be sustained as part of an overall management strategy, and must remain consistent year after year. Managers doing laundry can help change the culture, but not all managers can have this opportunity.

In 1972, 1976, 1979, and 1982 the Common Front conducted rounds of collective bargaining in which all public and para-public Quebec unions joined forces in Quebec-wide labour negotiations and strikes with the government. During the 1982 negotiations, all non-nursing staff at Verdun walked out and management had to cover as best as we could. The head of HR coordinated management's strike response and I found myself on cooking and laundry duty. I learned a lot about the kitchens as I spent time making soup, cutting vegetables, washing dishes and hosing down food carts. The work was hard and fast and I developed a much greater appreciation for our staff. The laundry service was certainly a new experience and taught me enough about what we were doing and how well we were doing it so that when, later, there was a move to close down the laundry services at the Hospital and move to a central laundry service, I was able to demonstrate for and commit the Hospital to producing a pound of clean laundry at a lower rate than was being offered, and in so doing, saved many jobs at the Hospital.

I left Verdun after 10 years and I have rarely felt more satisfied than when I first arrived at Notre-Dame Hospital and met the president of the local CSN. She said to me that she had received a call from the president of the union at Verdun and was told that Notre-Dame could look forward to a significant change for the better in labour relations.

Cutting Costs While Developing New Programs
I had no idea how much of my work life would be spent cutting costs. My first task at Verdun was to balance a budget that was $2.3 million in deficit out of a total of $33 million. I have been cutting ever since. The real challenge is how to maintain services for the people you are

serving while not reducing accessibility or quality. To understand the situation it is important to understand a bit about the budgets of hospitals.

Hospitals use about 40 percent of all health care dollars. This does not include physician payments or any medication and treatment outside the hospital. A hospital is given a budget based on its previous budget increased by a factor for inflation each year. The initial base budget was defined historically and is not based on the health care needs of the population being served. The budget year begins on the first of April and I would normally present the board with an operational plan and budget by the middle of March. This plan is based on a lot of guesswork, as the government does not tell hospitals what their budget will be until many months into the year. It is common to receive one's budget only in the fall, long after the budget year begins on April 1, and often it will not be finalized until the end of the budget year on March 31. No business could possibly work like this, yet we spend and manage billions of dollars in this very unorthodox way.

How to spend less and get more has been a daily concern for me for the last 30 years, and my first face-to-face contact with the consequence of cutting back taught me some important lessons. One way to cut costs is to see if there are programs that the hospital is offering that could be offered elsewhere at a lower cost or in better conditions. If the hospital is not the unique supplier of the service for the population, this is an approach worth considering.

A Strategy of Development While Cutting Costs

Verdun in the 1960s was accommodating between 3,500 and 4,000 births a year. By 1982, this was down to below 1,300 due to a major drop in the birth rate in Quebec, but also because other hospitals were providing the service. The regional council was looking at the regrouping of obstetric services and closing the service at Verdun. I saw an opportunity to help the bottom line and to develop something new at the Hospital. I had to convince the regional council to allow the Hospital to use part of the funds from closing Obstetrics to develop a new program for the community, as well as supporting the Hospital deficit. The Hospital's reaction was immediate and very negative, as birthing is not only a pleasant part of a hospital's role, but it is a way of ensuring a younger clientele for the hospital. Young families will use the hospital and the doctors they meet during birthing experiences for their future health care needs. Gynacology was especially concerned about losing their clientele of young mothers and, because they all had an obstetrics practice, it meant that they would have to work in two different sites or give up obstetrics. The teaching role of the hospital would be affected , since an important part of the training program for family physicians is the obstetrics component.

I argued that our community was aging and the number of births was going down dramatically. Young couples were moving farher west and were giving birth at a new, smaller hospital in their area about five miles from Verdun. Our cost per birth was rising as our fixed costs were remaining the same. Regrouping birthing made sense but the impact was gut-wrenching. A very important argument was that, as the number of births continued to decrease, we would lose the critical mass needed to maintain quality and full coverage. This argument is one that applies to many situations in which programs and even hospitals are being closed. It is important that physicians and staff have the opportunity to treat sufficient numbers of cases in each area of medicine to keep up their expertise, and hospitals often find themselves below the normally required numbers, especially in small, rural hospitals.

I had to come up with something new to replace the sense of loss and, as our elderly clientele was growing in number, I suggested a specialized program for the elderly: an active evaluation-and-treatment geriatric service. At the time, the idea of a dedicated unit for acute geriatric care was new. The specialty of geriatric medicine was only beginning to be recognized in the faculties of medicine. I suggested the program be run by family physicians with specialty consultation. The specialists liked the idea because it freed them from being the direct caregivers to very demanding patients while maintaining their involvement and revenue stream, and it gave GPs active-care beds in the Hospital. There werc many elderly patients in the Hospital and because their care was not well managed they spent much more time there than was necessary. Not only would the new program provide better and more focused care for the elderly, it would also save money and reduce bed utilization.

This strategy of developing something new and exciting at the same time as a service was being closed proved to be what was needed to soften the blow of the closure of Obstetrics, and I have used this approach ever since.

Once the decision had been made, it was necessary to tell the whole organization, beginning with staff immediately affected. I began towards the end of the day shift and went to tell the nurses in the nursery. This was still before the time when babies went back to their mother's room and babies remained in the nursery until discharge. The staff who took care of the babies were not registered nurses but were specially trained at the diploma level to take care of babies. Some of them had been in the unit for over 25 years, in what was considered one of the most enjoyable and pleasant positions in the Hospital. Taking care of the babies was very important to these women and I was about to tell them that the unit was closing. I had never experienced so much emotion all at one time. Many started crying and others were in shock as the life they had known and loved was coming to an end.

Witnessing the impact that decisions for cost-cutting had on the lives of my staff taught me a lesson that I will never forget. No decision is made in a vacuum, without consequences. I realized that it was important to take care of the staff being displaced, and offered the full support of the Hospital to all who wanted to return to school to get a nursing degree. Many of the younger staff took this opportunity, while others who did not want to go back to school were offered retraining to work with the new geriatric team or elsewhere in the Hospital.

Another cost-cutting measure that I used was the reduction of management staff. This is a measure that is often demanded by the physicians, the public and the media, since it does not affect direct patient care. I would like to say that management must be efficient and streamlined, with as few layers of control as possible, yet there are limits to this approach and those limits are defined by the quality and ability of management. If management becomes too thin or the situation is beyond the capacity of individual managers to cope, not only will money not be saved, it will be lost through loss of control. The removal of too many management staff can also lead to a situation where the quality of care can be put into peril as the supervision and leadership that management provides at the clinical level is not sufficient to monitor and adjust the quality of care.

Better purchasing was also a target of my efforts and there was much to be done here. There was no group buying at the time, or long-term commitments on the part of the Hospital or the suppliers, and there was a great deal of room for negotiation. Much of this has been done over the past 20 years, but most hospitals are still capable of negotiating better deals with their suppliers.

Bed closures were the next approach and the logic was simple. If it is possible to reduce the length of time a patient spends in the hospital, then the same number of patients can be treated in fewer beds and beds can be closed. Bed closure is the largest, most immediate saving in a hospital because there is a direct saving from staff costs. Many physicians were shocked at the idea since beds were their livelihood and they were always demanding more beds from the Hospital. How could I possibly be suggesting this? There followed long hours with the physician leadership, asking them what they needed to maintain volume if the beds were cut. This was my development side of the strategy and they were beginning to see the opportunity. Some of the suggestions included the development of day surgery, updating dialysis equipment, creating a palliative-care team and creating the position of discharge planner (to help physicians discharge their patients in a timely way). Primary-care services in the community were still weak and the move to ambulatory care, which was to become the buzzword of the 1990s, had not yet begun. But the ideas put forward to help find solutions showed initiative, involvement and commitment on the part of the doctors.

I believe the Hospital grew stronger from this first cost-cutting exercise, even though it was traumatic for many employees and demanded major change. We attempted to be as innovative as possible and to develop new programs where there was a need. We made every effort to make sure appropriate sections of the Hospital were aware of all the measures and that as much opportunity as possible was given to affected staff. Good relations were developed with the regional council and the government through the development of the active geriatric-care unit. The population's need for more services for the elderly were addressed. The Hospital's vision to be innovative and to develop a specialized community teaching hospital was put into place.

A Strategy of Innovation

The 1980s were the middle years in Quebec's health care system. The 1970s saw the introduction of Medicare and a new payment scheme for physicians, the first attempts to implant a primary-care system, and the building and development of new institutions. The 1980s brought the oil crisis, reduced tax revenue, and the first impact of all the money that had been borrowed to pay for the 1970s. Health care was going through the first in a long series of financial constraints. For me it was a fertile time for new, innovative programs. I have always been a hyperactive person and have always been anxious to try new things.

I like change, new ideas, new challenges, and search constantly for ways to improve things. As part of the strategy to develop a hospital and bring it recognition as an innovator in health care, I was always looking for new initiatives. Quality of care and the development of a managerial model that would focus management's energy in this direction was the area of innovation that interested me the most.

How do we measure quality? Do we offer good care to our patients? How do we improve the quality of care we offer? How do we report the quality of care provided to the population?

A Model of Management Through Quality Improvement

Quality in a hospital has many different components. Availability of the service is one aspect. At Verdun in 1982, there was no CT scanner, though this technology existed and had proved its worth many years earlier. All our patients needing this type of exam were sent to the downtown teaching hospitals, and the numbers were regularly increasing because more and more physicians were not prepared to make a diagnosis without the added information a CT scan could provide. It took three years and the hospital foundation raising the money needed to buy the CT scanner before authorization from the government was received.

Access to existing services is another example of quality. Waiting in the emergency room for a bed, having a scheduled surgery cancelled or having to wait months for cancer surgery are all examples of problems of quality.

The quality of direct medical and nursing services to patients is the cornerstone of the hospital's mission. Has the right diagnosis been made, and then, has the course of treatment prescribed led to the desired results?

Quality also means evaluating how well resources are being used and ensuring that they are used in the most efficient way possible. For example, it is important to continually evaluate the quality of staffing, purchasing, financing and to ensure that the processes are in place to get the work done. The quality of the physical environment as well as the psychological well-being of the hospital must be ensured. Air passageways have to be clean to prevent the spread of infection, and isolation rooms must be in perfect condition. The levels of stress in the hospital have to be kept to a minimum as they contribute to medical errors, on-the-job accidents and unhappy staff. All these factors are part of a hospital quality management program.

These issues must be foremost in the CEO's mind. The first systematic program of quality assessment in health care began at the beginning of the 1980s, following the work of Dr. W. Edwards Deming on quality in Japan. The concept was very new and there were few hospital boards that had put a complete quality-assessment program into place.

I became very interested in finding a model of management that would provide a clear focus for managers in the hospital. Management covers a variety of positions and in most hospitals a large percentage of managers are in direct contact with the patients. The head nurse on a ward, the chief technician in Radiology, the supervisor of Housecleaning or the night coordinator of the emergency room are all part of the management team. I wanted to find a way to inspire management and get everybody's efforts focused in the same direction.

I was reading a great deal about quality management, especially Deming's work, and how a quality approach had been integrated into the management culture of organizations. Managing through a focus on quality and quality improvement was very new and there were few hospitals that had developed this approach to management. I wanted to provide a systematic method and a common set of goals that would rally all of management. Managing through a focus on quality improvement was the theme of industry and I believed it could and must be introduced into the health care sector.

At Verdun, a quality-assurance program was first introduced measuring the state of quality at the Hospital. Next there was a move to the concept of total quality management whereby all aspects of the organization are considered part of the final outcome. This then evolved to total quality improvement whereby quality objectives are given to each unit in the Hospital and, at the end of the year, the achievement of the objectives are measured. Finally, a continuous quality-improvement process was put into place that focused on an ongoing exercise that monitored quality on a monthly and quarterly basis and responded as rapidly as possible in those areas where the quality measure was below target. Patient satisfaction was introduced as an important component of the quality-measurement process and has evolved over the years, such that today this is a very important component of quality measurement.

The challenge was how to design a model of management that integrated the concern for quality into the daily management of the Hospital. The model also needed to encourage the Board to look at the Hospital through a prism of quality and make decisions consistent with this concern. Once again, as with labour relations, we were considering a change in attitude, a change in culture of the organization—in this case, the managerial culture of the Hospital. Managers often feel that this is extra work added to what they already have to do, as opposed to a new way of doing the work they have to accomplish.

I believed that to begin to change the managerial culture of the hospital it was important to provide an ongoing program of training and development for management, and this became my first attempt in a hospital to provide to all management staff a program of training supported by an outside facilitator. The main focus of the training was to make quality concerns the guiding principle of management. This meant we had to set up structures that allowed for input and involvement from staff so we could establish a process to collect data on quality measures, analyze the data in each unit, focus on the levels of quality agreed upon and then, with broad participation, look at ways to do things differently.

There are many different models of management and we administrators in the field sometimes talk of the flavour of the month. Total quality management, internal auditing, risk management, process management, quality circles, lean management, *kaizen* (Japanese for "good change") and, most recently, change management are some of the models presented as the program that will solve all your problems.

It does not matter which model is chosen as the tool for training, although they each focus on a different aspect of quality, as long as the model is focused on improving quality and is flexible enough to adapt to change from within or change imposed on the organization. There must be a continuous program of training and development of management staff to ensure an understanding and acceptance of the organization's values and to build the quality culture.

Each hospital is unique and has its own personality, often defined by the CEO and senior staff. That is why stability in senior staff is so important in a hospital. The overall state of management in a hospital affects the direct care given to patients, and the drastic changes brought about by governments trying new strategies of cost-savings can put management into a very unstable situation, especially when those strategies include merging many hospitals across the country. This instability affects the building of a new culture and forces management to focus on solving the daily problems of the hospital.

The Emergency Room

There were many opportunities for innovation at Verdun and as the emergency room became more and more of a problem for the Hospital, and our patients were waiting longer and longer in brightly lit corridors, it became a priority for me to use the emergency room as an opportunity for change. While beds in the hospital were reduced and patients returned home earlier, those that remained were sicker and required more attention. This made the Hospital much less flexible. When the emergency room began to fill up, there were no longer patients who could be discharged because the patients remaining in hospital were sicker and were not able to be sent home.

This meant holding patients in the emergency room. Soon there was no room left and we had to place patients in the corridors. Normally, four hours after arriving in the emergency room, a decision should be made to discharge or admit the patient. If the decision is to admit, the patient should then be admitted within the next eight hours. This provides a guideline to the hospital and, though some patients are under observation in the emergency room, most patients are waiting because there is no bed available on the wards. In Quebec, this became a major problem in the 1980s and Mme. Thérèse Lavoie-Roux, then minister of health, was looking for solutions.

Dr. Bélanger, the Hospital's head of Surgery, had been working very closely with the emergency room to better coordinate movement of cases to the operating room. He believed that an important part of the solution to the emergency room problem was better coordination of activity through more rapid access to lab services and radiology results, as well as from specialists responding more rapidly to consultations. He recommended that a position of emergency room coordinator be created, along with the appointment of a liaison nurse and a social worker. The coordinator would be a physician with the power to strongly encourage doctors to discharge their patients and a mechanism to review length of stay. The liaison nurse would manage admissions to the wards as well as discharges to the home, and a social worker would work with home care and placement agencies to find alternative accommodations for patients who no longer needed acute care but could not take care of themselves. I saw the merits of this program and moved quickly to put it into place. The results were very positive and the strategy was picked up by the regional council and introduced into other hospitals, with Dr. Bélanger acting as a consultant.

A second program dealing with the emergency room was the development of a program for which the Hospital became known in the rest of Canada and in many countries around the world. I was at a conference in Toronto and one of the sessions dealt with a program in New Brunswick called the "extra-mural hospital." It was presented by Dr. Gordon Ferguson, the program's founder, and dealt with providing home-care services throughout New Brunswick, especially in outlying areas where there were no hospitals. This "hospital without walls" would have teams of physicians and nurses who would visit the homes of patients to provide them with the treatment they required, instead of having them remain in a hospital. I found the idea fascinating and, as I had a rule that I had to come back with at least one idea from a conference for it to have been worthwhile, I began to think of different possibilities.

The overcrowding in the emergency room was mainly due to lack of beds in the Hospital and since no new beds were going to be created I wondered whether it would be possible to open up a certain number of acute-care beds in the community. This meant that the Hospital had to have the ability to treat a patient in his or her own home as though they were in a bed inside the Hospital.

This was not home care whereby a patient was discharged from the hospital after receiving treatment, with follow-up at home. This was a program where a treating physician admits the patient to a bed, follows the patient through the treatment process and then discharges the patient when it is safe to do so.

An example of this is a patient arriving at the emergency room with a major systemic infection. This is life-threatening and requires intravenous antibiotic therapy for anywhere from seven to 21 days. Until this time, the patient would have been admitted to hospital and a course of treatment implemented. The question I asked was whether the patient could be treated at home under the care of a physician, with the appropriate nursing care and medical equipment. Could this be done more cost-effectively than in the Hospital and could the patient's safety be assured? I began to discuss the idea with physicians and nurses to gather information about the type of cases that could be treated in this way. I brought up the idea at the regional council and at some of my public appearances but knew that this was a costly project that would need a great deal of research before I might be able to make a solid proposal.

Politics plays a very important role in health care—most of the time, to the detriment of health-service delivery. But sometimes through a series of coincidences, opportunities arise. I was sitting in my office on a Thursday afternoon in 1986 when my secretary opened my door to say that I had a call from the chief of staff of the minister of health.

I was sure this was about our overcrowded emergency room because there was much media coverage around this issue. I was right, but also way off track. He began by saying that the minister was very concerned about the emergency room overcrowding problems and was looking for a series of measures that could help ease the situation. I started thinking about better coordination, the work of Dr. Bélanger, or more beds for the chronically ill to free up acute beds. "I heard you had a new idea about a hospital in the home and that this could alleviate pressure on the emergency rooms," he said to me. I was a bit taken aback as I had not written anything on the project and had only begun presenting the idea. He said the minister had heard about the idea and would it be possible for me to write up a proposal for the program. I became quite excited and, though I knew we had little data and hadn't done any planning on the feasibility of the project, I wanted to sound as positive as possible and said I could get something prepared in a couple of weeks.

There was a pause on the line, and he said the minister needed a document for the next day. It was my turn to be silent, until I finally asked what was really required. A program definition, a budget, expected results, advantages for the patients, hospital and emergency services, as well as a time frame for implementation, if you would be so kind, the gentleman responded. I was flabbergasted, but knew this was an opportunity that occurs once in a lifetime. I agreed and said I would fax the material by the end of the following day.

After getting off the phone I sat quite still for a few moments, which was rare for me, before I grabbed the phone, cancelled my meetings for the day and called in some of my key players. That afternoon and late into the evening we put together a program that sounded good, and asked for the development of 60 beds and a budget of $3.2 million. We all thought it was somewhat crazy, but it sounded good. The document was finalized and at the end of the following day it was faxed to the minister.

By Monday morning we hoped to hear something as we listened to the news coverage of the press conference the minister had just held. Nothing was mentioned in the clip and we were all a bit disappointed, though no one really thought the proposal would have been approved. A few minutes later, Anne-Marie Tardif, the director of communications, came into the office saying that a journalist had called to see if we had any information about a project that had been mentioned briefly by the minister during the press conference. We had the journalist fax over a copy of the press release and, at the bottom of a long list of measures, saw the title, "The Hospital in the Home Project" at the Verdun General Hospital. The budget allocated was $3.2 million and the project was to be up and running in six months. We were all stunned that a series of coincidences had put Verdun on the map and we had been given the chance to design and implement a brand-new program for our patients.

The ideal size of the program turned out to be 20 beds and I was able to set up two other programs, one at Claude Desjardins' hospital, Maisonneuve-Rosemont, and another at Cité-de-la-Santé. Many papers were written on the design, set-up and evaluation of the project, and six pilot projects were set up in Ontario. I spoke about the program in England, France, Germany and Australia, as well as in the United States. The CLSCs started lobbying from the very beginning that this was their jurisdiction of expertise as they were responsible for home care and saw the hospital intrusion into their domain as a threat to their budget. Eventually, as their political lobby grew, the hospital-in-the-home program was moved to the CLSC's home-care program.

It does not matter who offers the program as long as there is a close relationship between the physicians in the hospital and the nurses and physicians on the home-care team. What has happened is that as money in home care has become tighter, more expensive home-care services have diminished to be able to provide lighter care to a larger group of patients. As a consequence, the care needed for more serious, hospitalized patients is not available and these patients remain in hospital. I have found that as soon as the program is not attached to the hospital, the physicians lose contact and confidence in the home-care team because they do not know them as well and do not feel secure enough to refer their patients to this service. I would recommend a much more direct relation between the hospitals and home care, and that home-care staff be trained in the hospital, getting to know the physicians in the different programs, and the nurses and other professional staff who support these programs.

Designated Beds for Long-Term Patients

Beds in a hospital are central to most issues. One of these issues, and possibly the most frustrating, is the use of acute hospital beds to house long-term or chronic patients. After a patient has been hospitalized, treated, and has recovered from the illness, it is time for the patient to be discharged and a new patient to be admitted. There are patients who require a level of continued care that they cannot receive at home, either due to age or the nature of their medical situation. These patients require placement in a nursing home, a rehabilitation centre, or a chronic-care hospital.

A process was developed for the evaluation and placement of patients, yet many patients could not leave the acute-care hospital because the types of services they required were not provided elsewhere, or there were no places available in existing facilities. Beginning in the 1980s, many patients had to remain in hospital after their discharge, waiting for placement in appropriate facilities. The number of new facilities was not keeping up with the number of patients requiring placement, and more and more acute beds in hospitals were being occupied by non-acute patients.

These were patients living in an environment not designed for their needs and taking up an acute-care bed that was no longer available for acute care. These patients were scattered all over the Hospital and it was not possible to benefit financially from the fact that they required less nursing care than acute patients. I believed that, as we had no choice but to keep these patients until they were placed, it would be wise to convert a ward to a long-term ward with the appropriate less costly staffing, and to develop services to meet these patients' special needs.

The idea seemed quite logical to me and I was able to convince the nursing director and staff that this was an innovation worth implementing. The resistance to this seemingly obvious solution to help reduce costs and provide better care came from the physicians, who saw the number of beds under the direct control of their department diminished. It took some convincing to get this idea accepted, as they also felt that these beds would become permanent chronic beds and the government would not move to build enough new beds in the community. This last fear has proved true and, over the last 20 years, the rate of new chronic beds has not kept pace so that, now, up to 10 percent of acute-care beds are not available because they are filled with chronically ill patients waiting for placement.

There were many other innovations during my 10 years at Verdun, coming from all quarters, including the physicians. One of the real successes at Verdun was the development of a culture of learning and innovation that supported new ideas and the seeking out of new programs. Conferences, professional development and forums for exchanging ideas were encouraged, and I am convinced that the Hospital and our patients benefited greatly from the investment the Hospital made in encouraging this management style.

The Importance of Communication
Standing up in front of 200 employees in the auditorium of the Hospital to explain the decision to close Obstetrics and cut 100 staff was neither easy nor pleasant, yet, as CEO, I knew I had to do it my-

self, as openly, honestly and sincerely as I could. Communicating to staff, being present and available, and ensuring that staff is aware of what is going on in the hospital has always been one of my daily concerns. I realized as early as my first position at the CLSC that communication was an indispensable tool in the toolbox of a CEO and any good manager.

Communication is never one-way and it is as important to listen as it is to speak or to make presentations. There are many reasons to communicate. The simplest is to convey information, instructions, facts or explanations. However, communications tools are also used to influence behaviour, change attitudes, and even change the culture of organizations. Through communications, decisions are explained and support is sought, staff can be mobilized and spirits raised, work can be appreciated and efforts rewarded. It is through communication that a CEO stays in contact with the organization and the organization stays in contact with the CEO.

A hospital relies on people interacting with people to provide good services, and on staff who are well informed, feel they are a part of the hospital, and that the hospital and its reputation belong to them. At Verdun I created a permanent, full-time communications position for the Hospital and I ensured that the resources to do the job were available. This was quite rare at the time for a hospital the size of Verdun. I brought the position into my office and spent the time to make sure the person was aware of all the issues going on in the Hospital.

A CEO must invest time in communicating and cannot pass this off entirely to a spokesperson. A leader must lead and to lead well it is important to be seen and heard. Internally, communication is used as a tool to communicate what is happening to staff as well as to get feedback from staff. The first tools that I used at Verdun were a hospital newspaper that came out once every two weeks and an annual report that described the year's activities and honoured the staff and their achievements.

As I moved from hospital to hospital during my career, the role of communications grew, and at both Notre-Dame and Ottawa I had a VP of communications position added to the senior management team. Two distinct functions developed within this area, one focused on internal communication and the other on external communication. Internal communication focused on the staff, physicians, volunteers, foundation and the board. External communications dealt with the media, the population at large, the regional bodies, other heath care institutions, the Ministry of Health and the minister's office. Direct communication was also established with the local deputies and ministers of all political parties surrounding and influencing the hospital.

Internally, different tools where developed and, along with the journal and the annual report, I developed a CEO letter which I wrote on hospital issues and sent directly to all staff. On average, there was one letter a week and this became one of the most-read documents at the Ottawa Hospital. Staff were encouraged to respond and present their comments to the CEO. Every comment was looked at and a response provided by the communications team after discussion with me.

I also set up a breakfast and an afternoon tea with the CEO on each campus in Ottawa where, for about an hour on an occasional basis, anyone who wanted to meet and discuss issues with the CEO could submit their name and be invited to the upcoming get-together. A member of the communications team was with me at the meetings, taking notes, and minutes were kept. Senior management was then asked to respond to the issues and ideas that were brought forward and each person at the meeting received a written response as to the action taken. Open forums were held on all campuses on a regular basis, but one of the most interesting tools of internal communication was walking around and speaking to people at random. As the hospital I managed grew from 1,400 to 5,000 to 12,000 employees on three different campuses, it became harder and harder to be present and to communicate on a personal level with staff. This is a very big handicap in very large merged hospitals, as the presence of leadership is essential in developing the culture of the organization. The nature of managing a hospital is changing as hospitals are merging and this is a part of the job that is becoming more and more difficult. This is why I designed an organizational structure wherein there was recognized leadership at each campus, though they also had corporate responsibilities.

Energy, time and money must be put into internal communi-cation if the hospital is to run well and develop a strong culture of belonging and participating. People need to be respected and this is accomplished through communication, dialogue and listening. Internally, the communications team is also the eyes and ears of the hospital, picking up rumours, listening for issues and the concerns of staff, and providing continual feedback to the CEO and senior management. A good communications team is used by the VPs of the hospital (as well as by other managers in the organization) to help them run their portfolios.

The communications team is well placed to stimulate the social life of the hospital, from the summer barbeques for staff to the Christmas parties and the long-term employee award ceremonies, which are all essential to a harmonious, well-run environment.

External communication is as important to the hospital and the CEO as is internal communication, but for very different reasons. The authority of the CEO is based not on the formal authority of the position, but on how well the CEO is able to accomplish the following three functions: manage conflict in the organization, obtain resources for the hospital, and provide leadership in the interface between the hospital and the external world. To do the latter well, a CEO needs a strong communications team. A CEO must know what to say, how to say it, when to say it and to whom.

It was not until I arrived at Notre-Dame that I began to learn the importance of and challenges facing external communication, and certainly not until the media event surrounding my arrival in Ottawa did I learn that one's very survival could depend on it.

Involvement Beyond the Hospital

After the first five years at Verdun, I started to look outside the Hospital to see what role I might play in the health care field and how a greater presence externally could help my role as CEO of the Hospital and my ability to accomplish my mission. At Claude Desjardins' suggestion, I joined the Canadian Council on Accreditation and began to visit hospitals across Canada to evaluate their compliance with the accreditation standards put forward by the council. This was a wonderful experience because I had the opportunity to learn what was being done in hospitals across the country and bring many new ideas back to Verdun. I learned from the people I worked with on the accreditation teams, as well as from the ongoing process of developing standards for health care administration. I also had the opportunity to join the Board of the Canadian Internal Auditing Foundation and met with the Canadian auditor general, the auditors from most of the provinces, and the leaders of most of the major auditing firms in Canada at regular Board meetings to discuss and promote the use of internal auditing in the public sector. I believe very strongly that all public institutions should have an internal auditing service.

I joined the Board and executive of the Quebec Hospital Association in 1986, as well as the Association of Health Care CEOs of Quebec, where I became president in 1989. This role of representing all CEOs of all health care institutions allowed me to take public positions on health issues that CEOs felt strongly about. It was through these roles that I learned the difficult lesson that one becomes extremely vulnerable when exposed to the media.

Following the annual meeting of the association there is always a lot of media presence. In 1989–90, one of the main management issues was the growing surplus of acute beds because hospitals were moving more and more to day surgery, ambulatory care and shorter lengths of stays. As this was the beginning of a concerted effort by all CEOs in these areas, there were beds closed in most hospitals. Following the annual meeting, in response to a journalist's question on how to save money in health care, I suggested that if we could concentrate beds in certain hospitals, using all beds available, we would be able to close some of the smaller hospitals and save money. It would be cheaper to run three hospitals at full occupancy than four at 75-percent occupancy. This sounded good to me and made a lot of sense to the media, so the line was played often over the following week.

The director of the association called and asked if I was crazy. He went on to explain that my brilliant suggestion would mean that hospitals would be closed and CEOs would lose their jobs. As president of the association of CEOs, I was supposed to increase membership and not make suggestions to decrease it. Over the next five years, with hospital closures and mergers, the number of CEO positions was cut 50 percent, but I can say that almost all of my CEO colleagues supported most of the moves that brought greater efficiency to the system.

[CHAPTER FOUR]

Entering the Major Leagues

AFTER ALMOST 10 YEARS at the Verdun General Hospital, I wanted a new challenge and I felt the next step in my career was to be the CEO of a teaching hospital. As positions in Montreal became available, I applied for them, and in 1992 I was fortunate enough to be hired at Notre-Dame Hospital. Affiliated with the Université de Montréal, it was Quebec's largest and most prestigious francophone teaching hospital.

I remember my interview with the Board of the Hospital, on an evening right before they made their final decision. The selection committee had recommended two candidates and the Board had decided to interview the two candidates themselves. I knew there was an assistant deputy minister seeking the position, and when I entered the boardroom I must admit I was intimidated. I had prepared for the interview by studying the Hospital history, the annual reports of the past five years, and the latest strategic plan that had been presented two years earlier. I remember little of the questions or my answers. I felt I was talking continuously and saying everything I could think of. I could not read the Board's response and I waited all that evening for a call. Normally, if the Board had made a decision, the chosen candidate would have been called the same evening. The following morning I left at 5:30 for what was then the Centre hospitalier de Lévis (originally the Hôtel-Dieu de Lévis and later the CHAU de Lévis) near Quebec City, where I had been appointed acting supervisor by the Quebec government. During the entire 300-kilometre drive, I kept going over and over all I could remember about the interview. I convinced myself that I had not gotten the job and that I was going to live through another rejection. I had been looking for a new position for a year; I had applied unsuccessfully to two other Montreal hospitals, neither of them as large or as prestigious as Notre-Dame.

At 10:30 a.m., during the senior management team meeting at

the Lévis hospital, I received a phone call from André Bisson, chair of the Board of Notre-Dame, telling me that I had been chosen and that I would have to immediately prepare a statement because somehow the media knew about it. I knew things were going to be very different from that moment on. I was living the truth of the old saying, "If at first you don't succeed, try, try, try again."

I began working at Notre-Dame in June, 1992. Many people felt it was a risky marriage for someone with my background to be running Quebec's largest francophone teaching hospital, affiliated with the Université de Montréal. It turned out to be a love affair. Mr. Bison told me later that he had been verifying my candidacy with Marc-Yvan Côté, the Liberal minister of health at the time, to see whether he had any objections, and was told that I had the minister's full support for the appointment.

My First Months

Like my tenure at Verdun, the first few months at Notre-Dame were essential for getting to know the organization and getting known by the organization. An event occurred that had an important impact on my rapport with the Hospital and the staff and, though all worked out in the end, I would not recommend it as a path to follow. In August, 1992, very shortly after my arrival at the Hospital, I was chopping down some trees in the woods at our country house about 100 kilometres north of Montreal, when the head of the axe I was using flew off the handle and landed squarely in the middle of my forehead. It slashed me from the bridge of my nose to the top of my head and there was a lot of blood pouring down my face. I got back to the house, tied a cloth around my head and called the medical clinic in Saint-Sauveur, about a 20-minute drive away. My wife drove me to the clinic, more anxious than I had ever seen her. The medical staff informed me I would need X-rays and stitches and that I would have a major scar in the middle of my forehead.

I called Notre-Dame and was able to speak to Dr. Denis Gravel, a general surgeon and head of the Department of Surgery, whom I had just recently met, and asked him what I should do. He told me to drive into Notre-Dame and he would take care of me. When I arrived at the Hospital, word was already out about the unusual accident and they were waiting for me! Denis did a great job patching me up and today there is no visible scar, unless one looks very closely. As a patient, I got to know the staff in the emergency room and the operating room, I met nurses and doctors, and I became acquainted with the Chief of Surgery, who became a close friend at the hospital over the next five years. But most of all, I learned about the Hospital and the people who worked there, and they got to know me. Despite these positive and unexpected benefits, it's not an approach I would recommend.

The Hospital

The institutional culture at Notre-Dame was very different from what I had experienced at Verdun. The physicians were leaders in their respective fields, and the Hospital had one of Quebec's largest cohorts of interns and residents, and the largest group of full professors. To be accepted on faculty, a physician had to have at least a two-year fellowship in medicine or research.

There were many respected and well-known physicians among the medical staff and many had made major, internationally recognized contributions to the science and art of medicine. There were also many equivalents to Verdun's Georges Bélanger, and my work was cut out for me getting to know them and developing a good working relationship with each one. The staff and physicians were proud of their Hospital and proud to be a part of it.

The institutional culture was quite formal and hierarchical, and the role of CEO was very different from my management style. I enjoyed throwing out ideas and having lively discussions about issues. At Notre-Dame, the CEO did not throw out ideas and was very careful about what he said in public. When the CEO presented an idea, it was assumed that the decision to implement was already almost a fait accompli.

I was entering the Hospital from the parking lot one day, when the head of the Division of Orthopedic Surgery approached me and started talking about a new piece of equipment he needed in order to pursue more extensive laparoscopic surgery. I said it was an interesting project and I would like to look at it. Two days later, the head of Surgery burst into my office fuming and asking me how I could approve a $300,000 piece of equipment for Orthopedics without even speaking to him. I explained what I had said but the damage was done. I learned I had to be very careful about what I said and to whom I said it.

The previous CEO had a conservative management style, and was organized and formal. He was authoritative, remained in his office most of the time and was not a public figure. Since my style of management was so different from his, I had to move far more slowly than I was used to. I believed in an open, accessible CEO who was available to staff and physicians. I discovered that the prevailing culture did not tolerate errors, but I liked trying out new things and believed that if there were no errors, there would be little innovation or progress.

A strategic planning exercise done before my arrival had laid out a clear vision for the Hospital, which was to develop a CHU (Centre hospitalier universitaire), that is, a University Health Centre, or teaching hospital, as defined by a recent Quebec law. This law was designed to reduce the number of teaching hospitals by differentiating which were full teaching hospitals and which were only affiliated teaching hospitals. The academic medical community hoped that the government had created these designations so that there would be more academic funding. Although there is still no new funding formula based on academic designation, the labelling exercise has caused unimaginable turmoil, competition and the merger of hospitals that, in my opinion, should have been more carefully thought out.

When I arrived at Verdun, my mandate was somewhat vague, but when I arrived at Notre-Dame, my mandate was very clear: Develop and maintain good external relations with the university, the regional council, the minister and the ministry, the community, business people and the Hospital's benefactors; obtain the university hospital designation from the minister; continue to manage resources well; and ensure a strong foundation that maintained its fundraising capacity.

The Key Players

Given the size of the Hospital and its prestige in Quebec, there were many more key actors influencing the Hospital than what I had been accustomed to. Mr. André Bisson was chair of the Board. He was a former bank executive who sat on the boards of many major corporations around the world. He was chancellor of the Université de Montréal, and he had been the Board chair at Notre-Dame for 15 years and remained in that position throughout my term there. A distinguished gentleman of the highest moral standards, Mr. Bisson knows how to chair a board. He knows the role of a CEO and how to use a CEO for the benefit of the board and the hospital. We spoke often and his ability to understand Hospital issues was remarkable. His love of Notre-Dame was infectious and he was instrumental in my quickly becoming very attached and loyal to the Hospital. A CEO can learn a great deal from an experienced board chair, especially how to develop relations with board members.

The members of the Board were influential people in their milieus elected by the community, designated by interest groups according to the law, or co-opted. These were individuals with strong personalities who were accustomed to being listened to when they spoke. The president of the women's auxiliary comes to mind, Mrs. Lyla Paquette. For many years she raised money through various enterprises and found volunteers to help take care of our patients. She was a volunteer with a very strong personality who knew how to get what she wanted and she had the knack of making everyone happy to give it to her. The physicians loved her, as she was always positive about raising funds to support their projects or equipment. Lyla came to my office often and I realized she knew everything that was going on at the Hospital: which physicians were having trouble with the residents, who was having an affair with whom and some of the delicate situations I should be taking care of. It was wonderful talking to her and she was very helpful in revealing to me the human side of the Hospital.

The Physicians

I walked into the small boardroom for my first meeting of the Council of Physicians, Dentists and Pharmacists and there were seven physicians, all in their white coats, sitting around the table. This council, elected by all the physicians in the hospital, is the medical executive and the political body of the physicians. The law governing health and social services in Quebec requires the creation of the council, which has the authority to oversee medical issues in the hospital. The council discusses matters such as quality of care, physician privileges, physician sanctions, medical coverage, resource allocation, new technology, new construction and recruitment. There is normally a meeting once a month and the CEO is always present. This is one meeting a CEO must not miss unless he or she is so sick as to be unable to get out of bed.

The members of the council are often the heads of the major

departments and this was the case at Notre-Dame. Some of the members were more academic and research-oriented, while others were more clinical. The less academic physicians tended to be the more political and they became the driving force for the building and development of the academic teaching hospital. As I had done at Verdun, I met with each head individually and with their departments and services so I could better understand their needs.

The Team

The management team I met when I arrived at the Hospital had been in place for a very long time and they were all much older than my 42 years. They had spent most of the past 10 years with the same CEO and all had a very conservative approach to managing the Hospital. The team became my biggest challenge and I had to spend considerable time working with each director to understand the administrative dynamics. I started in Finance, as the financial well-being of a hospital determines most of what the hospital can do in terms of development. Nursing was my next priority and it was here that issues of quality of care and the number of worked hours came under consideration. The director of Technical Services, Building and Maintenance, Pierre Chenier, had been my director for many years at Verdun and had been hired at Notre-Dame the year before I arrived; the department was very well managed with no particular problems so this area was not a primary concern.

One of the hardest jobs of a CEO is to have to ask someone to leave the organization or downgrade their role and responsibility. My approach is to be clear, factual and honest in presenting the reason for my decision. The most important attribute I recognize is loyalty to the organization and to the CEO, and if the level of confidence required is not present, it is time to break up the relationship. Where there is a well-established executive team, this loyalty is often the major factor upon the arrival of a new CEO.

The Unions

My approach with the unions had been one of no confrontation. I arrived at Notre-Dame with a fair respect for the role and importance of the unions in a hospital and I believe I had gained the respect of the union movement as well. As Notre-Dame was the flagship teaching hospital of Quebec, it was also the test hospital for the unions, especially the CSN, Quebec's most militant and politically oriented union. My strategy did not change and I experienced the same kind of resistance from the director of Labour Relations that I had met with at Verdun. The message was that the CSN often used Notre-Dame as a test case for what could be achieved in the rest of Quebec. The introduction of efficiency into the Hospital, either through a continuous quality-management strategy or through re-engineering, would be seen by the union as a threat to jobs and was something that had to be resisted for the time being. I took the approach that there were enough savings in administrative costs that would not only allow me to balance the budget but would also permit some development. Most hospital programs are mainly labour-intensive and in a teaching hospital labour is about 76 percent of the budget, so I was able to assure the unions that if a quality-management approach were introduced there would be no job losses and staff would be used in new programs. Against the recommendation of the director of HR, I encouraged the participation of the union in a formal way as part of my management strategy. The strategy did work out and subsequently the union used this model to encourage other hospitals to adopt the same practices.

I developed a good relationship with the president of the CSN, Mr. Gérald Larose, as well as the vice-president, Marc Laviolette, who ended up as one of my Board members. When I left Notre-Dame, the CSN national office presented me with a pen that they give to the members of their own executive when they leave. I was very proud of this and the pen sits on my desk today.

The Nature of the Hospital

My integration into the complex environment of Notre-Dame was a real challenge and my strategy was fundamentally the same as at Verdun. The difference, however, was the nature of Notre-Dame. I was a young leader with a certain public presence who was well respected by my peers. This suited Notre-Dame's need for a leader who could represent the Hospital well externally. Internally, the Hospital was very satisfied with what it was doing and the role played by the physicians and the administration. I remember hearing a head of department say, "Notre-Dame is looking for a captain to steer the boat, but not to change direction."

The Hospital operated through three constellations of power. The medical staff was strong and the Council of Physicians, Dentists and Pharmacists was led by a president with a great deal of political influence; the heads of departments were strong; and the physicians had a direct link to the Board of the Hospital through the medical positions they had on the Board.

The Board and its chair were very influential due to a long tradition of Board control and the quality of the Board members, all of whom were closely involved in and extremely proud of the Hospital. The senior management team also had a strong influence as they had managed to maintain a balanced budget and were involved in the implementation of a $100 million construction project. The director of Medical Affairs was a well-respected radiologist who had been VP medical services for many years. The challenge was to find my own authority as CEO and move into this constellation of authority.

After studying the strategic plan of the Hospital, the budget, and the direction the university was taking, I was convinced that the appropriate strategy was to develop the areas of excellence for which the Hospital was already recognized and to concentrate our energy and resources in developing these areas. Notre-Dame was an internationally recognized academic teaching hospital, but because the government had introduced the notion of the "designated teaching hospital," the medical staff wanted to develop all areas of academic medicine, 32 of them, on this one site and to become the centre of academic medicine at the university. The argument was that the synergy among the different disciplines, with all specialty services on one site, was the way of the future, especially since we were moving to a multidisciplinary approach to teaching and research.

I contended that the Hospital was not large enough and did not have the resources to do this. I believed specialization was the only way we could manage the investment of resources that would permit the Hospital to be internationally competitive. The physicians proposed that Notre-Dame should be a centre engaged in research and teaching in all specialties so that it could attract the best in each discipline, and to be able to achieve the critical mass needed to excel and to ensure the support needed to be in the forefront of medical research. Historically, this was the way the great teaching hospitals of the world had developed and it remained the dream for the physicians of Notre-Dame.

I realized that this issue was the key for my acceptance in the Hospital and that I would not get the required support to pursue my vision, even though I believed it was the only financially feasible solution in the existing context. Pursuing my vision of specialization would only lead to conflict within the medical and academic staff. I had no choice but to accept the vision for an academic health-science centre covering all areas of medical specialties, and I began to plan how this could be implemented. It is this vision that ultimately led me to support the mergers that were proposed a few years later as a way to achieve the resource base needed for this vision to be successful. In theory, there is merit to this approach; however, I learned afterwards, as did many others, that the cost of merger—both human and monetary—is huge. The merger of different teaching hospitals, with different levels of academic achievement and recognition, is very challenging. My argument that persuaded the physicians to accept the merger with two other hospitals, one they considered academically their equal and the other not academically very strong, was that this was the only way to achieve the critical mass needed to become a fully academic teaching hospital covering all the specialty areas. This led to the conclusion by the physicians that the only solution was the construction of a brand new mega-hospital that would excel in every area of academic medicine and be concentrated on one physical site. The collective vision led almost inexorably to this solution.

I am not sure that this is the right approach. I believe that if the appropriate conditions of leadership are present, the goals of academic medicine can be achieved through coordinated specialization, and that the coordination can happen through multiple sites that come under a single jurisdiction. The danger of the mega-hospital is the reduction in access to health care for the population. If the mega-centre is to be pursued, then it should be kept as small as possible while at the same time ensuring that there is a large tertiary (specialized services) community hospital that could provide almost all services to the population at a lower price per case than what is possible at a full teaching hospital. (I will explain later in this chapter how this might be achieved.)

But the immediate issue was my successful integration into Notre-Dame. The whole merger issue would only arise a few years later. My assimilation was much more difficult at Notre-Dame than at Verdun. I was seen as an ambitious administrator interested in innovation and change while the Hospital was conservative and set in its ways. Many people felt that my background in a small community hospital meant that I did not understand the complexities of a major academic centre. In the beginning, there was also certainly some resistance because I came from a different cultural background than the rest of the Hospital, but this never overtly manifested itself and very soon after my arrival it was not an issue.

Shortly after my arrival, the head of Maintenance and Technical Services came to my office to ask me if all was in order and if I needed anything. Notre-Dame was built in 1932 as a Catholic hospital and in my beautifully wood-panelled office there was a crucifix above the door. Knowing that I was Jewish, he asked me if I would like to have the cross removed. I said no immediately, since the cross was part of the hospital and would remain in place long after I was gone. The traditions and history of an organization must be respected and maintained, and the pride of an organization very often comes from its origins.

Winning My Place in the Hospital

My experience at Verdun served me well and I applied the same approach at Notre-Dame. I spent the first months getting to know and meeting the different groups and key players in the organization. Although my style was very different from the past CEO, I learned that as long as I was prudent with my comments and new ideas, and respected the formal lines of communication and the decision-making process, I was able to implement my new style of management. This adaptation on my part allowed for the subtle changes in culture that can occur over time but are resisted when they are introduced too rapidly.

Looking for Winners

As at Verdun, looking for winners was part of the strategy and, here, medical equipment was high on the list. The Division of Cardiology was strong, dynamic, and in competition with the Institute of Cardiology as the centre for academic cardiology in Montreal. They needed a new catheterization lab to do work in the field of cardiac stents, which at the time was the new non-invasive technology to repair blocked arteries without open-heart surgery. I supported their project immediately.

Government approval for a new lab was needed, as well as a financial plan. Radiology was asking for an MRI (magnetic resonance imaging) suite, which was essential for an academic hospital the size of Notre-Dame. Both projects were launched and led to the choosing of a new director of the foundation to help myself and the departments raise the funds for these projects.

The other winner was the establishment of a Communications Department that would guide internal communications and foster the Hospital's external presence. Almost immediately, all parts of the organization were provided with information they had never had before, and this resulted in a much greater sense of participation. Externally, meetings were held with the various journalists responsible for health issues; a team of physicians was chosen as spokespersons for the Hospital to answer the journalists' questions. The new VP communications became a very well-known and well-liked person in the Hospital and at times was even called The Confessor because the physicians, directors, Board and some of the staff liked to "confess" their problems to him, such as projects and issues affecting their work. One of my major mandates from the Board was to increase the public profile of the Hospital and this was done through a presence in the media both locally and nationally. The Hospital developed a strategy of communicating regularly with the media and being available to comment on health care issues. We began to measure the number of publications and the number of times the Hospital appeared positively in the media. As our successes increased and there was greater recognition of the Hospital in the media, acceptance of my leadership grew among staff and key players in the organization.

Becoming a Leader in a Complex Organization

I had never analyzed the process by which a new CEO was integrated into his or her organization, I just moved forward with what seemed right at the time. I got to know the hospital, the key players, spent the first months looking for the strengths and weaknesses, and whether there was a vision for the organization. I then planned a strategy based on these findings, all the while keeping in mind the attributes of leadership that I had learned. After I had been at Notre-Dame for six months I had a meeting with Ann Langley and Jean-Louis Denis, professors in health administration at the

Université du Québec à Montréal (UQAM) and the Université de Montréal respectively. They asked if they could do a case study on the integration of a new CEO into a complex organization. They would follow me for a period of time and carry out interviews with physicians, staff, and Board members as they attempted to develop a model that would describe the process. I was hesitant at first; the project would involve a degree of personal exposure for which I was not ready, and I did not know how the Hospital would receive the idea. I consulted both the physicians and the Board chair and they felt it was appropriate to go ahead since the hospital was an academic centre. I agreed to the proposed project and the article reporting its results appeared in the journal *Gestion.*

More than 15 years later, as I reread the article describing my first 18 months at Notre-Dame, I can see the process of integration much more clearly. A new CEO is either assimilated into the organization, transforms it, functions in parallel with it, or reaches a compromise. I realized quite quickly that if I wanted some of my ideas to be incorporated, I would have to find a way to seek out a compromise with the Hospital. As I've mentioned, the Hospital had very strong constellations of authority and a very clear vision of its future. I wanted to introduce a new style of management, open the organization to the outside world and introduce changes that would prepare the Hospital to manage the financial constraints and quality measures that I believed were coming.

New Initiatives | Board Committees

After getting to know the organization and testing its capacity to respond to changes and new ideas, I began to introduce a series of new initiatives. I remained convinced that the Board was an important tool and created Board committees to look at different aspects of the Hospital. We created the following committees: Finance and Auditing, Quality, Construction and Equipment Acquisition, Human Resources, and Planning. This allowed for greater participation of Board members but also shifted the influence of power. Members of senior management would be more present at Board committees that they were responsible to manage and ensure a greater circulation of information. This removed authority from a small group, the traditional executive of a board, and distributed decision-making to a larger community through Board committees, thus encouraging greater discussion of issues.

Changing Managerial Culture

The next effort was to change management practice and focus managerial culture on continual quality improvement. This move met with a great deal of resistance. Management already considered itself efficient and they interpreted my focus on quality as a case of the CEO not recognizing the quality that already existed because he did not know the Hospital well enough. I introduced a management-training program whereby managers themselves became trainers of other managers. I led training sessions for physicians to demonstrate my commitment to this approach to management. It was clear that I was touching a very sensitive chord in the Hospital and the program of continual quality improvement evolved into a program of re-engineering that was more adaptable to the vision that management had of itself.

Re-engineering in a hospital meant creating multidisciplinary teams that included physicians, nurses, professionals, and non-professional staff to look at ways of improving the performance and quality of specific programs or services in the Hospital. But it takes years to influence the culture of a large organization and the way things are done. The previous CEO had been in place for 10 years and the existing culture was entrenched. Slowly, however, the quality approach to management was becoming part of daily life and, in my opinion, the Hospital was on the right track. Unfortunately, three years into this change of direction discussions began about the merger of Notre-Dame with two other hospitals, and the focus of management energy shifted to dealing with the merger and its consequences. The merger took up so much energy just in trying to cope with the new discussions on merging and its consequences that the managerial culture I was trying to instill was no longer a priority and it was pushed aside. The turmoil the merger caused did not allow this new managerial culture of continual quality improvement to evolve as fully as I had hoped.

Changing the Office of the CEO

I added a series of positions to the CEO's office: a position responsible for quality control, an internal auditor, and an assistant to the CEO responsible for new initiatives, in addition to the new director of communications and public affairs. Once again, there was resistance because directors saw these actions as removing them from the CEO's circle of influence. It took some time before they realized how they could use these professionals to support their activities. There is a warning here for CEOs not to surround themselves with an inner circle and make senior management or the physicians feel there is a barrier between themselves and the CEO. The strengthening of the CEO's office allowed for the germination and refinement of ideas and I chose people who already favoured this approach due to their personalities and their interests.

Ambulatory Services

I took a special interest in promoting a new, strengthened focus on ambulatory services for the Hospital. At Notre-Dame this was applied not only to surgical services but to all services where patients could be seen, evaluated and treated without being admitted to the hospital and occupying a bed. The physicians felt they were already quite involved in ambulatory activity and at first did not see the need to create a unit specifically dedicated to ambulatory care. I was finally able to persuade the medical staff that this was the right approach, based on results of such moves elsewhere, especially in the United States, and I was able to demonstrate the savings such an approach would have for the Hospital's finances. I encouraged innovation in new ambulatory activity and the physicians came to see this as a challenge and opportunity to develop new technology; they embraced the idea with much enthusiasm as this was seen as an important component of an academic health-science centre.

The Board approved the design of a new ambulatory centre to be built adjacent to the existing physical plant. This project disappeared with the announcement of the merger of Notre-Dame with two other hospitals in Montreal and, through a multitude of political manoeuvres among the players in the new merged hospital, the ambulatory centre has not yet seen the light of day. It is now 20 years since the first project was put on the table in 1994.

The process of integration was certainly one of compromise, as I had bought into the academic vision that the physicians were supporting while trying to change the managerial culture of the Hospital and introduce innovation into a conservative milieu. I was redistributing the power from a small group to a much wider group of key players, thus ensuring broader participation.

Within three years, by 1995, I had firmly established my position in the Hospital and gained the full confidence of the organization.

New Technology

There is probably no field other than medicine where so much work is being done to develop new understanding, new techniques, new equipment and new technology. Health care is growing more costly not because people are getting sicker but because they are getting better. Pharmaceutical companies are driven to discover, design and produce new medication to better treat known problems more effectively, as well as responding to new issues as they arise. The new strains of antibiotic-resistant bacteria are a good example and it is literally a race between the pharmaceutical companies and Nature to see who will win the day.

Some of the latest figures indicate that to bring a new drug to market with full approval takes about 12 years and costs about $800 million U.S. in today's dollars. This cost is being transferred to our health care systems. Diagnostic tools to look inside the body are regularly being discovered, refined and upgraded, and the pressure to use the new technology is enormous. New technology, however, does not always have to be an add-on cost; it can sometimes save a great deal of money.

At Notre-Dame, the move to ambulatory medicine was well underway and we were looking at new ways of reducing length of stay in the Hospital when an unexpected event occurred that demonstrated how useful this new technology could be. I was working in the garden, pulling out weeds, when I cut my elbow on a piece of glass buried in the soil. I washed the cut but after a few days my elbow was sore and the wound was infected. I went to the emergency room at Notre-Dame for treatment. They took a sample and I was given antibiotics. The wound healed on the outside but the elbow was still sore. A few days later, I was with the head of Medicine to whom I mentioned the soreness in my arm. He then noticed that the infection was producing a reddish path up to my shoulder. I was hospitalized immediately and was told the infection had become systemic, and after moving up the arm it would spread to the whole body. If not stopped immediately, my life would be in danger.

I was more frightened than I had ever been and very soon the whole Hospital knew what was happening. The specialist from Microbiology came to see me, took some samples and put me on massive antibiotic intravenous treatment. Since the results of the test would not be available for a couple of days, they were concerned whether or not they had used the right antibiotic, as time was critical, and I am allergic to penicillin. I would have to wait 48 hours before I knew if the treatment was working. My wife and I watched the red path moving up my arm. Everyone was nervous as it reached my shoulder by the following morning; the nurses were monitoring me constantly. After 36 hours, there was no further advance of the infection and we felt enormous relief when the doctor said he felt that the infection was responding well to the treatment.

After three days, he was sure the treatment was working and I was then told that I would need antibiotic intravenous therapy for 21 days. I was already restless and wanted to get back to work, so I was put on a program of therapy that allowed for one hour of intravenous therapy every seven hours. I would be able to work in my office downstairs but I knew I would be taking up a bed and sleeping in the Hospital for the next three weeks. My microbiologist saw my frustration and asked me if I would like to experiment with a new ambulatory pump that the Hospital was testing to see if it could be used as part of the ambulatory program.

This is a pump that you wear around your waist and you are permanently connected to a sack of antibiotic medication being continuously pumped into the body through a shunt placed in your arm. The bag had to be changed every 24 hours, which meant coming to the clinic once a day for a replacement. This meant I would free up a bed in the Hospital and be able to work and to go home as I would normally do. I accepted and went through the training. I learned about all the connections, how to read and program the rates of flow, and what to do when the alarms went off. It all sounded complicated, but in the end it was quite simple and straightforward.

I learned how to take a shower with the pump hung on the shower-curtain rod and how one sleeps at night by hanging the pump on a hook in the wall over your bed. Everybody saw me walking around the Hospital with the pump and I was the best salesperson for the program. Eighteen days of hospitalization were saved. The pumps cost $5,000 each but it was clear to me that the program was worthwhile not only for the savings to the Hospital, but more so for the patient who could return to a normal life while still under absolutely essential medical treatment. These tests led to a full-blown program at Notre-Dame and many patients have benefited.

The University

Notre-Dame was my first opportunity to enter the world of academic medicine, a world that was filled with tradition, with high expectations for success, and with people seeking prestige, recognition and excellence. It is a complicated, highly political world that is as difficult to manage as any hospital. I learned very quickly that the university and the faculty of medicine have a vested interest in the Hospital and in all decisions that might affect their objectives. About 40 percent of the research in a university derives from the faculty of medicine. There are 16 faculties of medicine in Canada and each has one or more affiliated teaching hospital.

A CEO in an academic hospital must develop a strong relationship with the dean of the faculty of medicine and the principal of the university. A consensus has to be reached as to the vision and direction the faculty and the hospital are taking. Both the CEO of the hospital and the dean of the faculty of medicine must have confidence and trust in each other in order to avoid the situation whereby the physicians could easily play one off against the other to achieve their objectives. This relationship of trust and mutual benefit depends very much on the personalities of the players, as well as the number of teaching hospitals within the university. The Université de Montréal included five major teaching hospitals and two community teaching hospitals. Notre-Dame was the largest, with the greatest number of professors, programs and residents. The relationship among the hospitals was competitive and the dean was often caught in the middle, trying to arbitrate among the players. Cliques and alliances formed and much energy was expended in this competition for professors, resources and programs. This sometimes led to all-out conflict among the competing hospitals, and long-standing animosities grew up among the medical staff. Each hospital wanted to be a leader in their particular specialty and often two hospitals were trying to excel in the same area. The support of the university was crucial to the success of the hospitals' efforts, and strong, decisive deans were important to this exercise.

The Role of Government in Health Care Delivery

Health care is a provincial-government responsibility in Canada. Close to 45 percent of all our provincial taxes are spent on health care. Seventy percent of health care expenditure is publicly funded, for those services covered by the public Medicare system, and 30 percent is funded by individual spending, either out of pocket or through an employer or private insurance plan. Initially, the public system covered all physician expenses and all services offered in hospitals and other health care institutions. If you are hospitalized and need medication, it is paid for by the hospital. Once you are discharged and need to continue the medication, you have to pay for it out of your own pocket. This artificial distinction is part of the Canadian health care system and most provinces have developed additional programs, such as home care, community clinics, medication-insurance programs, to name but a few. Since provincial governments spend so much of their budget on health, and since this percentage is increasing each year, financing the system is of major public and political concern, and I will look at this issue in detail in later chapters. For now, I would like to concentrate on how the system is currently managed.

At Verdun, I was not aware of the extent of government involvement in health care management but I became much more aware through my experiences at Notre-Dame. Politicians are elected in local ridings and are always looking for ways to invest in their riding. Health care is always on everybody's mind and most ridings have a hospital, clinic, CLSC, nursing home or other health service nearby. Investment in new buildings, new equipment, new programs and new services is an important way in which ministers and local deputies gain recognition for their efforts.

Since health care uses up such a large part of the provincial budget and all requests for development and growth in health care have a political impact, many decisions are made not in relation to the needs of the population but for political needs and interests. Hospitals put pressure on elected officials to block projects from competing hospitals and, through their associations, different categories of institutions politically block projects when they do not want to lose jurisdiction or authority in certain areas. The CLSCs in Quebec argued against the "Hospital in the Home" project at Verdun because they did not want the hospital sector involved in home care. One hospital lobbied government to prevent a new catheterization lab for a rival hospital because they did not want to lose their control of the specialty.

An example of this type of non-constructive activity occurred while I was at Notre-Dame and I believe it had serious consequences for me. Notre-Dame covered almost all of the very high-end, complicated aspects of acute medicine. We were doing most of the organ transplants in Montreal, with the exception of lung transplants, which were done at the Montreal General Hospital. The total number of lung transplants for Quebec, or any province for that matter, is very limited and they tend to be concentrated in one teaching hospital, if the province does them at all. There are very few surgeons prepared for or capable of undertaking these extremely complicated cases, and the pre-operative work and post-operative care are extensive.

The Montreal General was beginning to have problems with their program, and the success rate was below what was normally expected. The surgeons doing the transplants at Notre-Dame very slowly and prudently began to do a number of cases. The program at the General continued to deteriorate and, in my discussions with the CEO of the Hospital, a decision was made to transfer the program to Notre-Dame, with the funds per case to support the program. The regional board and the minister were involved in the file from the beginning and were well aware of these discussions. I was very vigilant to ensure that all the quality-control measures were in place and that the cases attempted were medically appropriate, with a reasonable chance of success. The decision was also a logical one, on the grounds that in cases where both a heart and a lung are transplanted at the same time, the transplants should take place in a hospital that can do both.

The largest number of lung-transplant cases comes from the areas of densest population, which is the Montreal area. A maison des greffes (transplant hospice) was established close to the Hospital, where out-of-town patients and their families could wait until a lung became available.

The program had been running for about 10 months and was

showing a very acceptable success rate when I received a call from the office of the minister of health to come to Quebec City for a meeting with the minister. I was told that the CEO of the regional council was also invited. He was a good friend and we drove to Quebec together, not knowing the subject of the meeting.

The minister told us that he had decided to transfer the lung-transplant program from Montreal to Quebec City and that they would be done at a small hospital that specialized in heart and lung diseases. We were both stunned and could not understand what was happening. The vast majority of cases came from Montreal. There were surgeons in Montreal who had the competency to do the work, while at the Laval Hospital in Quebec City—indeed, in all of the rest of Quebec—there were no physicians trained to do lung transplants. We gave every argument possible to explain why this was not a good idea and how there would be a very negative response from the population, the physicians, the hospitals in Montreal, and the media, as there was no logic or rationale for this move from Montreal, where there was proven capacity, to Quebec City, where there was not the required expertise to do the procedures. The minister was firm in his position and we drove back to Montreal not believing what we had just been told. We found out later that the minister was also the minister for the region of Quebec City and his regional responsibility was to see to the development of his region. We also found out later that the CEO of the Laval Hospital in Quebec was a good friend of the minister's.

The minister scheduled a meeting in Montreal to make the official announcement to the hospitals and to the public. As predicted, the response from all was extremely negative and the minister was criticized for the decision. This was a difficult time for me, as I truly believed this was the wrong move for health care and services to patients needing lung transplants. Patients have to be near the hospital—sometimes for a long period of time—while they are waiting for a lung to become available. This would mean the majority of patients and their families would have to move to Quebec City, when most of the patients came from the Montreal area. This kind of transplantation requires specialized expertise and, although Notre-Dame was already doing a lot of transplants and research into anti-rejection medication, it had taken Notre-Dame about 12 months to be comfortable and successful with the program.

At a meeting with journalists present, I expressed my concerns—not realizing at that time that I was breaking one of the cardinal rules of a CEO in a provincial health care system: Never publicly criticize the hand that feeds you. A CEO is responsible for obtaining resources for the hospital and functioning as the interface between the hospital and the external environment. It is not recommended that a CEO of a major teaching hospital criticize a minister's decision. I was so caught up in the file and the media was in such frenzy over the issue that, although it had not been my intention, journalists quickly picked up my comments. I was not able to sleep that entire night because I was concerned about the next day's headlines. After my position became public, I sensed a tension in my relations with the minister's cabinet, even though my predictions of the consequences of the minister's decision came to pass.

From the start, the projected move had problems and the media criticism did not abate. The media had a field day when it became known that there were no surgeons in Quebec City capable of performing the operation and that the Hospital and the minister were trying to recruit surgeons from Toronto to come to Quebec City when there were surgeons in Montreal capable of doing the transplants. In the end, the program never left Notre-Dame and was never transferred to Quebec City. But I had learned an important lesson!

There are many much less spectacular examples of political involvement in the administration of health care and they occur throughout Canada in every province. The question I have been asking myself is whether the direct administration of health care should be at arm's length from government. Governments must be responsible for the basket of services covered, as well as the level of funding they are prepared to invest. They must also be responsible for monitoring the quality and efficiency of the system but I believe that if the administration of the system were given to a public agency, the system would be better planned and better managed. There would be less local lobbying and the decisions taken would be in line with the health needs of the different communities and their population. I believe that the health system should be population-based, with territorial-based responsibilities given to a health care organization capable of providing the majority of primary and secondary services required by both health and social needs. This idea was part of the work I was able to do later as junior minister of health in Quebec and it became a reality in 2005 with the implementation of the territorial-based Centre de santé et de services sociaux (CSSS) system.

A Forced Merger and a Strategic Retreat

In 1990, the Government of Quebec brought in legislation to define and award status to teaching hospitals in Quebec. There were 44 health organizations in Quebec that claimed to be teaching institutions, and the government and the universities felt it was time to put a framework and specific criteria into place that would better define what a teaching institution actually was. Nineteen criteria were established to define a university teaching hospital or institute.

It was this new approach to naming official teaching hospitals that defined Notre-Dame's strategic plan of 1990 and the plan I was to put into place. The competition among the hospitals was becoming much more intense due to this labelling exercise and it was clear that all the hospitals wanted to be full teaching institutions and not just affiliated teaching hospitals.

Notre-Dame believed, with the support of the dean of medicine, that it was clearly destined to be designated the official university hospital and chose a vision that would develop all specialty programs, instead of concentrating their energy on areas of excellence. The dynamic among the five hospitals of the Université de Montréal (Notre-Dame, Hôtel-Dieu, Saint-Luc, Sacré-Coeur and Maisonneuve-Rosemont) was not good, and the faculty of medicine decided to hire a consultant to carry out a planning exercise that would look at the possible solutions.

I remember sitting around a table with the other teaching hospitals and the dean of medicine, listening to the recommendations of the consultant. The first was the merger of Notre-Dame and Hôtel-Dieu on the existing site of Notre-Dame, with the building of a new ambulatory centre. This was a proposal I had strongly supported since both hospitals were already academic with a strong research base. This new hospital would be designated CHU (Centre hospitalier Universitaire). The second recommendation was an affiliation of Maisonneuve-Rosemont and Saint-Luc on their respective sites, sharing the academic programs and also designated a CHU. Sacré-Coeur would be designated an affiliated teaching hospital. There were other com-binations possible but I believed that the merger of Notre-Dame and Hôtel-Dieu on one campus would provide the critical mass needed to develop a teaching hospital covering all the specialties. The other advantage was that this could be done quickly. The volume of activities, as well as emergency coverage, would be maintained and access for the population would be assured. The space was available on the Notre-Dame campus and the construction could be done for around $500 million.

Hôtel-Dieu rejected the idea because they felt it would be a take-over by Notre-Dame, what with the new hospital being located on the Notre-Dame campus. And Saint-Luc refused as well, saying it was totally unacceptable for them to lose some of the programs they currently had since they might end up only an affiliated hospital. The dean was not strong enough to impose his will and the exercise ended in total failure. During this time, McGill University realized the need to merge in order to achieve the required critical mass and, with the strong, almost directive leadership of the dean of the faculty of medicine, it was able to achieve the desired objective. McGill suc-ceeded in getting the two rival hospitals, the Montreal General and the Royal Victoria, to merge by recommending building a brand new mega-hospital that would cover all specialties. This way, they avoided the difficult discussion about who would get which service, who would be seen as the winner and who the loser. The Montreal Children's Hospital was to be included in the merger, as well as the Montreal Chest Hospital and the Montreal Neurological Institute, and the plan also included the new building of the privately owned Shriners Hospital on the new campus.

Because of the inability of the francophone teaching hospitals to define a clear direction for themselves, and the indecision of the faculty of medicine, the government imposed the merger of Notre-Dame, Saint-Luc and Hôtel-Dieu. This imposition was a political solution influenced by Hôtel-Dieu and Saint-Luc. The intention was that Hôtel-Dieu would not feel it was being taken over by Notre-Dame, it would have the support of Saint-Luc in the power struggle that would evolve, and Saint-Luc would be assured it would be part of the full teaching hospital and not be left out as only an affiliated teaching hospital. Mr. Guy Coulombe, a very well- known and respected civil servant, was chosen to facilitate the merger and get the parties to agree. I had clearly supported the idea of a merger between Hôtel-Dieu and Notre-Dame on one campus, bringing together two hospitals with the same level of excellence. I projected a budget of about $500 million for new construction to provide the beds and ambulatory space needed for a modern hospital. This could have been achieved in a five-year period, with all the objectives of academic medicine being respected. The compromise solution, for political reasons, was to begin a 20-year saga that the province hopes will be partially completed by 2016 and fully completed in 2019 at a cost of over $2.5 billion, more than two and a half times the original projected cost of $800 million.

The first meeting of the Board of the new Centre hospitalier de l'Université de Montreal (CHUM) was held on October 16, 1996. It was clear from the very beginning that Hôtel-Dieu and Saint-Luc would combine their forces on the Board to ensure that Notre-Dame did not take a leadership role. To this end, the Board decided to open the search to outside candidates and I realized that I would not be chosen as the CEO.

In my opinion, a fundamental error was made in the designation of the Board. The government appointed a Board divided evenly among the three merging hospitals. The three chairs of the existing hospitals were also appointed as Board members and the lines of battle were drawn. In a newly merged hospital, the board should be made up of mostly new members who have not been on the previous boards. This was the case later in Ottawa, with the creation of the Ottawa Hospital, where the Board chosen by the government to manage the affairs of the Hospital came from well-known representatives of the business, government, financial and judicial spheres, and from the community.

As was also the case in Ottawa, the chairman should be appointed by the government for his or her proven ability and competence in running large, complex organizations because the role at the beginning of a merger, before the new CEO is appointed, is crucial to the success of the merger.

I was truly disappointed at the time that I was not chosen as CEO because I felt I had the leadership skills to succeed in a merger this multifaceted, and because I understood the physicians, the university and the needs of academic medicine. But I realize now, especially after merging the five hospitals in Ottawa and closing two of them, that choosing a CEO from one of the campuses in an imposed merger that is resisted by many of the players is the wrong way to go. Rather, the choice should be a strong, new leader with a solid track record in managing hospitals. A new merged hospital requires a person with a great deal of experience in managing a professional bureaucracy in which the authority of the CEO comes from the credibility he or she can acquire from the professionals in the organization. Physicians who are paid separately by the government and not by the hospital, and who have their license to practice from the College of Physicians (the professional medical body that confers legal certification), are not under the authority of the CEO. Choosing a CEO who had never been in a hospital management position and had no experience in health care or academic medicine or in working with physicians was a recipe for failure, and one must ask what the objectives of the selection committee actually were. The CEO who was chosen to run Quebec's largest hospital had no hospital experience and was removed two years later. But the damage to the organization and to its employees and staff was already done. The single most important job of the Board is to select the CEO and in this case the Board made a major error.

Following this, a series of interim CEOs were appointed and it was not until 2002 that a permanent CEO was chosen. He was removed by the government in 2008 and a new CEO was chosen, who was subsequently removed for political reasons in 2013. The merger began a 20-year saga with five CEOs, three of whom were removed from their position by the government.

As a result of the 1990 legislation to designate teaching hospitals and affiliate hospitals, by 1995 there was tremendous upheaval in the entire Quebec health care system and the jockeying for power and influence was most strongly evidenced in Montreal.

The story of the CHUM is a fascinating one, and I was involved for the next 15 years, in a variety of ways, in the evolution of the Hospital. When I was CEO of the Ottawa Hospital in 1998, the minister of health of Quebec asked for my advice on the evolution of the CHUM. Later, as junior minister of health in Quebec, I was responsible for the file on the teaching hospitals. Between 2002 and 2012, as president and CEO of the Montreal Health and Social Services Agency, I was responsible for all health care activity, including the teaching hospitals in Montreal.

I was managing the merger at the Ottawa Hospital when I was asked to comment on a proposition to merge all the services of Hôtel-Dieu, Saint-Luc and Notre-Dame on one campus. By 1998, Pauline Marois, then minister of health and social services, was looking at the option of regrouping all services in one large organi-zation on a single site, to compete with the proposition of the anglophone McGill hospitals. The McGill hospitals had chosen this route as a way to gain support for the merging of the Montreal General, the Royal Victoria Hospital, the Montreal Children's Hospital, the Montreal Neurological Institute, and the Montreal Chest Institute.

The hardest thing to do in an academic merger is to achieve con-sensus regarding which specialty programs will be located on which site. Each hospital wants to handle the program they feel they are best in, but as these teaching hospitals are always in competition with each other, it is very difficult to arrive at a plan that satisfies all the players. At the time, the CHUM in Montreal was managing over 1,000 beds among the three hospitals, and putting all activities together on one site would be quite a challenge. I supported the idea of a new site, given the decision to merge the three hospitals, instead of just Notre-Dame and Hôtel-Dieu. But I believed that not all services should be on one site, and that there should be a secondary site with a community hospital with 400 beds and a large, busy emergency room, and also a tertiary site with 600 beds and a small speciality emergency room to which other hospitals would refer cases. Both of these proposed sites would be academic, to cover the needs of specialty and family physicians, while maintaining research and teaching at the highest level. These were the same arguments that I presented to the McGill Hospital and the CHUM when I became Junior Minister of Health in Quebec. The McGill Hospital decided to use two campuses for the delivery of care: the Montreal General, with more of a trauma and surgical focus, and the new construction at the Glen site for the more medical campus, to include the Montreal Children's and the Neurological Institute. The CHUM, instead of choosing a two-site model, decided to give up 300 of its academic beds to be able to have 700 beds all on one site.

The mega-hospitals file remains one of the most complex and expensive projects ever undertaken in health care and it is taking place at a time when there is consensus to develop primary care and move away from a hospital-centred model of care. Once the construction is finished, the real issue will be how to control the pressure to expand curative services and pay the greatly increased operating cost of running two such mega-hospitals.

There are moments in a health care system when major changes can occur that will reorient the system and allow it to better respond to the emerging needs of the population. Quebec's own commissions (the Rochon Commission and the Clair Commission) both recommended realignment of our health care system through the development of a strong community-based family-practice service. The opportunity arose to make the investments required for this change and redirect an existing hospital curative system to a more population-based system focused on chronic-care management, management of elder health care, mental health issues in the population, public health and increased accessibility, without diminishing the curative-care capacity of the system. Instead, government chose to invest massively in hospital buildings and services with no investment in any primary-care infrastructure. We have opted for major investment with ongoing debt cost, but with no added advantage for the population or the health care services they are being offered. Was it lack of understanding of the issues by the government? Political pressure from the vested interest groups, such as the universities and physicians? Or business interests wanting to support massive building projects? Competition between the Anglophone and Francophone communities? Prestige or the desire to build monuments? Or all of these? It is hard to say, but the consequences are that Quebec will maintain an existing, inefficient, hospital-centred system that is not responding to the overall needs of the population.

Lessons I Learned

This first experience in an academic health-science centre taught me many new lessons. These were sometimes hard lessons that helped me subsequently to put together a merger that is considered one of the most complicated ever to take place in Canada, and to understand and manage effectively in the academic hospital environment.

Academic physicians have very strong egos and, at a certain point, once their careers are established and they have international recognition, they can become a group apart that has a great deal of influence with their university and the research community. I learned also that the most political physicians are rarely the most academic and, though they enjoy teaching, they are not scientists. They enjoy power and recognition in their organization and they are involved in helping the more academic physicians expand and develop. They have very strong personalities and enjoy being respected and sought after. Their concern and dedication for their hospital is very real and a CEO must learn how to work well with this group, who are often very active clinically and concerned about issues of volume and clinical activity.

An academic medical institution needs to grow continually if it is to keep up with other academic institutions at home and internationally. This means looking to acquire the most modern technology, the latest procedures, the newest treatments, and having as many people as possible be involved in as many clinical trials as possible. A CEO in this environment must make choices with the limited resources available and the need to have the physicians as satisfied as possible.

I learned that decisions must always be patient-centred and they should work to improve the quality of patient care. This is the strongest argument for the board and will win good support from the foundation. Academic concerns come next in a teaching hospital, followed by the cost considerations, which must be reasonable and manageable. This balanced approach is a good guideline when it is necessary to choose between competing programs.

The rivalry among different departments for resources, students and status must be managed well in an academic hospital centre. The rivalry among competing hospitals can be very vicious, and good political connections are often more important than logical and rational arguments.

Changing the culture in a hospital begins at the top, which is often the hardest change to implement. Each director feels they are CEO in their own area, and if they have been there for a while they are reluctant to change because they feel they are admitting to not having done the right things in the past. It's important for academic hospital CEOs to respect these concerns, go slowly, show the benefits, and if in the end this does not work, it might be time for a change of directors.

In every hospital there are people who I like to think of as hidden jewels. They are loved by the organization, respected by all, aware of what is happening among the staff and physicians, and are very important allies for the CEO.

My experience at Notre-Dame certainly taught me to never be surprised by the extent of political involvement in health care, or by the many bad decisions that are made through ignorance or not listening to knowledgeable advisors. Governments always want to be re-elected and in Quebec this occurs riding by riding. This can lead to decisions linked to the most powerful politicians rather than to the wisest course of action. It is important to be aware, however, of how far one is prepared to go in terms of public criticism of a political decision. Since a CEO is responsible for many issues, as well as for the staff of his or her organization, it is not usually desirable to engage in such public criticism. At the end of the day, whatever the issue, accept losing the battle if it helps to keep your organization moving forward.

Mergers are useful and allow for certain economies and the development of the critical mass that is often needed to improve quality and services. But mergers must be done well, with appropriate upfront investment. Board and CEO leadership are the most important factors in a successful merger, and errors here can have negative consequences for thousands of staff, for quality of care, and in the cost of operations for many years.

CHAPTER FIVE

Quebec's Delegate General in New York

An Interesting Consolation Prize

DURING THE SELECTION PROCESS for CEO of the CHUM, the Government of Quebec had offered me the position of delegate general in New York City, Quebec's second-largest delegation abroad, after Paris. It was an honour to be chosen as Quebec's representative but it was also an elegant way for me to take my leave from the merged hospital. When I first brought home the idea of going to live in New York, my family was quite taken aback. My son was 18 and my twin daughters 15; they would have to leave their friends and their school. My wife was a CEGEP professor and she would have to take a sabbatical. We discussed this at length and, in the end, the family was ready for an adventure. I went to New York at the beginning of 1997 to look for a place to live as the current delegate had a few months left in his mandate, and the apartment that belonged to the Government of Quebec in the Museum of Modern Art Tower was not large enough for a family with three kids. The idea was to rent a place for our stay in New York that would serve as the delegate's residence. It had to be large enough for receptions and to accommodate the delegate general's full-time chef. The chef was always a student or past student from Montreal's Institut de tourisme et d'hotellerie du Québec, and the Quebec delegation had a reputation for having one of the finest chefs of all the consulates in New York.

We found a beautiful apartment in a newly renovated, prestigious old building on the Upper West Side, at 86th Street and Broadway. It included a one-room rooftop studio with easy access to the apartment. The furniture from our home in Montreal would fill about half the apartment, but we needed new living-room and dining-room furniture. The space was then filled with Quebec art from the Musée national des beaux-arts du Québec in Quebec City, and when my family arrived they felt like they were living in a palace. We could seat 18 in the dining room, where we held many receptions for diplomats,

Quebec artists hoping to advance their careers, and Quebec ministers who were holding meetings with industry, municipal and state leaders. Our daughters were enrolled in excellent high schools and our son entered New York University. My wife was a gracious hostess and became very involved in the activities of the delegation.

I was well known in Quebec and had worked with each of my hospitals to gain respect, and I had a certain media presence in the health care community. In New York, one becomes completely anonymous. I kept receiving mail addressed to "David Levine" that was nevertheless not mine, and after this had happened a number of times I went to the building management office to find out what the trouble was. They informed me that there were four David Levines living in the building and problems arose when the apartment number was not indicated on the mail. There is both a comfort and frustration in anonymity, and I began to realize how important being recognized can be to one's sense of self. I later learned how important this is for politicians—being recognized is one of the very important attributes of a political career.

Learning to be a Diplomat

Quebec had made the decision many years earlier to maintain a presence in a number of countries around the word to support trade and immigration. As a province, Quebec has no legal status in other countries. The close relations between Quebec and France has allowed Quebec to maintain a large delegation in Paris that has been given full diplomatic status by the French government, with the privileges that go along with this status for the head of the delegation and the employees. In other countries, however, no official status is given to Quebec or any of the other provinces, and the delegations or trade offices have no official government link except as extensions of the Canadian embassies in that country.

The role of Quebec's delegation can be compared to that of consulates established by embassies in the major cities of the countries where they are based. The consulates engage in more diverse trade and immigration issues, and they make contact with local, city and state politicians and leaders. Connecting with the other consuls in their jurisdiction is also part of the mandate.

New York City has the largest number of consulates in the world, representing virtually every country, so there were many contacts for Quebec's delegate general to make. Building relations is one of the most important roles of the delegate and this is done through many different approaches. I would invite the consul general of Australia to lunch at the apartment and get to know the person and some of the interests and concerns of their country. We might then get together with our wives for a concert featuring a Québécois artist who had been invited to perform in New York. A reciprocal invitation would cement the relationship and a new contact would be made.

Along with making contacts, the delegation was responsible for organizing activities and events to make New Yorkers more aware of Quebec's presence in order to stimulate tourism, trade and immigration. We would help companies look for new markets, seek out investment of American companies in Quebec, and promote Quebec culture.

Quebec's culture is its biggest selling point and many activities were organized for well-known Quebec modern-dance groups, the symphony orchestra, the Cirque du Soleil, and artists and performers such as Robert Lepage. We held receptions for the artists, invited the media and promoters, and created as much of a happening as possible. It's not an easy task because there is always a great deal of activity in New York and the competition for attention is ferocious. Fortunately, however, Quebec has developed such a strong reputation and is so recognized for its cultural achievements that our activities were always well received and very well attended.

Managing the Delegation

I was 48 years old when I arrived at the delegation and this was clearly not the career path I had chosen. I did not know at the time that there were other reasons why I had been sent to New York by the Quebec government, nor that things would develop in the way they did concerning my future career. But I was still the administrator I had always been, and my approach to managing the delegation was the same as managing a hospital or any other organization. I set up a management committee of my directors and we met each week, developing a common vision with a series of objectives for each department. I met regularly with each department to discuss their plans, strategy and activities to achieve their objective. I was far more hands-on than previous delegates, but I made sure not to take away the authority or the initiative of my staff. Let us say they were not used to this style of management of a delegation, but with time they began to really feel they were a strong team that had good support from their leader.

During a discussion with the economic development team, the New York food fairs were mentioned. The James Beard Society is an important gourmet food organization in the city and in their facilities gastronomic evenings are organized to showcase chefs, new cookbooks, and other food or wine products. We organized a gastronomic evening with the James Beard Foundation at which the chef and his team from the Casino de Montréal provided a meal for 75 invited guests, including food journalists from all media, tourism agencies, local politicians, consuls general, and artists. The food was made with Quebec products but the creativity of the chef and his team were the real sensation. Media coverage was excellent and this initiative helped promote both the Casino and Quebec tourism in general.

New York has food carts on street corners throughout the city. I was walking to work one day when I noticed a slogan on the side of one of the carts: "We Answer to a Higher Order." This was in reference to the kosher hot dogs they were selling. This reminded me that New York has the largest Jewish population outside of Israel. "Kosher" has the image of being cleaner or safer, although I imagine there is no solid basis for this belief; it is used as an advertising tool. I began to think of Quebec products and the idea of putting kosher labels on those products that could be considered as such. Coke puts a kosher sticker on its bottles and this is done through an accreditation body that evaluates the manufacturing plant, the work process and the ingredients of the product. For Coke, the ingredients are not a problem but their manufacturing process has to meet certain required conditions as well. As I pondered this, maple syrup came to mind and I reasoned that if we could get a kosher label put on our maple syrup there would be a larger market in New York and probably elsewhere in the U.S.A. I spoke to the team and they proceeded to do the research, contact the kosher labelling agencies, contact the maple syrup associations of Quebec, and start to get kosher labelling. This is an example of the type of work a delegate general can do and, in my opinion, it is very important for the economic, cultural and political development of Quebec.

I was getting more and more involved in my role—yet there was something missing. There was no shortage of excitement or intellectual stimulation in New York and I was certainly not bored since there was always something interesting to do. Still—something was missing.

In February, I received a call from Mike Moga, a headhunter working on the selection for a new CEO for the recently merged Ottawa Hospital. He asked if I would be interested in the job. My first response was no. I had recently arrived in New York, my family was now well settled into the new life, and I knew they would not want to go to Ottawa. He asked if he could fly down and take me out for lunch just to talk about health care and the issues concerning mergers and academic health-science centres. I had no objection to going out to lunch and we met a week later.

The lunch lasted more than a couple of hours and I talked a great deal about health care. After he left, I realized how passionate I still was about health care issues and how much I missed dealing with doctors, nurses, the faculty of medicine and, most of all, hearing about patients. Mike called back in the middle of March asking if I would go to Ottawa to talk to the selection committee about mergers and running a hospital. They would pay all expenses; I thought I could take the opportunity to travel through Montreal and see my mother.

To my surprise, I liked the members of the committee, especially the dean of the faculty of medicine, Dr. Peter Walker, and I really enjoyed explaining hospital strategy. A second interview was organized in April, where I met the newly chosen Board chair for the first time, Nick Mulder. He was a past deputy minister in the federal government and had run several different ministries, including Transport, where he was responsible for the privatization of the airports across Canada. He was then running Stentor Telecom Policy Inc., an alliance of very large communication companies. He was a highly respected, dynamic person and I liked him when we met. By this time, I had finally admitted to myself that I was getting more and more interested in the idea of being CEO of the Hospital, although I had not said a word to anyone about my meetings.

I had a long discussion with the committee concerning my past political activity because I was concerned that this would be an issue and I wanted the committee members to be fully aware of all the facts. The committee asked many questions and it was clear to them that my interests were solely in health care and that I had not been involved in politics for the past 20 years, not since I had been a candidate for the Parti Québécois in the 1979 by-election in Montreal.

After the second interview, I gave a talk to the business community in Rochester, New York. Raymond Chrétien, Canada's ambassador to the U.S.A., was also speaking at the same event. During the lunch, I received a call from the Board offering me the position of CEO of the new Ottawa Hospital. I was asked to think about the offer and call back after the weekend.

My family was opposed to me leaving my position in New York, saying this was a once-in-a-lifetime opportunity and I would be foolish to give it up. I also knew that the response from my friends and colleagues in Quebec would be negative to me moving to Ottawa, and that the Quebec government would not be pleased as they had made a significant investment to move my family to New York. Even my mother thought I was crazy not to finish my mandate in New York.

Another issue came up at the same time and it made my decision that much harder. Bernard Landry, then Quebec's minister of finance, had come to New York on an economic mission and, when we had a moment alone, had asked me if I was interested in being minister of health of Quebec. Lucien Bouchard was the premier of the province at the time; Bernard had discussed the possibility with him, and told me that Bouchard was in agreement. I told Bernard I was not interested in going into politics, yet the idea of being minister of health was tremendously exciting and I kept imagining the possibilities of what I could do.

I did not have an easy weekend and was truly torn. On the one hand, taking the position in Ottawa would have a serious impact on those I loved and cared about. There was also the negative impact of such a choice on people for whom I had great respect. On the other hand, I had a strong desire to use all the skill and knowledge I had gained over the years to try to succeed in a very complex situation and to build a new academic health-science centre.

It was still an issue for me that I had not been given the opportunity to be the CEO of the newly merged CHUM, and the challenge of a career—to see if I could manage a difficult and contentious merger—was something I could not resist. Though my family did not agree with my decision, they understood why I made it. When I called Bernard and Lorraine and explained that I had decided to accept the Ottawa offer, and why, their response was cold and negative. I felt bad, as I admired them both for their commitment to and passion for Quebec, and I felt that I had let them down.

We left New York in June, 1998, and headed to Ottawa. None of us, however, could have expected what would follow.

[CHAPTER SIX]

A Surprising Return
The Ottawa Hospital

A Decision that was Not Well Received

THE ANNOUNCEMENT of my appointment as president and CEO of the Ottawa Hospital was planned for May, 1 1998, and I was to begin at the end of July. Before the announcement, *The Ottawa Citizen*, Ottawa's main English daily, published a headline, "PQ Envoy to Head Hospital." Thus began a firestorm that no one had predicted. The article indicated that as I had been a candidate for the Parti Québécois 20 years earlier, I was a separatist with the desire to break up Canada. There were statements that I intended to hire only French-speaking people and that unilingual Anglophones would be fired.

The issue made front-page headlines in Ottawa for a month, papers across Canada carried the story, it was written about in New York, and even *Le Monde* in France carried it. Jean Chrétien, then prime minister, made a statement during a trip to Italy, and both Premier Lucien Bouchard in Quebec and Premier Mike Harris in Ontario also commented. All the Ottawa media, including the talk shows, were filled with discussion of my having been a PQ candidate in Montreal in a 1979 by-election and questioning how the Ottawa Hospital could hire a separatist as head of the Hospital.

There was absolutely no consideration for the fact that I had not been involved in any politics for 20 years, that I had been president of the association of CEOs of Quebec health and social services organizations (L'Association des directeurs généraux des services de santé et des services sociaux du Québec) for more than five years, and the president of the Association of Canadian Teaching Hospitals for four years, or that I had been hired in Quebec during the mandate of a Liberal government, and with the approval of Minister of Health Marc-Yvan Côté to head Notre-Dame Hospital, Quebec's largest and most prestigious teaching hospital. None of these things seemed to have any impact on the rage that was expressed by some of the media, the general public, and even some elected officials. Premier Harris of Ontario said, "Surely there is administrative capability within Ontario, or at least a Canadian or even a non-Canadian who believes in Canada and keeping Canada together."

An Unexpected Scandal

There was such an outcry in the media that on May 20 the Hospital Board held an open meeting to respond to questions from the public; it was strongly suggested that I not attend. I followed the events from my home in New York as Jean Pigott, a well-known and very well-respected Ottawa public figure, chaired the public meeting with more than 300 people packed into an overflowing auditorium. The meeting shocked many and aroused the underlying tensions that still exist in Canada for many people over the Quebec sovereignty issue. The meeting got out of hand and became violent, with yelling, pushing and shoving, all captured by the television cameras and transmitted across the country on every news service. This is not something one sees often in Canada.

People in Quebec were shocked and nobody could believe what was being said about Quebec in such a public fashion. The debate in Quebec that has been going on since 1976, when the PQ first came to power, is open, frank and honest, with none of the hatred that was being expressed in Ottawa by what was clearly a very angry segment of the population. There are differences of opinion in all layers of Quebec society, but the debate does not descend to hatred. There is even a family in Quebec in which two brothers have been premier of the province, one for the Liberal party and the other for the PQ.

I believe there were many issues that had been lying dormant and for which I became the lightning rod. The Ottawa community was still recovering from the shock of a very close 1995 referendum on Quebec sovereignty in which the Yes side lost by one-half of one percent. This issue is very disturbing for people in Ottawa as so much of their lives is intertwined with Quebec, and so many work side by side with people from Quebec. Adding fuel to the fire, the health care restructuring committee had recommended the merger of the English and French hospitals in Ottawa, as well as the closure of two much-loved institutions. Emotions ran very high!

Rumour and speculation abounded. There were even concerns that the Ottawa Hospital would become completely bilingual, and unilingual English-speaking employees would all lose their jobs. I was told that the bilingualism policies of the Trudeau era were still resented by certain groups in Ottawa as it prevented their sons and daughters from holding prominent civil-service positions if they didn't speak French. A right-wing group under the banner led the charge, protesting my appointment even before I arrived in town. The media were relentless in their campaign to have me fired, community members were lobbying the Board members, and it took courage for the Board to keep me on as CEO.

Even before my appointment began officially I had become a very public figure and the media did everything they could to dig up information about me. Journalists called our unlisted number in New York, speaking to anyone answering the phone, including our children. Whenever I came to Ottawa, somehow the journalists knew about my arrival and would be waiting for me at the airport, with questions about my political allegiances.

The Board held a press conference in Ottawa and I was asked to renounce any ties to the PQ and reaffirm my allegiance to Canada. I had not been a member of any political party since I left government 20 years earlier and had not participated in any political activities during that time. At the press conference, I refused to comment on any political issues and I would not make any statements about my past or present political interests, insisting that one's political past should not be an issue if one has been judged competent to do the job, and if the job has nothing to do with politics. I was being hired to run a hospital, not to get involved in politics. I clarified that I had clearly said all this to the Board, who had confidence in me to do the job for which they had hired me. I assured the media and the public that I would not be involved in politics and that I should be judged by my work at the Hospital. Randal Marlin, a philosophy professor from Carleton University and a specialist in the study of propaganda, wrote a book about this very public uproar, *The David Levine Affair: Separatist Betrayal or McCarthyism North?* The book documents the media coverage and it attempts to examine this very emotional and highly charged controversy.

I quickly became visible, not only in the Hospital, but throughout the Ottawa area. I had learned from previous experiences that a new CEO should try to enter his new position as quietly as possible and then build up his credibility and visibility—and it was obvious I was not starting out on the right foot. There was, however, a positive side to the scandal that surrounded my hiring, and that was the impact on the Board and the staff of the Hospital. Normally for a newly merged hospital, where some of the board members come from the merging organizations, there is a considerable lapse of time before the members can move out of the past and focus on the best direction for the new organization. In Montreal, at the CHUM, this has taken many years and has been a major barrier to moving the merger forward in a positive manner.

The need for the Board to rally against a common external threat acted as a catalyst to bring the members together as a team and to focus their efforts on the best direction for the Hospital. Board members from different sites supported some issues based on whether or not their site was perceived to have gained or lost in the decision, but the best overall interests of the Hospital prevailed under the leadership of a strong chair, Nick Mulder.

The media events gave the Board a strong sense of unity and purpose, and the need to prove that they could make the merger work. I had great support from the staff of the Hospital, who I believe felt the injustice and inappropriateness of the media attention and criticism. This helped me in my first contacts with the Hospital, the physicians and staff, and then helped in building the confidence and credibility that new leadership needs to move things forward.

My First Months
Few people have the challenging opportunity to create a new hospital, a new academic health-science centre. The Board of the Ottawa Hospital was created on April 1, 1998, and I began as CEO on June 15, a month and a half earlier than planned, because of the controversy. This was very different from my first months at Verdun or Notre-Dame and I knew that things had to move much more quickly. Every decision made by the Board or by me was scrutinized by the media, the community, the medical staff, and employees. It was like being a fish in a fishbowl.

The Merger

Before discussing my strategy and what I did during these first months, it is important to understand how the merger came to be and some of the key issues at play. In 1996, the Government of Ontario set up a restructuring commission that was to look at the redesign of the Ontario health care system. This was done in response to the cutbacks the government was imposing to balance their budget. In 1995 and 1996, the government cut six percent and seven percent respectively from the global health care budget. The mandate of the restructuring commission was to reduce costs by closing certain hospitals, regrouping some activities in others and, finally, merging hospitals into larger organizations in the hope there would be economies of scale in these larger organizations.

Merger mania, as some of my colleagues called this period, stemmed from the belief—with no proof or data to support it—that large, merged hospitals would save money. The theory went that if the private sector was merging and consolidating then the public sector could do the same thing. Data from studying hundreds of hospital mergers in the United States now suggest that the only cases that are successful are those that are able to regroup medical specialty services on one site to create the critical mass and expertise needed to carry out all aspects of the specialty safely, while maintaining the critical mass necessary for teaching. Economic savings were not realized by mergers over and above what could have been achieved with measures such as group buying, outsourcing and other administrative cost reductions. The cost of mergers was far greater than anyone had estimated and delays in investment always led to a deterioration of quality in the merged hospitals.

The restructuring commission visited communities across Ontario and, after a very brief analysis, made recommendations for restructuring. In Ottawa, after much debate and public outcry, the commission recommended that the General, Civic, Riverside, Grace and Montfort hospitals and the Ottawa Heart Institute be merged into one large hospital and that the Riverside, Grace and Montfort sites be closed. The implications of this recommendation were huge as it completely changed the existing dynamic among the hospitals and the way the community received hospital services. The Civic was the English teaching hospital of Ottawa and the General was the bilingual hospital serving the French community for tertiary services. The Salvation Army Grace was a small, efficient community hospital, which covered mainly obstetrics and ophthalmology, some general medicine, and surgery. The Riverside was a 200-bed community hospital with an emergency room covering the full range of primary and secondary services, as well as a fair bit of specialty work in medicine and surgery. The Montfort Hospital was the francophone community hospital serving the Francophone community entirely in French, with full bilingual capacity. The Heart Institute was a world-recognized speciality cardiac centre led by the well-loved Dr. Willie Keon.

The first outcry was from the Montfort Hospital. It launched a very public campaign to protest the projected closure, including a court action against the provincial government to prevent the closure. The issue again brought into the open the unspoken French-English tension in Ottawa. For the Francophone community, the merger of the Montfort Hospital was an issue of survival of the French language and French-language services to Francophones outside Quebec. Montfort's campaign succeeded, and that part of the recommendations of the restructuring committee was put on hold. This was not the case for the other hospitals required to merge and be closed. The court case was eventually settled and the merger was rejected, ensuring that Montfort would remain an independent francophone hospital. (The Montfort Hospital has since been completely renovated and increased in size, and it continues to play a very important role in the Ottawa health care community.)

Some physicians at the Civic Hospital feared that all specialty and academic activity would move to the newer General Hospital and they helped organize a group called Patients First, which included leading citizens of Ottawa, to fight against the possible closure or even the downgrading of the Civic.

The Civic and the General had been fighting with each other for years and the two CEOs of the hospitals would not even sit in the same room together. Doctors in the hospitals talked about the "baby wars" when both hospitals were battling for control of the level-three neo-natal unit, which is the intensive-care unit for babies. Most people believed that the idea of putting both hospitals under one leadership was an impossible challenge.

The closure of the Riverside was also viewed very badly as this was a low-cost, efficient 200-bed hospital that was serving its community very well. It had been built in the 1970s and expanded and refurbished at the beginning of the 1990s. If this site were shuttered, 280,000 square feet of excellent space would be removed from health care. I remember on one of my visits to Ottawa, before beginning the job, driving past the Riverside site. I remarked how new the building looked and how well placed it was, with city buses passing directly under the building and stopping to let off passengers in an enclosed area. An elevator right at the bus stop took people directly to the main floor of the Hospital. I realized immediately that something had to be done to prevent the closure of the Riverside. At the CHUM in Montreal, one of the solutions that I had strongly supported was building a freestanding ambulatory-care centre at Hôtel-Dieu and using Saint-Luc and Notre-Dame as the bedded campuses. Had this plan been put into practice right away, the whole dynamic of the CHUM merger would have been different and the turmoil and deterioration that followed the merger could have been greatly reduced. Instead of a $2.5-billion project, with an ongoing debt cost of $125 million a year, we could have spent $1 billion and saved 10 years with a debt of $50 million a year. In order to avoid the consequences of this kind of costly decision-making, it seemed obvious to me that the Riverside Hospital should be converted into a freestanding ambulatory centre and that this could easily be done.

I had to test out the idea with the physicians, the group that would be most affected by the upcoming changes. I asked the dean of the faculty of medicine, Dr. Peter Walker, if he could organize a dinner for me to meet all the heads of departments of the Hospital. The evening reminded me of the dinner with Georges Bélanger at Les Halles in Montreal 16 years earlier, with the Verdun department heads, but this time I was no longer the naïve CEO just beginning his career in hospitals. During the meal, as we were discussing a multitude of topics concerning the Hospital, I asked them what they thought of the idea of keeping the Riverside open as an ambulatory centre.

They told me the idea was not new and had already been suggested and rejected by the restructuring commission. I said I was interested in their opinion of the value of a freestanding ambulatory centre if it were possible to change the commission's directives. The response was very positive and right away I could see each department head thinking about how they could use the facility. Knowing there would be physician support for the idea, I started to test this out with some Board members. They also felt it was worth a try, although most felt we would not be able to convince the commission or the government.

As it was necessary to respond to the commission directives to close both the Riverside and the Grace sites, the Hospital set in motion a multi-level planning process involving well over 600 people at the Hospital. A preliminary analysis indicated that the impact of the closure of the Riverside and the Grace on the Civic and General campuses, mainly for new construction and renovation projects, would be far more costly than the predictions of the restructuring commission. In addition, the completion of these projects would take up to four years.

Time delays are very dangerous to the success of a merger. The longer it takes to positively move forward, the less the chance for success, with consequent deterioration of the existing services, morale and the spirit of the organization. The projected cost of closing the Riverside and Grace sites and rebuilding the needed clinical and academic space was $166 million. When our planning team analyzed keeping the Riverside open as a freestanding ambulatory centre, the cost dropped to about $122 million. This became the basis of the argument I put forward for changing the function of the Riverside. We were also able to demonstrate that the cost per case at the Riverside would be less than at the more complex Civic and General campuses. The Hospital was responsible for a great deal of clinical activity. Putting all of that activity in an academic environment would both slow down productivity for teaching purposes, and require more staff.

I used the example of cataract eye surgery to demonstrate this argument. The General site housed the Eye Institute, which was doing teaching and research in ophthalmology. They were doing about 2,000 cataract surgeries a year, an amount evaluated as sufficient for teaching and research needs. The Grace had a team of ophthalmologists who had developed a major cataract surgery activity, performing 6,000 surgeries a year. With the closure of the Grace, it was necessary to move this activity onto the General campus, expand the Eye Institute, and create a dynamic between an academic and a non-academic group of physicians, each with very different objectives. The proposition of the Riverside ambulatory centre allowed me to suggest including in it a dedicated high-volume cataract surgery centre, which the literature had recently demonstrated was both lower cost and higher quality due to increased volumes in a dedicated environment. Eventually, the new centre performed 10,000 cataract surgeries a year, covering almost all of Eastern Ontario, at the lowest cost per case and lowest infection rates.

Under this new proposal, the Riverside Hospital could be closed much sooner than expected since we would be able to keep the emergency room open and there would be no need to expand the emergency rooms at the Civic and General. In addition, the shifting of more ambulatory surgery to the Riverside would make room at the Civic and the General for the increase in surgeries resulting from the closure of the beds at the Riverside. The physicians, staff and community became very enthusiastic about the idea and it gave me the issue I needed to help rally the Hospital around a common cause that was not a threat to anyone and was seen as saving the Riverside. This was a project everyone could feel good about.

The risk I was taking was enormous because, after building up hope in the Hospital, if I was not able to deliver and convince the commission and the government to change their decision, my authority as leader of the Hospital would be greatly diminished. I now had to convince the commission that they should change their previous direction to adopt this new one. The commission was being asked by most communities to change something in their directives and they were very reluctant to make any changes as this would set a precedent and possibly start a chain reaction throughout Ontario. The Hospital's arguments were very solid from both a monetary and timing point of view, and I made many trips to Toronto and had many meetings with local politicians to put as much political pressure on the commission as possible. The commission finally accepted the argument that the economic savings warranted the change. The newspapers picked up a phrase I presented in one of my talks and the Riverside was labelled "The Mayo Clinic of the North."

Today the Riverside is a crucial part of the Ottawa Hospital. The development of the ophthalmology centre at the Riverside allowed the

Grace to close earlier than had been planned. The Riverside became a dedicated ambulatory environment with four operating rooms performing 10,000 cataracts and other ambulatory eye surgery. This large volume has allowed for the most cost-effective service possible and I am convinced that there is no facility in Canada, public or private, that is as cost-effective, with the highest quality of care and lowest infection rates. This experience has shown me that dedicated centres performing a large volume of different types of surgery that do not require hospitalization in an acute-care centre are the most efficient way of providing the highest-quality, lowest-cost services.

The Riverside would also house the women's health centre, the dialysis centre, almost all ambulatory surgery, and a major walk-in clinic to preclude visits to the emergency room at the Civic and the General. It would become a major diagnostic centre with the latest technology and focus on rapid access to diagnostic services and medical decision-making.

This project was a real winner and had a very important im-pact on the morale and positive spirit of the Hospital. We were building and developing something new and this was exciting. This achievement set the stage for a much more difficult battle over the final distribution of services in the Hospital.

The Senior Management Team

In each hospital I have managed, the senior management team is vital to the position of the CEO and the hospital. Choosing the team can be challenging and, in Ottawa, the challenge was compounded by the fact that I needed to provide a balance among the campuses with my VPs. Too many from one campus would not be well received. In forming the team, I understood one of the important differences between Quebec and Ontario in managing hospitals. In Ontario, each VP has a signed contract that defines the role and responsibilities, as well as the salary and all benefits. In Quebec, government directives define these conditions and there is no discussion. My Ottawa VPs had their contracts checked by their lawyers and came back to me to negotiate certain clauses. I had never dealt with this before and it represented a completely different approach to managing a hospital. This was a much healthier, more businesslike approach to hospital management, an approach completely different from the civil service model adopted by Quebec.

Salaries in Ontario are significantly higher than in Quebec. Excluding the salaries paid to CEOs of hospitals—which are at least double those paid in Quebec—the salaries of my VPs were at least 50 percent higher than the equivalent positions in Quebec. Benefits were also much higher, more in line with the private sector than what is usually allowed in the public sector.

Senior managers are paid higher salaries but can be removed from their position much more easily than in Quebec. In Ontario, every contract has a buyout clause and there is no need for justification if the CEO decides that he or she is no longer satisfied with the work being performed. Normally, the buyout is one year's salary plus one month for every year worked. The same clause applies if the position is cut or if there is a merger that results in a major change in the nature of the job description.

With the merger, every VP was eligible for a buyout as the number of VP positions was reduced and job descriptions changed. Most VPs had been in their hospital from five to 10 years; I met with each one to determine their interests and skills so that I could ascertain whether or not I had a position for them in the new organization. I discovered most were interested in taking their package and leaving their position. The reason for this is that in Ontario, as opposed to Quebec, there are no restrictions to being rehired by a different health care organization, with no loss of the package benefits. In Quebec, if one's position is abolished there is a three-year support clause that guarantees salary until a new position is found in the system. Once a new position is found, the salary support stops. If the position is cut and the employee seeks a buyout—which is two years' salary in Quebec—the employee is barred from working in the health care field for a period double the buyout period.

The Quebec practices are more logical when positions are being abolished, since they provide salary support while managers find a new position. Ontario, however, has a much more generous and flexible approach that allows institutions to determine the salaries to be paid to management and also includes a buyout clause that kicks in when the organization or the CEO decides it is time for a change.

Under these conditions, I was able to define an organization chart and put a first team in place a month and a half after my arrival. During the following 12 months, I asked two members of the team to leave as I was not satisfied with their work. This is one of the hardest things a CEO has to do and it is one of the defining moments when the CEO is no longer just a part of the team but clearly the leader and person responsible for the team.

In our merger situation it was more urgent than would normally be the case to build strong relationships among the members of the team. They came from different organizations and brought with them old allegiances to the physicians and staff of their past hospitals. In the early fall—barely three months after my arrival—I brought the entire team of 17 directors to my country house in the Laurentians for a three-day, two-night planning session where we prepared our meals together, made beds, cleaned house and worked very hard in a structured way to arrive at a collective vision for the new Hospital. Everybody was very enthusiastic about the exercise and I believe that this activity at this time was a key element in the development of the strongest management team I have ever had. People slept two to a room and I believe the close contact allowed them to get to know each other in a way that prepared the ground for much closer relations in the future. We did our retreat in the country each year I managed the Hospital and this became a special activity looked forward to by everyone.

Communication is Still the Key

Communication continued to be especially important to me and I created the position of VP communications, bringing another new player to the senior management table. I cannot stress enough how important internal communication is to the success of a hospital merger, and the larger the merger the more important communication becomes. We quickly implemented a proper program that included new logos, a journal, a new website, a senior management weekly update, a CEO's letter, an employee telephone talkback line, monthly meetings with all directors, open forums on all campuses, and a program of breakfast or tea with the CEO.

This last initiative was one of the most exciting because it provided the opportunity for me to meet and talk to about 15 staff members at a time, on each campus, each month, for about an hour and a half, and thus to take the pulse of the complex workplace.

There was one issue that came up at every meeting and it was one I never expected, but which taught me how important it is to take care of problems that are of persistent concern to staff. The issue was parking. That's right, parking! Employees were on a waiting list to get parking and some of the lots were so far away from the buildings that transport had to be provided. Some lots did not have paved surfaces and the path to the Hospital went through a field that became muddy when it rained. The lighting was poor and at night staff were very nervous about walking to their cars alone. Our ability to deal with the parking problems would be a test of our ability to deal with other issues. I put a team on it right away.

Another issue on which I was getting considerable feedback from employees, patients and doctors was the cleanliness of the Hospital. Cleanliness came to represent so many things—good-quality patient care, infection control, a safe environment, a well-managed organization, and even a successful merger. I brought this to senior management as an important item and we initiated a major and highly visible campaign for cleanliness in the Hospital. We purchased new cleaning equipment, initiated new cleaning techniques, redid bathrooms, painted walls, and a sense of pride returned to the cleaning staff of the Hospital. Cleanliness became everyone's concern. I mentioned the issue in all my letters, meetings and talks to the staff. We cut down on cleaning of administrative areas to focus on those areas of greatest patient concentration. The pre-merger cutbacks had affected all non-direct patient services; cleaning services were one of the hardest hit and it showed. As the Hospital got cleaner and washrooms were redone, attitudes changed and staff regained pride in their workplace. "Pick It Up, Keep It Clean" and "I Love My Hospital" were a couple of the slogans used on posters and soon everyone was conscious of and concerned about keeping the Hospital clean.

Y2K: The Year 2000

The term Y2K was not part of my personal vocabulary when I arrived at the Ottawa Hospital but it became an important topic of discussion in my first year on the job. The non-event, as this became known after the fact, was a very big deal before December 31, 1999. For a Hospital this was particularly so, as the possibility of failure of our computer systems or medical equipment that was dependent on a computer component was a very real concern. Most of the team was on standby that evening. A year of preparation and many millions of dollars went into ensuring as best we could that all would go smoothly. There was an update of Y2K activities every month with some Board members from industry, who were also very concerned.

From the time I began as CEO we had 18 months until D-Day, and this was in the middle of merging five hospitals into a single institution with one financial system, one payroll system, and some form of integration of medical records. We tested all systems with appropriate simulations, followed all the vendor recommendations for their equipment and waited with fingers crossed. The world breathed a sigh of relief as the New Year came and went but the exercise for the Hospital had been quite a challenge. The lesson learned was how a team effort with a clear focus could achieve a great deal. In this case it was to ensure that Y2K was a non-event.

The CEO and Politics

A few months after arriving at Ottawa Hospital, I was asked to speak to an association of health care managers on the subject of the CEO and politics. I assumed this had to do with the political ramifications of my arrival in Ottawa and how I managed the situation. The more I looked into the subject, however, and what the word politics really meant, the more I realized that a political perspective was a completely new and different way of looking at managing, especially managing in the health care field.

From a sociological perspective, politics is about the relationships of power. The politics of the family is about the power relationships that exist within the family. There are many different references to politics: political systems, political parties, political intrigue, playing politics, political dynamics—and all refer to the relationships of power. "The CEO and Politics" is a look at the relationships of power that exist and are continually interacting with the CEO as he or she is trying to achieve a mandate. What is the political situation in which a CEO is likely to find him or herself? What are some of the strategies that will help navigate these often stormy waters?

If politics is the interaction between different zones of power, could I then develop a model that would help navigate those zones of power in a very complex organization such as a hospital? I divided the zones of power into two categories: those that are internal to and those that are external to the organization.

The Internal Zones of Political Power
THE MEDICAL STAFF

In a hospital, one of the most important zones of political power lies with the medical professionals. Physicians receive their authority to practice from their licensing body and are given a billing number by the province in which they work. In the Canadian system, medical professionals receive their remuneration directly from the government on a fee-for-service basis and much of their activity is volume- and revenue-driven. This group forms an association in each institution and sends elected representatives to the board of the hospital. Their role is very political as they represent the interests of the physicians. In certain provinces they also have a legal mandate to ensure the medical quality and medical coverage in the hospital. Other provinces create a medical advisory council (MAC) and choose a chief of staff who also sits on the board of directors and is directly responsible to the board, not the CEO, for the quality of medical care and medical coverage in the hospital. The MAC is made up of the heads of departments, who each in their own right have a degree of political power in relation to the size and importance of their department. The VP medical represents the administration among the medical groups of the hospital and establishes the formal link between the CEO and the physicians.

I have discovered that the merger of hospitals adds many dimensions to the power of the medical staff as each merging hospital has a medical structure that defends their institution in the merger process. Even though these structures are merged into new bodies, the perception of winners and losers is very strong because the medical staff have invested their lives in the development of the hospital and the programs for which they have been responsible. There are a multitude of vested interests that must be taken into consideration, ranging from practice plans to research and teaching arrangements.

For example, the physicians at the General wanted their campus to become the main teaching campus and were convinced that this would be the case, given their interpretation of the restructuring commission's directives. The physicians at the Civic were not going to allow this and their first objective was to take control of the medical staff. This was done through the election process of the officers of the medical staff. It was agreed that the General and the Civic should each provide a member of the executive; if the president came from one campus, the vice-president would come from the other. All doctors voted together and, since the Civic had the greatest number of medical staff, their candidate became the president. In response to this situation, a number of physicians at the General formed an unofficial group, the Association of Physicians from the General Campus, and presented themselves as a formal body in the Hospital. This set the stage for direct confrontation between the official and informal medical groups. Recalling management expert Henry Mintzberg's three roles the CEO must play well to develop the credibility and respect needed to manage a hospital, the first is to be able to manage conflict in a fair and honest way. In a hostile merger, the difficulties are multiplied manifold, particularly with the medical staff. Once again, there is the need to develop a collective vision and use it to help guide decisions in a conflictual environment.

The Professional Staff

The professionals of the hospital, nurses, therapists, psychologists, etc., form another zone of power along much the same lines as the physicians, though with much less political power. These professionals are employees of the hospital and have limited representation on the board of directors. They represent many different groups, but nursing is by far the largest and the best recognized by the population. Nurses are in direct and continual contact with patients and their families. They are the most affected by budgetary constraints and merging services, and find themselves constantly being asked to give more and better care with fewer resources. They are the first to notice the reduction in quality care to patients due to restructuring. The issue of quality care is the most important to this group and it is essential for the CEO to ensure that quality care is a cornerstone of the vision, with very concrete measures and investment.

The Board

In a merged hospital, the board of directors is as important as the physicians group. Even if the board is mostly composed of new members who have not been part of the merging hospitals, there are always a few representatives from each of the merging hospitals who are there as part of the merger agreement. These people tend to be strong, knowledgeable board members who often have a vested interest in defending their site and the physicians and staff with whom they worked in the past. It is very important to work closely with the board chair and the executive and to ensure board communication is well developed so board members hear about all new issues and plans from the CEO first. Gaining board support is essential for the success of the merger and the new vision of the hospital. If board support is not strong and consistent, the sea will be much rougher.

The Merging Sites

In a merger situation, each of the merging sites becomes a zone of power and influence, and senior management must take special care to recognize the contribution of each site and make sure that the sense of loss is kept to an absolute minimum. Saving the Riverside was a good example of turning a loss into a win. Closing the Grace but building a new ophthalmology centre at the Riverside to accommodate this former Grace activity was also a win. Sometimes it is best to move very slowly and let time and the departure of certain persons allow change to happen. This was the case for the Heart Institute of Ottawa. Cardiac specialist Dr. William Keon developed the Heart Institute and was recognized as the father of cardiac care in Ottawa. He had become a senator as well as the director of the Institute and was very much opposed to it becoming part of the Ottawa Hospital. This was a very delicate situation and I highly recommended to the Board that the integration, from a management point of view, could wait until the other requirements of the merger were completed and then we could set up a negotiation committee to discuss the nature and the extent of the integration.

The Unions

The union environment in Ontario was very different from what I was accustomed to in Quebec. Unlike Quebec, Ontario has no common salary agreement between the government and the unions. Each hospital negotiates its own salary scale and there are multiple union accreditations in each hospital. In a merger, the highest pay scale in a category, no matter the union, becomes the new salary level for all the employees in that category. Since the Ottawa Hospital merged teaching hospitals with non-teaching hospitals with lower pay scales, the result was a payroll increase of over $30 million—not easy to accept when government is aiming for and expecting cost reductions. But the real sticking point was seniority, since the new institution was required to recognize everyone's seniority. Expertise and competence were still the main criteria for filling positions, but due to seniority there was a very strong risk of bumping and this is always disruptive to an organization. Buyouts and early retirements were always a possibility, but as far as nursing was concerned there was a shortage of qualified nurses and new training programs were introduced to raise the level of competency of the nurses from the non-teaching hospitals. These training programs added new costs to the Hospital.

External Zones of Power
THE MEDIA

It seems superfluous to mention the influence of the media because, after their coverage of my arrival in Ottawa, they felt they had not only a license but also a responsibility to report on everything that happened in the Hospital. They seized on every change, every new hiring, the movement of services, and they sought out comments by staff, physicians and those members of the Board who were not content with the merger or the new direction of the Hospital. My response was to always be available for the media, answer all questions with well-prepared responses, and do the talk shows and TV interviews, hold press conferences on a regular basis to update the public on the merger progress, and to actively demonstrate our focus on patient care and what the Hospital and staff were doing for the people of Ottawa.

We paid special attention to local politicians at the provincial and municipal level and maintained good contact with the politicians at the federal level. We developed relations with the ministry not only in Toronto but with the regional director who played a very strong support role for the Hospital. The university was always a close partner and, from the very beginning, I developed a personal relationship with the dean of the faculty of medicine. The other regional health care institutions in the Ottawa valley were very important and efforts were continually undertaken to include them in the Hospital planning and to develop partnerships with them that could be mutually beneficial, facilitating transfers and services for our clientele.

I participated in all the social activities and accepted all invitations to speak. Given the controversy over my arrival, it was important to be very present and open with the community. Being present with your community is something I would suggest to any CEO of a health care institution.

Defining a Collective Vision

One of the most important steps a leader must take to gain both credibility and the respect of his or her organization is to develop a collective vision for the organization. This is the most important exercise for establishing its direction; if there is a strong consensus on this direction, the health and well-being of the institution will be established.

To develop a collective vision the CEO must put into place and lead a process that ensures inclusion of all the key stakeholders. Define the environment, understand the key players and the leadership roles they play, clearly identify the key issues, recognize the zones of power and influence, and clearly enunciate the mission of the organization.

With these steps in mind, I set up the planning structure needed to guide this most important exercise. Developing this type of common vision in the context of a merger determines many of the elements that must be put into place from the beginning. All administrative services must be integrated and all clinical services must be rationalized. The first is complex but fairly straightforward; the second can be very dangerous to a hospital merger. There was a strong desire to succeed and this would bode well for the successful development of a collective vision. The Riverside strategy was very well accepted and was considered a winner, and this gave hope to the community and allowed me to establish a measure of credibility and support from senior management. But the forces against success were the past rivalries between the General and the Civic, the rivalries between the two medical staffs and the rivalries between certain individuals.

I learned very quickly how influential individual rivalries can impact an entire hospital. I was told the story of two Francophone classmates who at an early age began competing with each other. Their rivalry began in school and they maintain it to this day. They were on opposing teams in football, both went to medical school, both became neurosurgeons. One became the head of Surgery at the Civic Hospital while the other became head at the General Hospital. Both were very political, had very strong personalities and leadership skills. After the merger, it was clear that a confrontation was in the works. Much of the change in a merger is around the regrouping of medical services, and battle lines were drawn as to which campus would dominate which specialties, and how this would affect the medical staff and where they had been working. Both hospitals would still be full-service general hospitals but the concentration of every speciality service would be on one site or the other, affecting the academic program and the placement of interns and residents.

The Strategy

The strategy for moving forward took on three main dimensions. First was the regrouping of service, the second was the building of new expanded facilities to support the concentration of activities, and the third was a focus on improving the academic and research status of the Hospital. After consultation and a great deal of negotiation, a plan was prepared and presented to the Board. I will mention just one element of the plan that created much division among the doctors and consequently among Board members.

The "neuroscience wars," as they were known, became a focal point. As I have mentioned, two of the key players were both neurosurgeons. The Civic had developed very strong neurosurgical activity while the General had developed a similarly strong Neurology Department headed by a well-known researcher in neuroscience. The plan was to concentrate cardiology and neuroscience at the Civic, where the Heart Institute was located, while concentrating oncology cancer surgery and orthopedics at the General campus, where the Cancer Institute was located. This would allow for the complementary development of strengths on each campus while providing the critical mass for the academic development that was a key component of the vision. The reaction of the physicians at the General was swift and very aggressive. The General had invested in new facilities for neurology and the head of the Department of Neurology refused to allow the service to move to the Civic as this would impact the role of neurosurgery and force it to also move to the Civic campus. Since the issue was to go to the Board for a decision, there were many phone calls to Board members and the atmosphere became more and more tense. This was a showdown and it was a test of my ability to lead the Hospital in a new direction. It was also a test of the Board's ability to deal with conflict. The Board, especially with the leadership of the chair Nick Mulder, had already shown its courage with the issues over my arrival, the approval of the Riverside project against the recommendations of the restructuring committee, and the constant interruptions of Board meetings by angry protesters. It now had to deal with the most important of all the issues, the direction of the new, merged Hospital. A Board retreat had been planned to deal with the issues and I met with the chair and the executive committee a number of times before the meeting to plan our approach. After much discussion, and even argument, the Board made a large majority decision to accept the vision and strategic plan for the new Hospital. For me and for the senior management, this was the real test of the success of the new hospital team. This original plan has remained the backbone of the Hospital and all its components have been achieved. Services were regrouped, new facilities were built and others renovated, while the academic and research ambitions of the Hospital were initiated. Dr. Michel Chrétien, brother of then prime minister Jean Chrétien, was brought from Montreal to head the research institute and lead the research in genetics and proteomics. Though there was some dissension on the Board, this decision made it clear that the Board was in charge and would be able to lead the Hospital into the future.

The End Game

By 2001, the merger was three years old and the financial impact of merging large hospitals, combining services, implementing new information systems, and planning the building of new facilities was becoming more and more evident. Harmonizing staff salaries to the highest pay level had added a recurring cost of over $30 million a year; there was an additional cost of $18 million for a new information system, the regrouping of departments, and reorganization of the delivery of care to integrate non-academic activity into a more costly academic environment. New investments for new programs and expanded activity came to another $29 million, which would be recuperated by the economies of scale that we were now beginning to achieve. The Hospital budget at that time was about $700 million and, under the direction of the regional director, the minister sent in a team to evaluate the situation. The external evaluation confirmed that the salary increases and the unavoidable merger investments amounted to $48 million and that this should be covered by the ministry, with the remaining amount to be recuperated by the Hospital through economies of scale. This was all presented to the Board, who approved the reduction plan.

Once the report was submitted, the Hospital, the Board and I all waited for the response while we implemented the new balanced budget, presuming the $48 million injection of funds from the ministry was assured. A couple of months later I received a call from the minister's chief of staff asking for a meeting. At this very private meeting I was told that because of the Hospital's deficit, the minister had made the decision to remove the Board and to replace it with a supervisor. I was shocked by this news and immediately asked why I was not being replaced if there was a crisis serious enough to remove the Board. I was told that the minister was asking if I would stay on to run the Hospital, as the government was very satisfied with my leadership there. This was a unique situation—the Board was to be removed but the CEO was asked to stay on. There were clearly political issues. I was ready to leave right away and said I would speak to the Board and get back to him with my decision. As I left the meeting, I tried to figure out the reason for such a clearly political move. The Conservative government in power under Mike Harris had had to accept the Board decision to keep me as CEO of the Hospital at the beginning of my mandate when the controversy broke out around my hiring. The group of angry protesters that had been present from the announcement of my appointment came from the riding of one of the only elected Conservative members from the Ottawa region and he was the only minister from the region in the Harris government. The Hospital was situated in the riding of Dalton McGuinty, the leader of the opposition Liberal Party of Ontario, who would later become the premier of Ontario. It had been announced that Mike Harris would be stepping down before the next election and that there would be a leadership race before the upcoming election. The Board had been critical of the government's management of health care, of the long delays for approval of projects, which had caused increased cost, and of the lack of acceptance of the merger costs, which had led to the Hospital absorbing the cost, thus running up a deficit. The Board included community leaders, industry CEOs, business people, former deputy-ministers, an assistant auditor-general of Canada, retired judges, professionals and prominent citizens respected in their fields. I knew they would be shocked and angry.

With all this in mind, I called the Board chair to relate my conversation with the minister's chief of staff and to call an emergency Board meeting. All the Board members were taken by surprise and reacted as I anticipated. The decision was clearly a political one. They were angry, I was angry, and I indicated quite clearly that I was not ready to stay on if the Board was removed. Discussion turned quickly to the Hospital and what would be best for the staff, the physicians and, certainly, for the senior management team—and the Board asked me to stay on to help the organization get through this crisis. Two weeks later, the minister announced the removal of the Board to the shocked response of the Hospital and the public. I agreed to remain in order to provide leadership for the organization, under certain conditions that were accepted by the minister. The most important condition was that the supervisor's role would be to replace the Board but that I would continue to be fully responsible for managing the Hospital. This condition was not respected; the supervisor hired his own staff and began to run the Hospital. An agreement was negotiated and I left the Hospital three months after the arrival of the supervisor. A week after I left, the government gave the hospital the $48 million that had been promised.

From the moment of my arrival—and even before my arrival—to the time of my departure from the Ottawa Hospital three and a half years later, there was never a dull moment. All my leadership skills were tested in this complex situation. I am proud that the entire team, including the Board, skillfully managed a difficult, but very successful, merger. Despite the problems that marked its beginnings, the Ottawa Hospital is recognized today as one of Canada's major academic health and science centres.

Lessons I Learned

The Ottawa experience taught me many new things and reinforced others I was already aware of. We are never free of our past and must always remember that what we do can have future consequences. If we are true to our values and believe in what we are doing, we have a good chance of successfully getting through difficulties. Politics and health care do not mix well, yet they are inseparable in the Canadian universal health care system. The media use health care as a tool to generate controversy and not always for the benefit of the population, but sometimes for the benefit of the newspaper and its drive to attract public attention. Once in a position, the CEO of a public institution must stay out of politics and refrain from making political comments. A CEO must fully understand the community in which he or she is working. This sometimes means looking for underlying reasons for issues that erupt unexpectedly. It is important to understand the background to these issues in order to deal with them appropriately and effectively.

In any community large or small, the written, spoken and visual media are very present. An important lesson is to get to know the media—the journalists, the editors, the talk-show hosts and the television personalities—and what they write about, talk about and show most often. Understand what they like, who they are friendly with, who they support and who they are against. With this knowledge, be ready to respond on all issues. Be available, open, honest and upfront, and understand that everything will come out in some story no matter what you do or say. I learned to present the story before the media presented it, and hence set the tone. This means being aware of what is going on throughout the hospital, in government, and throughout the community. Develop a network of eyes and ears so you are aware of issues as they arise, rather than being taken by surprise. When errors are made known, own up to them. Never do anything you would not be comfortable explaining on the front page of the newspaper, next to a very unflattering photo of yourself.

Finding a winner has always been important to gain credibility, but the size of the winner needs to be in direct proportion to the gap in credibility. Saving the Riverside by converting it into "the Mayo Clinic of the North" was the type of winner I needed in Ottawa. If the win is big, usually, so is the risk. I learned that sometimes you must take serious risks if you want to succeed badly enough. It's a leap of faith.

One of the most important lessons I learned at the Ottawa Hospital was the distinction between the Ontario business model of managing health care and Quebec's much more centralized model. Both systems function in the public domain but the role of management in Ontario is left to the hospital, and a well-paid CEO is fully responsible for the results of the organization, along with the hospital board. In Quebec, it is hard to determine who is responsible for the institution as there is so much intervention by government and the regional agencies in the daily managing of the hospital, and there exists a culture where nothing can be done without permission.

People issues are always the root cause of conflict. I had learned that it was important to understand an organization's zones of power and influence and their leadership. In Ottawa, I learned that personal, individual rivalries can influence the direction of an organization if the people involved are powerful enough.

I learned that strong, factual, well-researched and logical arguments are important in order to give politicians justification for making decisions they will need to present to the public, but the most important arguments are the financial arguments. Governments try hard to avoid public criticism and will always be interested in ensuring they have arguments they can comfortably present to the public to defend their decisions before they give their approval to a project or a plan.

A good vision stands the test of time; the Ottawa strategy for the merged hospital on multiple sites with regrouped services has proven to be very successful and the least costly over a long period of time.

The more planned services that ambulatory centres offer really do provide greater and less costly access to care that is separate from the more complex bedded environment, which is often at the mercy of unplanned emergencies. Both environments are academic but they do not necessarily get in each other's way.

One of the last lessons I learned is that unforeseen things

happen. None of us—not the Board, the Hospital or me—had even the slightest premonition that the Board would be removed. Perhaps the most important lesson I learned was never to underestimate the influence of politics.

CHAPTER SEVEN

Internship in Politics

How I Became a Minister in a Parti Québécois Government

BEING NAMED A MINISTER of health was by far one of the most unexpected chapters in my life and it came to be in a most roundabout way. As a CEO, I had witnessed many health care decisions that were made for political reasons and were not necessarily in the best interests of the patients or about the ability of the health care system to deliver the care that was needed by the population. I believed that it was important to dissociate health care and health care management from politics and I began to look at ways to better understand this issue and how one could go about implementing a new approach to managing health care in a public system. I believed that health care should be run by an agency that is at arm's length from government and that this agency should be funded from taxes that are specifically designated to health care. The agency would have a public board, it would be open and transparent, and would be charged with the mission of administering health care to the population. Government would be responsible for defining the health and social services offered by the public sector, it would determine the level of financing it was prepared to provide for these services, and it would be responsible for implementing the measures necessary to ensure the quality and efficiency of the services offered. This idea was presented to the Clair Commission in Quebec and was baptized as "Hydro-Health," to mimic Hydro-Québec, the Quebec hydroelectric company that is considered by many to be a well-run and efficient state-owned corporation.

With this idea in mind, I asked for a meeting with Bernard Landry, now premier of Quebec. I wanted to propose a research project that would examine different health care systems and the impact of their different governance models on the delivery and outcomes of health and social services. Mr. Landry was interested in this approach to health care and after some discussion and some quiet moments on his part, I realized he was coming up with some ideas of his own. He asked me if I would be interested in becoming minister of health in his government. He was planning a new cabinet at that time and felt that I could contribute to improving health care in Quebec. This was the third time I had been asked to take on this position and my initial reaction remained the same. I was not interested in politics and saw myself as a health care administrator, not the minister of health. Landry was very persuasive and insisted that as minister I could set up the study group to look much more closely at the idea of a health care agency, and if the ideas proved interesting and feasible I would then have the opportunity to bring a proposal to cabinet and try to persuade my colleagues to introduce the change.

I was being asked if I was prepared to help develop and improve the health care system of Quebec and address some of the many pressing issues confronting health care. There were problems of accessibility, quality of care, wait times, whether to see either a generalist or a specialist, overcrowded emergency rooms, inefficiencies in the operations of the system, in addition to many problems with care for the elderly, mental health and home care. The recent Clair Commission had underlined each of these issues and it was now time to deal with them. The public was losing confidence in the system and turning more and more to private services to reduce wait times and increase access to diagnostic testing, and even for certain surgeries (hip and knee replacements). The financial constraints and increasing deficit of the health care budget was a growing financial burden on the province, and the morale of everyone working in health care was very low.

If the confidence of the general public in the ability of the public sector to run and manage the health care system does not improve, the public will demand a way to access the health care they want. The public health care system is based on the belief that we will have a level of economic growth that will allow for appropriate public funding of the system. However, there is increasing pressure on public funding of health care, not because we are not generating the wealth to cover the cost, but the wealth we are generating is being concentrated and not equally distributed across the population. The concentration of wealth in the upper middle class and the increasing gap between those who have disposable income and those who do not is a major problem for health care because, as the public system becomes unable to cope due to limited resources, those who can afford to purchase high-quality rapid access to ser-vices will do so, and this will leave the rest of the population to manage with what remains of the public system. The danger here is not that those who can pay extra for their own services will do so, thereby liberating space in the public system; rather, the danger is that we will lose the lobby and influence of this group in ensuring the strength and viability of the public system. The very serious consequence will be that, as the pressure on government to provide services diminishes, there will be a tendency to shift priorities away from the public health system, thereby leading to its slow but inevitable deterioration.

With these thoughts in mind, and because I realized the impor-tance of building confidence in our health care system, I began to see the incredible challenge that I was being offered and I told Bernard that I would have to think about the offer and discuss it with my wife, friends and colleagues. Until that time I had been running large hospitals, but this was an opportunity to help run the health care system itself.

I had remained far from politics for 20 years, and my involvement back in the late 1970s had not been at all from the perspective of an active political life. Accepting a ministerial position as a non-elected person would mean I would not be able to respond to questions from the Opposition in the National Assembly. It also meant that I would have to seek a seat in the legislature within six months, as is the tradition of non-sitting ministers.

Premier Landry asked me to meet him at his home on Monday, January 28, at 10:30 a.m. I arrived on time, parked beside four other cars already there, and went in. I had been to this house many times before, for birthday parties and weddings, but this was the very first time I'd been there in a role other than as a friend of the family. Landry got right to the point and asked me if I would accept the position of junior minister of health responsible for the management of the health care system. Right away I knew that something had changed because we had never discussed anything other than my being minister of health with another minister answering questions for me in the National Assembly. I must have appeared very confused, for he went on to explain very rapidly that choosing a cabinet was complex and in itself a very political activity. There were two very strong ministers in the government: Pauline Marois, who later became the premier, and François Legault, today leader of a new opposition party. At the time, however, Landry needed Legault to balance the power in cabinet. Legault had recently been the minister of education and he wanted a high-profile cabinet position that would keep him in the public eye. Health and Social Services was the one ministry that was in the newspapers every day and the minister of health became a very well-known public figure to every Quebecer. I told the premier that I understood his needs for a balanced cabinet, then thanked him for the offer and explained that I was not interested in being the junior minister. Considerable discussion followed my response and it was clear that it was important for Landry that I enter politics. Over the previous two weeks, I had been thinking of all the things I could do as minister of health and social services; I was excited by the idea, and was very disappointed with the turn of events.

Thinking about it more, eventually I said I would like to meet Legault, who was in the other room, to hear his ideas. So I met with him and we discussed the role we would each play. It was clear that he knew what it meant to be a minister while I certainly did not. I knew a lot about health care, whereas Legault had only a general knowledge since he had never worked in this field. I was interested in managing the system and he was interested in being the minister. I was not as comfortable as I wished after our discussion but I accepted the position and rationalized to myself that this was an experience I was not likely to get in any other way. I was very aware that, although I was entering politics through the back door, I was going forward with eyes wide open and the desire and passion to change the way things were managed.

Many things I did not realize at that time became clear over the next few months, particularly why people go into politics and why they want to become a minister. Many of the reasons have to do with representing their riding and introducing change, but other reasons are more to do with ambition, notoriety, visibility and the power of a minister. The role of a member of the National Assembly is a difficult one, but the role of minister is far more complex. A minister is on the job from the moment when he or she wakes until turning in at the end of the day, often very late. It is a seven-days-a-week job with risks around every corner. The public has less and less confidence in their political leaders and the media are not very friendly to politicians. I learned many of these things very quickly when I took on this new job. A few days after I agreed to take it, the new cabinet was sworn in at the National Assembly and from the moment of the swearing-in until the moment I left the government, each day of my life was orchestrated, not something I was very happy about.

The first order of the day was to be assigned chauffeurs who would become my bodyguards, drivers, helpers, and even facilitators for many of the activities I was called upon to undertake. Very close relationships develop between the team of chauffeurs and the minister as they become part of your life, going out to every meal with you, driving you everywhere, and being with you every waking minute. I was not permitted to take my own car to the country or simply to go out to dinner alone with my wife. When I asked why, I was told that it began after René Lévesque had an accident while driving his own car when he was premier. Following this incident, it became mandatory that a chauffeur be responsible for the transport of all ministers to avoid potential incidents.

After chauffeurs were in place, offices were assigned in Quebec City and Montreal, and the briefing sessions began with the staff of the deputy minister. At each of the briefing sessions I asked many questions and assumed the role of a CEO meeting his team of directors. It was immediately clear to me that Legault was not very comfortable that someone else who knew the health care system very well was asking detailed questions about the issues, problems and potential solutions that were being considered. We divided up some of the major files and, given my experience, I took on the responsibility for academic medicine and the teaching hospitals.

We each chose our cabinet, a chief of staff and political advisers, and it was the responsibility of these staffers to manage the activities, agenda and dynamic among the ministers, as well as with the machine of government. From the start, the media had a field day; caricatures appeared in the papers with Legault and me in a limousine with two drivers, each trying to go in a different direction. Few people realize the importance of the media in a minister's life.

Impact of the Media and the Addiction to Notoriety

If someone had told me before I entered the political arena that I would become addicted to the media and my presence in the media, I would not have understood what they meant. I had considerable experience with the media, both before and after my Ottawa experience, and I never gave it a second thought. It had always been gratifying when a friend or colleague said, "I saw you on TV the other day and I liked your comments." I have always believed in the importance of communication, and the media in all forms are important communication tools. The role of the media in the life of a politician is far more present and much more intense than most of us can imagine. Once elected, politicians must always consider their re-election, and many decisions governments make reflect this concern. The image of a premier, a minister or an M.N.A. that is in the mind of the public is an ever-present concern because the prevailing public image is represented principally by the media. In the back seat of my car each morning, I found all that day's newspapers and all the media clippings concerning the government and the Ministry of Health and Social Services. This scenario is repeated for every minister, and every minister is expected to stay on top of all media coverage. The very first thing one looks for is whether or not you have been mentioned, how any of your public appearances or press conferences have been reported, and whether the editorialists are making any comment about you, your actions, or your ministry. Starting early in the day, Opposition questions are being formulated for Question Period in the National Assembly and government staffers are already preparing answers to likely questions. The power and influence of the media is enormous in politics and this has always been so. I was already aware of this, so this part of the media presence was not unexpected. What was unexpected was the impact of the media on ministers themselves—and this is something I was to learn from personal experience.

I soon learned that the communication section of the premier's cabinet had set up a tracking mechanism for the number and nature of every minister's appearances in the media. Staff scanned national and local newspapers, television and radio channels, and every time a minister's name was mentioned they did an evaluation of the context as well as the extent of the coverage and a score was assigned. Reports were given to each minister, ranking him or her among his or her colleagues for presence in the media. In the first few months after the swearing-in of the new cabinet, I received a very high ranking—much to the chagrin and frustration of Legault. I am sure this situation did not help relations between Legault and me, and our respective staff.

Name recognition, or even simple presence in the public eye, is very important to most politicians, and especially to ministers, and they become more attached to these things than they sometimes realize. My personal experience arrived after only three months as junior minister. I had often been in the media in my previous positions, dealing with various issues concerning health care. But now, as part of a government in power, my relationship with the media took on a new importance. I checked the newspapers each day, looking for any article in which I was mentioned, and was very pleased to see that most of the coverage was positive. One Monday morning I looked through the media and found no articles. The next day again I found no mention of or reference to me anywhere. I didn't really think much about this at the beginning, but noticed after the regular cabinet meeting on Wednesday morning that I was more irritable than usual. I had meetings with my own staff in the afternoon and they kept asking me what was wrong. I kept saying, "Nothing," but I knew that I was becoming more irritable. The following day was worse and I still had no idea what was happening. The week's agenda was interesting—we were doing a number of hospital visits and reviewing work on part of a new health reform stemming from the Clair Commission. My press secretary came to see me and said what I found to be a most surprising thing: "David, you have all the systems of withdrawal." I have never smoked, I drink lots of coffee, but alcohol only moderately, and yet I was being told I was suffering from withdrawal. When I asked what I was withdrawing from, I was told it was withdrawal from my dose of presence in the media. I could not believe that after so short a time I was so affected by something most ministers must learn to manage one way or another. The adrenalin of being present in the media, of a certain recognition, was a form of addiction and I had to learn to control the consequences. When one asks what people get out of entering politics, one of the answers is the "high" of a public profile and presence, along with the considerable satisfaction of doing a very difficult but important job.

A Minister is Not the CEO

My experience in management until that time had been that of the CEO in charge of and responsible for my organization. I looked at the Ministry of Health as my new organization and assumed I was responsible for making sure that it worked well and answered the needs of the population. At the early briefing sessions I took on the role of CEO, and through my questions it was clear that my interests lay in the running of the system. After about two weeks in my new role, my deputy minister, Pierre Gabriel, came to my office and asked to speak to me in private. He was very polite but quite firm in his comments. He said, "Minister, you have been a CEO all your working life and, in fact, you have been recognized as a good health care administrator. But now you have a new job—that of minister—and the job description is not the same. You are no longer the CEO. You must not try to manage at the operational level but function within government to define the policies that will allow the system to be the most efficient. Your job is to obtain from the Treasury Board the resources that will allow for the development of the services most needed throughout Quebec." He went on to explain that if I tried to manage the system I would short-circuit the traditional lines of authority and, in the end, undermine the authority and initiative of the team of deputy and assistant deputy ministers, as well as the CEOs and managers in the system. My responsibility was to be the minister and not a manager of the system. I was now in politics and I had to think like a politician whose first priority is to get elected and re-elected, and I had to remember that decisions are made with this priority in mind. Get health care administrators on your side, gain the respect and credibility of the public and the media as much as is possible, and you will be able to do more for health care as a minister than dealing with any one specific problem or managerial concern. His comments and my interpretation of their meaning allowed me to better understand the dynamics of politics.

Health Care is Political

The Parti Québécois had indicated that they planned to reduce taxes, always a popular political decision, and the Ministry of Finance had announced they would do this in the budget before the next election. After being on the job for only a short period of time, it was clear to me that the health care system needed about $500 million more than the current allocation to be able to respond to the needs of the population, especially in home care and care for the elderly. I made the suggestion that instead of reducing taxes, which were about $500 million, or $100 on average per taxpayer, the tax reduction could be held off and the money invested in health care. I argued that this would be better appreciated by the public and could even gain greater support than a tax deduction if it was well presented. The government's choice was to reduce taxes rather than use the money to support health care. This was a political decision and one I did not feel was the most responsive to the needs of the population.

The ministry had been working on the recommendations of the Clair Commission and had already introduced the concept of family-practice groups in response to the recommendation to develop primary care. This also tied into the federal government's decision in 2000 to invest and develop primary care across Canada. The reform being discussed was very significant; it would create population-based geographic territories and then merge almost all of the health and social-service institutions in the territory into one single organization. This model of care was designed to respond to the issues of accessibility, continuity of care, a single medical record, and better patient management. As minister, I supported this model and worked very hard for its implementation. It was clear that merging the CLSC system (which covered primary care and front-line social and community services) with the hospital into one organization would generate resistance from the CLSC sector, since they would immediately assume a guaranteed takeover by the hospitals. An election was imminent and the political decision was to not introduce any change even if there was agreement that this was the right direction in which to move because it would generate resistance in one of the power bases of the Parti Québécois: The CLSC and the community sector were traditionally supporters of the PQ and had been for many years.

These examples of how party politics and strategy affect health care decision-making were eye-openers for me and made me think carefully about my place in politics.

The Teaching Hospital File

In 2002, I was responsible for the files of both the CHUM (Centre hospitalier de l'Université de Montréal) and the CUSM (Centre universitaire de santé de McGill), also known as the MUHC (McGill University Health Centre). I decided to meet regularly with the two hospitals to follow the progress of their development and to deal with the many issues that would arise. I met with board members and the CEOs to discuss the financing and development of their respective new building projects. I believed the merger of Hôtel-Dieu, Saint-Luc and Notre-Dame to form the CHUM and the merger of the McGill hospitals was the right approach, not only to create the critical mass that teaching and research required, but also as a way to reduce a hospital-centred system and move into the community with more primary care.

A practice plan for physician remuneration was an essential reuirement for the development of university teaching hospitals. The objective of a practice plan is to provide physician remuneration for teaching and research, as well as for clinical activity. It is also a way to pool resources so those physicians who do more clinical work can support those physicians who do more teaching and research. This approach is essential for a true academic health-science centre. In Quebec, payment is fee-for-service with no additional funds for teaching or research. Thus, there is no distinction if one works in an academic or non-academic centre. An evaluation was done of what would be required to finance academic activity, and it was calculated at about a 17 percent increase in the fee-for-service rates at the time. Government did not accept this approach, and one of the most important factors for the creation of real academic health-science centres was not put into place. Quebec has invested $5 billion in building two new academic health-science centres for McGill and the Université de Montréal, with another billion dollars going to the Sainte-Justine teaching hospital in Montreal, without resolving the question of appropriate remuneration for academic medicine by the introduction of a practice plan.

Fee-for-service or payment-for-volume with no academic component has led to academic physicians demanding very large volumes of activity to enable them to generate the funds needed to support their academic activity. This has led to the current reality where out of the total activities of teaching hospitals, only 15 to 20 per-cent is tertiary activity, while more than 50 percent of their activity could be done in a non-teaching hospital at a lower cost per case.

The cost of finding and purchasing a site for the new hospitals and the increasing cost of construction as each week went by was beginning to put a strain on the projects and was creating many government worries that the original $800 million planned for each project would get well out of hand. Sixteen years later, as the hospital building projects are nearing completion, the cost is estimated at $2.5 billion for each hospital, with no real idea or understanding of the new operating costs that will be required.

The number of beds and its academic standing are what define a hospital. The CHUM was awarded 1,000 beds and the MUHC 832, based on the existing capacity of the merged hospitals and taking into account reductions in the average length of stay and the transfer of community cases to community hospitals. When the cases treated in the teaching hospitals were analyzed, only 15 percent were considered to be tertiary care. The objective for the new facilities was to move closer to 50 percent tertiary cases and to off-load less intense activity to the other community hospitals in Montreal and the surrounding regions of Montérégie, Laval, Lanaudière and Lauren-tides. In my discussion with both hospitals, and as a strategy to con-trol construction costs, I suggested keeping two sites for each new hospital. Both sites would be academic, with one to be a speciality site with a very small emergency room that mainly received referrals from other hospitals, and the other to be a community site that would have a very large, active emergency room. I began discussions with the CEOs and their boards with this objective in mind. The discussions were finalized later, while I was head of the Montreal Health and Social Services Agency. In the end, the MUHC accepted the two sites, kept all their beds but kept both sites as speciality sites, dividing up the main academic activity between them, while the CHUM decided to reduce their beds to 700 in order to remain together on one site. The CHUM will be the only major university teaching hospital in Canada on only one site with a very large emergency room that risks clogging up the hospital, and many patients who are sick but do not require the tertiary care that only a specialized teaching hos-pital can provide.

The By-Election in Berthier

The months flew by and the issue of my being elected could no longer be ignored. It had been put aside, as Bernard Landry had not been able to find an M.N.A. who was willing to give up his or her seat in a safe riding for me, but by now the situation was becoming an embarrassment for the government. During this period, there was a scandal in Quebec concerning lobbying in which a minister in the government had played a major role. The minister was obliged to leave the government and resign his seat, leaving the Berthier riding vacant. This riding was a safe PQ riding that had elected PQ candidates for the past few elections. It is a rural, agricultural riding that stretches north along the St. Lawrence River for about 200 kilometres, between Montreal and Trois-Rivières. I became the Parti Québécois candidate for the by-election, which angered many in the riding, still upset that their much-liked M.N.A. of eight years had been forced to resign. Matters were further complicated because I was an Anglophone from Montreal who was parachuted into a riding that was overwhelmingly French-speaking. To top it all off, this was a very politically risky time for the PQ. The poll numbers were not very good and I was far from the ideal candidate for this particular community. Nevertheless, in June, 2002, I took on with a passion the task of getting elected. I met the mayors of all the 26 municipalities in the riding; 13 came out publicly in my favour. I visited pig farms, chicken-slaughtering facilities, beef and dairy producers, and learned about the issues in the community. I realized for the first time how important deputies are to a riding and how, during their time in office, they play such an important role in their community. They are the community's most important advocate for development and growth, for new jobs, for building new schools and health care facilities, and for dealing with the many diverse issues and conflicts that may arise.

As the campaign began, I found myself in a rainstorm in the very small town of Sainte-Élisabeth at 9 p.m. with two of my close friends, climbing a telephone pole to put up campaign posters. At one point I looked down from the top of the ladder, water dripping off my face, to see my friends looking up at me and we all burst out laughing at the situation we found ourselves in.

People who volunteer their time and energy to help politicians get elected are a very special group. No matter which party you are

148

running for, you cannot get elected without their help and support. Although my campaign in Berthier was well run and highly organized, as expected, I lost to the daughter of a former mayor of the largest city in the riding who was quite well known and lived in the riding. In the general election about 10 months later, a 26-year-old student won the election for the PQ, demonstrating that the riding was still a PQ stronghold that clearly did not want to be manipulated.

I was both sad and happy at the turn of events. I was sad for the team that had worked so hard for me, but I was not sad about leaving politics. I knew at heart I was an administrator and I liked the hands-on feeling of producing and offering health care to the population. The government had recently restructured the Regional Health Authorities (Régies régionales) and it was the minister of health who recommended the head of the new authorities to cabinet. After discussion with Landry and Legault, I was recommended for the position of head of the Montreal Regional Health Authority, and two months after the by-election, in mid-August, 2002, I took up my new position as President and Executive Director

I had been a minister for only six months but I learned more in that short period than at any other time in my life. Politics, with all its flaws and all the media criticism it receives, includes many men and women who are dedicated and devoted to their ridings and the important mandates for which they are responsible. They work seven days a week and are constantly at risk. Errors in judgement are made, comments are made and regretted afterwards, and the media and the public are not forgiving. We need good politicians, yet we make the job harder and more difficult. As with any field, there will always be those who seek personal advantage and whose ethics are not what we would expect, but it is important to remember this is a very small portion of those who decide to go into politics, and we need good, devoted people to take on this responsibility.

CHAPTER EIGHT

Caught in the Middle
The Montreal Health and Social Service Agency

Arriving at the Agency: New Rules of the Game

I BECAME President and Executive Director of the Regional Health Authority of Montreal on August 18, 2002. My first contact with a Quebec regional health authority had been in 1975 when I was elected by the Montreal CLSCs as their representative on the Board of the Montreal regional authority. The law on health and social services mandated the "Conseil régional" (as it was called at that time) to evaluate the health needs of the region and present those needs to the government. The conseil at that time was solely a consultative body to the ministry, while the health care institutions dealt directly with the different departments of the ministry. At this point, the Quebec governance model was still a two-tier model run by the Ministry of Health and the health care institutions in each region.

By 1990, after a number of reforms, the "Conseil régional" became the "Régie régionale," a body with more responsibility and some authority, and for which there was a board of directors. Boards were partially elected by the population and partially nominated, with representation coming from different sectors in the health and social-services system, such as hospitals, universities, users, foundations, and community organizations. For the next 10 years, the régies régionales were responsible for recommending regional health projects to the ministry and ensuring the application of government directives. The régie in each region was also responsible by law for public health and the director of public health in the régie had distinct powers to intervene in health crises and to evaluate the impact of new projects, such as the construction of new roads or buildings. With time, the régies and their boards became defenders and lobbyists for their region, and they often supported their regional needs very publicly. The régies régionales set up their own association and became a political entity in health care. This evolution of the role of the régie régionale annoyed government, which saw the régie as an extension of government authority in each region, not an independent body that could publicly lobby the government.

In 2001, the government introduced Bill 28 to realign the role of the régie. Although they were given more responsibility for the management of their regions, the bill removed most of their autonomous authority. The law came into effect in 2002, and with it the boards were no longer elected or nominated by different groups of institutions and community organizations, they were appointed by the minister of health. The CEO was no longer chosen and evaluated by his or her board, but by the minister of health. The sole spokesperson for the régie was the CEO. The board chair, who in the past had been the spokesperson, was no longer the person in front of the cameras. This was the context of my new position as head of the Regional Health Authority of Montreal. By the next election in 2003, eight months later, there were calls to abolish the régies and move back to a two-tier model of governance for health care.

By the mid-1990s, across Canada, governments had be-gun to look at better integration of care. Reorganization followed, mainly through the regionalization of services. Health services in a given geographic area were put under the jurisdiction of a single governance structure, with one CEO and a single board responsible for the delivery of services in their geographic territory. British Columbia regrouped all hospitals into five regions; a sixth entity handled certain province-wide services. Alberta started out with a large number of regions for their population and, over time and in different stages, they consolidated the regions until now there is a single entity, the Alberta Health Authority, with a CEO and a single board responsible for the delivery of all health care in the province. This was a possible example of the "Hydro-health formula" that I had been interested in investigating as a possible way of removing government, hence political involvement, from the direct running of the health care system. The Alberta model did not achieve this, as it became clear that for almost all the important decisions, the level of ministerial involvement in the Alberta model was not only present, it was even more involved. Manitoba, Saskatchewan, New Brunswick, Prince Edward Island and Newfoundland followed the trend to regionalization, while Quebec and Ontario developed their own regional models for managing the health system. Ontario created 14 local, integrated health networks (LINS) that were responsible mainly for the coordination of services; health care institutions were responsible for the delivery of services and each had its own board and CEO.

In 2004, Quebec had 18 regions. There have been many attempts to reduce the number in order to give each region the critical mass and staff necessary to do the work the law requires, but politics in the regions have prevented this rationalization. In addition, the extent of duplication of services between the agences and the ministry is continually growing. It is important to understand that the civil service is a very structured, top-down organization with well-defined authority. The ministry bureaucrats see themselves as the managers of the health care system, and with the changes in the law in 2001 and the increased authority of the agence régionale, a competition and power struggle began between the ministry and the agences. Resources were to be transferred from the ministry to the agence along with certain mandates. This transfer never happened, however, and, consequently, there was no reduction in ministerial staff but rather the proliferation of duplication where the ministry systematically redid the analysis that had already been done by the agence.

Surviving a Change in Government
On April 14, 2003, the Quebec Liberal party, under Jean Charest, was elected and Dr. Philippe Couillard (currently premier of Quebec) was named minister of health. I had been on the job for eight months and, though I considered myself a good administrator, I had been junior minister of health named by the Parti Québécois. I was in charge of the largest region of Quebec with over one third of the province's health budget under my jurisdiction. Everyone in the health care sector expected there would be changes and everyone, including me, was wondering if I would keep my job. The government was planning to introduce a major reform in health care. In the early weeks of the new Liberal government I had had no contact with the new minister and I became increasingly convinced that he would want to give the job of running the Montreal régie to someone else. My first encounter with Minister Couillard was at a news conference at the Verdun General Hospital, where he announced new facilities for the family medicine

teaching unit at the Hospital. I was invited not only as head of the region but also because this was the family-medicine unit I had started at Verdun 20 years earlier, during my time as CEO there.

My only previous contact with Minister Couillard had been when I was minister visiting the Université de Sherbrooke Hospital in a meeting with the CEO of the hospital, the dean of the faculty of medicine and the principal of the Université de Sherbrooke. The head of the Department of Neuroscience made a presentation on the need for a new technology that could be used to remove a brain tumour without surgical intervention. This was neurosurgeon Dr. Philippe Couillard, and he presented the request for a Gamma Knife. He explained the technology and the advantages to patients with inoperable tumours: a Gamma Knife produces a beam of gamma rays that focuses on the brain tumour and literally burns it away. I was a biomedical engineer and had been involved in this type of presentation many times with physicians seeking new technology, and I engaged in a detailed exchange with Dr. Couillard. There was a potential for about 350 cases a year in Quebec and it was clear that we did not need more than one piece of equipment. The Montreal Neurological Institute had a worldwide reputation in neuroscience, they were attached to McGill University and they expected they would be the first to get the new technology. At the end of the meeting, I thanked all the participants and said I would think about the proposal.

Shortly thereafter, I received a phone call from Jean Charest, the M.N.A. from Sherbrooke and leader of the Liberal Party of Quebec. He was doing his job as member for his riding, indicating he was very concerned about the Hospital's request for the Gamma Knife. He asked for my thoughts on the request and I was very honest with him. I said that I thought the Gamma Knife would be a good complement to the recent acquisition of the positron emission technology that is used to image activity in the brain and the heart, and to detect cancer. The two technologies would give Sherbrooke an area of excellence that would raise their profile. If a decision were made to introduce the Gamma Knife, I would recommend Sherbrooke. As I left politics shortly thereafter, I did not have the chance to follow through on the project.

On May 15, 2003, barely a month after the election, Minister Couillard and I met at the Verdun Hospital. He began the conference by announcing a $133 million health care investment, with a priority directed towards lower wait times in the emergency room and to reduce wait lists for surgery. Then to everyone's surprise, especially mine, he went on to announce that he had full confidence in the leadership of David Levine and he supported the projects I was introducing in Montreal: network clinics, more radiology in the community, and the creation of high-volume surgical centres that would increase surgical capacity and reduce wait times, especially for hip, knee and cataract surgery. He indicated that my position was not in danger and he publicly expressed his admiration. He said, "Partisan consideration would never play a role in the appreciation of people's competency."

I was quite taken aback and very pleased, especially with the open support for my ideas and orientation for Montreal. I had worked hard to establish the respect and credibility needed to bring change into the system, and Dr. Couillard's brief comments went a very long way to giving both myself and the regional authority support to implement the needed changes. Dr. Couillard was elected Premier of Quebec in 2014.

Managing a Health System, Not an Institution

As CEO of different health care institutions, I had the responsibility of directly managing the provision of services to the population in the most efficient and effective manner possible. I was responsible to my board to ensure the mandate we were given was carried out. I learned, as I went along and developed strategies, to effectively manage those organizations. When I became a minister it was clear that, though I had a leadership role, it was not a CEO role and to do it well I had to change strategies. My newest role was to manage a region, the second-largest in Canada after the Alberta Health Authority, yet very different from the Alberta model. Alberta has a two-tier model wherein the regional authority is the direct manager of the institutions under its jurisdiction. It is run like a large corporation, with direct reports to the CEO.

The Quebec model at that time was a three-tier model wherein the central authority was supposed to define provincial objectives and standards, ensure equity among the different regions, define the extent of health and social services to be offered, and help determine the level of funding that the government is prepared to allocate to health. The role of the regional authority is to produce a strategic plan that defines the needs of the population being served, ascertains what services should be offered and where and how they should be provided, and determines which services can and cannot be met and with what delays. In the Quebec model, the regional agency did not have direct responsibility to manage the health services being provided since each institution was an autonomous organization with its own board and CEO. This created a very special situation, much like that of a CEO in a professional bureaucracy, where the authority of the regional agency must be won.

The Montreal region covers 1.9 million people on the Island of Montreal, as well as another 500,000 from outside the region who seek health services of one kind or another in Montreal. The health budget of Montreal, at $6.3 billion, is 35 percent of the province's expenditure, although the region includes only 24 percent of the population of Quebec. The difference in spending is due to the concentration of specialty teaching hospitals in Montreal that offer services to the population at large, not just Montreal residents.

The Role of the Agency

The role of the regional agency was to:

Coordinate services in its region to ensure access, quality and the continuum of care required by its population.

Provide funding to the institutions in its territory, as well as to the community groups that have been accredited to provide services.

Sign an annual management contract with the Ministry of Health that defines the funding available, the objectives to be achieved, volume targets, population health objectives, and a strategic plan that is to be implemented over the year.

Sign an annual management contract with each institution in its region containing the same elements as the contract signed with the ministry but now adapted to each institution.

Administer an accreditation process for private long-term residencies.

Evaluate and recommend to government clinical development relating to new services, new equipment, new construction, new technology (I.T. services).

Evaluate the performance of the institutions in the region relating to financial performance, quality of care, accessibility to care (wait times), client satisfaction, and security and safety of care.

Plan disaster and emergency services for the region in partnership with local authorities.

Evaluate the state of health of the population and determine the health needs of the population in the region.

Implement a strategy of public health, health promotion and prevention.

Ensure the optimization of services through regional efforts that use economies of scale, and implement an optimization strategy to ensure the best care at the best price.

Develop and implement a manpower strategy.

The role of the regional authority was very different from that of the ministry. Even if the regional authorities in Quebec are eliminated—as had been suggested many times in the past and is now being implemented with the passage of Bill 10 (as discussed in chapter 11), the work carried out by the regional authorities must still be done. I believe that what should have been done is to first streamline the system, eliminating the duplication that exists between the ministry and the agencies, and then reduce the number of agencies by consolidation, so each agency would have the critical mass needed to do its work efficiently, leaving the existing institutions to manage the offering of services.

For many years now, there has been political debate in Quebec, especially around elections, about demands to eliminate the regional authorities and move to a two-tier system. But simply eliminating the regional governance model does not eliminate the work to be done or the number of people to do it. I believe that it only changes the labels, while increasing the risk of much greater centralized decision-making and shifting the focus towards administrative and political issues and away from clinical and patient issues.

Social Services

One of the unique features of Quebec's health care system is that it is a health and social-service system, integrating the notion that social services play a very important part in the health and well-being of a population. A single medical record that contains not only the health data but also the social information and needs of both individuals and families is a very important tool in understanding the health and well-being of a person. Poverty, unemployment, problems in school, problems with the police, drug abuse, poor housing, and lifestyle issues are but a few of the factors that affect the health of a population. The regional authority's public-health teams also look at issues of infectious diseases, occupational health and safety, the impact of the environment on the health of the population, scholastic maturity in young children entering grade one, and many other issues affecting the well-being of the community.

The unique nature of including care for the elderly, the handicapped, youth protection, the intellectually handicapped, and community services into one ministry has made Quebec a leader in integrated care. This orientation was introduced in the 1970s when the Medicare system we know today was established in Quebec. The introduction of local community centres in the reform responsible for primary care and social services to the population was very innovative and avant-garde, and though all the objectives of the CLSC system were not achieved, the social role they played in the health care system was crucial.

The system in Quebec is to give regional responsibility for the health and well-being of the population to the regional authority, or as with the new law, to a regional institution, the CISSS (Centre integré de santé et de services sociaux/Integrated Health and Social

Service Centre—in this book the term CISS also includes CIUSSSs, which are the university-affiliated CISSSs). Social services are part of all care programs, (acute, home, long term, psychiatric), and are also offered by community groups that are supported by the regional institution. The integration of health and social services into one organization allows all of the dimensions of the person's well-being to be evaluated and addressed, but since under the new reform these services will not be delivered by distinct institutions with their own boards and CEO it is important to ensure that the social component of care will not be subordinated to the acute needs of the population offered mainly in the hospitals.

There is still a widespread lack of understanding of how important a person's social and family situation is to their health and well-being. For example, it is much harder to remain in a healthy state after an illness or an accident if social issues that cause stress are not taken into consideration. It is only by integrating these concerns into a single integrated vision of health that we can truly serve our population by serving the citizen within his or her whole social context.

Managing a Structural "Professional Bureaucracy"

The management approach I adopted for the management of the Montréal region is the same approach that I believe a CEO would need to use in the direct managing of regional health care. Managing a region meant for me working with the CEOs of the different institutions who are responsible to their boards. In Montreal it meant working with the community associations that bring together most of the 700 community groups on the island, the medical federations, the national unions based in Montreal, the police, the city government, and especially the population, who see the regional authority as the body they can go to when they are not satisfied with care. It also meant being available to the media to respond to the many issues that arise, mostly critical issues concerning health care. This role will now be filled by the CEO of the new regional institutions, the CISSSs.

This was a new environment for me and the skills I had acquired working in hospitals with physicians came in very handy, as did the communications skills I had acquired over time in Ottawa and in politics. I was now working in a professional bureaucracy that was far larger and more complex than any single hospital. One of my major tasks was to develop consensus among different stakeholders on a variety of projects, even though the level of the regional agency's direct authority over them was more persuasive than legal. Henry Mintzberg's principles for managing a professional bureaucracy in a hospital are also applicable in the management of health care in a region:

- ▶ Manage conflict and make decisions in a fair, honest and transparent way.

- ▶ Obtain the maximum resources possible for your region, through new clinical programs, new equipment, new construction and renovation, pilot projects, and research projects.

- ▶ Pay close attention and work on the interface between the region and the ministry, the other regions, the public, and especially the media.

- ▶ Succeeding in these three arenas will gain the credibility and respect needed to move change forward.

The first months at the Régie régionale were as demanding as the early days of any of my other positions. I had to put my team together, find the key issues for my staff and understand the internal zones of power, but I also had to do the same thing with the ministry and the many diverse institutions in the region. The agency was the focal point for all issues touching health care and this meant there was now a more direct relation between my organization and the external environment. The communications unit became my eyes and ears and was essential to keeping me abreast of all that was happening politically and within the different organizations and the community groups. We held daily briefings to define and investigate the issues that were making the headlines and for which I and/or the minister would be responsible. First thing every day, I received the newspaper clippings and scanned the headlines. Unlike the task when I was a minister, now I most wanted NOT to find my name in the news! One of my concerns was whether the régie (later the agence) would have real authority to introduce and implement the changes needed to improve health care delivery, social services and the health of the population. For the first seven years of my mandate I was able to lead the region, implement reform, introduce a city-wide information system and initiate many pilot projects. In the latter part of my mandate, the ministry often asked, "Who gave you permission to do that?" I will discuss the impact of ministry control in chapter nine, when I go into more detail on managing in the public sector.

Health Reform in Quebec: A Second Quiet Revolution

In my opinion, since 2004 Quebec has been undergoing a "quiet revolution" in health care as important as the first one 35 years previously, when Medicare came into effect in 1969. This revolution is not in structure, although there has been important structural change, but in the philosophy of how health care is provided to the population. This reform is now more than 10 years in the making and in these early stages we have created health care organizations that can provide integrated care more efficiently. The challenge now is to fully implement the reform by reallocating funds from the acute-care hospital sector to primary-care front-line services so that we can actually provide integrated care in an efficient fashion. Unfortunately, the power and lobbying of interest groups, especially the federation of specialists, has put up many roadblocks and, up to the time of this writing, government has not moved forward with the major reallocation of funds required to adequately support an integrated-care network. In December 2003, the Government of Quebec adopted Bill 25, which launched a major reorganization of Quebec's health and social-services system. Initially, the regional boards were abolished and replaced by the same number, 18, of new regional bodies called Agencies for the Development of Health and Social Services Networks. In January, 2004, these agencies were given the mandate to propose a new way of organizing services in their territory, based on the concept of integrated networks, with the goals of bringing services closer to the population, facilitating case management, and helping vulnerable patients obtain the care and the follow-up they required.

In the spring of 2004, the Montreal agency held a widespread public consultation involving the general public, health care service providers, and other partners in health care delivery. In April, 2004, the agency made a proposal to the then minister of health, Dr. Philippe Couillard, based on an organizational model of 12 Health and Social Service Centres (HSSCs) on the Island of Montreal. In June, 2004, the agency's final proposal was approved, establishing in Montreal 12 out of the existing total of 93 HSSCs across Quebec. In July 2004, letters patents were issued and the minister appointed the members of the boards of directors of the new HSSCs for a two-year transition period. This set in place the framework required to deploy a new way of seeing and doing things in the area of health and social services in Quebec.

Initially, the agency (including myself) supported a much smaller number of HSSCs on the Island of Montreal in order to properly integrate the teaching hospitals into the framework. I believed that the university-designated teaching hospitals should have been excluded from the HSSCs but that all the other hospitals should have been included as this would have provided a much greater integration of care. In those HSSCs where the acute-care hospital is integrated, the support for family medicine is much easier to develop and the corridors of service for the different specialities are easier to establish. At the time however, certain community hospitals applied political pressure to remain autonomous and, as a result, when the changes were made in 2004 only five of the networks on the Island of Montreal included an acute-care hospital, while seven HSSCs were orphans and had to rely on agreements with their neighbourhood hospitals for their acute-care needs. There were eight acute-care hospitals in Montreal that were not integrated into an HSSC. In September 2014 the government introduced a bill in the National Assembly to regroup all the institutions on the island into five integrated centres of Health and Social Services (HSSCs) leaving the McGill Hospital, the Université de Montréal Hospital, Sainte-Justine children's hospital and the Montreal Heart Institute as the only independent institutions in Quebec.

The 12 new HSSCs of Montreal came into being with the merger of 54 institutions, the abolition of their separate boards, and the selection of 12 new CEOs. The HSSCs were the result of the merger of local community health centres, local community hospitals, long-term care centres, and certain rehabilitation centres, such that each HSSC would have the necessary resources to carry out its new mandate. With responsibility for a population ranging from 100,000 to 220,000, the 1.9 million people were divided among the 12 new networks.

Although this structure was replaced in April 2015 at the time of the abolition of the regional agencies, and the disappearance of the HSSC groupings, with the creation of the CISSSs, the overall move to a population approach remains the goal of the Quebec health care system.

Guiding Principles: A Population Approach and Hierarchical Provision of Services

In the last 30 years, Quebec, like other industrialized regions, has moved from a health care context dominated by infectious diseases such as influenza, meningitis and tuberculosis, to an unprecedented situation marked by the appearance of new "epidemics" such as obesity, smoking, suicide, chronic illness and mental illness. While these contemporary health problems are causes of illness and mortality within the population as a whole, the situation is even more worrisome for certain groups. These health problems are currently responsible for almost 60 percent of deaths worldwide and it goes without saying that they cannot be ignored in the health care profile of the coming decades. The impact of these diseases is no longer measured only in the number of deaths, but also in terms of the quality of life of the persons who suffer from them.

With ever-increasing life expectancy, the chronic-disease phenomenon is progressing apace, and in its wake creating a new challenge for the health care system: meeting the needs of an aging population often suffering from chronic diseases requiring long-term case management. In order to face these new challenges, it is necessary to leave behind the current system, which is based mainly on a curative approach, and move to a population approach to health care, to manage a continuum of interventions aimed at developing and maintaining health and optimizing individual personal and social autonomy. Our health system must be designed so it can intervene at the right time to prevent an illness from progressing to those more advanced stages where the curative aspect will play a greater part in treatment. This approach will not only eliminate human suffering, it will also lower health care costs.

Finally, technological and pharmacological progress is resulting in mushrooming costs. A health care system that is better adapted to the current situation would ensure that all our initiatives have a real impact on the population's health. In our search for efficiency, decision-making must be solidly based on professional and organizational practices that have been scientifically proven or are the object of a consensus at the regional level. Interventions at the community level and the way in which health care is organized can have a very positive effect on the population's health—going well beyond treatment provided by a physician to an individual. For a number of years, various initiatives have produced encouraging results, notably, innovative projects aimed at increasing clinicians' mobility in order to ensure better coordination of care, and the setting up of integrated service networks.

The guiding principles with which we should move forward are a population approach to health care and the hierarchical provision of services.

The Concept of Responsibility for the Population

The ultimate goal of the health-system reform that was begun in 2004 was to optimize the impact of services on the health of the population by introducing the concept of responsibility for a given part of the population. This population approach is essentially based on the conviction that health is a collective asset that must be maintained and developed. In this respect, it both recognizes the various individual factors that influence health, and seeks to reduce social inequalities, which constitute another obstacle to well-being and health. The objective of this reform is to ensure a maximum state of health in the population of a given territory by taking into account available resources, and globally coordinating the services offered to a given population, rather than defining the service offer according to the individuals who consume the services. This kind of approach takes for granted that regional and local authorities are responsible for the health of the individuals in their territory and must provide access to the services that are appropriate to that territory, taking into account the effectiveness of interventions and actions in living environments rather than in theoretical vacuums.

According to the population-approach principle, HSSCs and now CISSSs their local partners have an acknowledged collective responsibility to the population in their territory. They assume this responsibility by ensuring that efforts converge to maintain and improve the health and well-being of the population. They do this by making the necessary services available, and by providing support and case management for persons within the health and social-service system.

This approach means that it is up to the CISSS (and earlier to the HSSC) to rally the personnel, physicians and resources of its territory around an organizational and clinical project that will enable it to fulfill its responsibility to the local population. As indicated in the draft guide for implementation of the clinical project, developed by the Ministry of Health of Quebec, the HSSC was required to:

▸ Establish the health and well-being profile of the territory's population;

▸ Conduct an inventory of the resources and services currently available to meet those needs;

▸ Analyze the gaps that must be filled in order to meet access, continuity and quality objectives;

▸ Identify clinical models and fruitful collaborations that are already in place and that must be maintained and strengthened;

▸ Choose, if appropriate, other models that can be incorporated to fill the gaps in terms of reaching the chosen objectives;

▸ Specify the elements of the service offer, and the parameters that must appear in the service agreements;

▸ Specify actors' roles and responsibilities;

▸ Mesh service programs with all of the services offered;

▸ Follow up on the impact of services on the health of the population.

Source: *Guide pour l'implantation du projet clinique*, MSSS, consultation document.

An important element to this model was that a new resource allocation based on an evaluation of the health needs of the population would support the implementation of this new approach over the coming years.

Added Value

Our health care system has traditionally been dominated by the logic of service production. Each institution was responsible for its clientele and planned its service offer by allocating resources according to the demands expressed by that clientele. Needs were generally identified using a combination of a record of service use and waiting lists.

Today, the need to redefine objectives in the health world—with the relevant parameters being service accessibility, continuity, quality and efficiency—has made it imperative to revise professional practices and forms of organization. The population approach, service integration, the development of networks, comprehensive and personalized case management, personalized medicine and result-based management offer promising ways forward, as testified by several recent experiences in Quebec and elsewhere in the world.

In the chart following on the next page I have compared certain components of a health care system that is based on user needs to a system based on a population approach, showing how this new approach in Quebec will change certain dynamics in our organizations. The chart includes some of the changes we hope to realize with the new population approach.

Hierarchical Service Provision

The goal of hierarchical service provision in health care is to ensure that the right service is provided to the right person at the right place, at the right time and by the right service provider. Hierarchical service provision is aimed at guaranteeing that services complement each other, and at facilitating the ways users navigate between front-line, secondary and tertiary services, as appropriate.

The HSSC was made responsible for the front-line health and social services required for the population in its territory. If it was not in a position to provide the entire range of front-line services, the HSSC had to enter into agreements with other institutions or partners, notably with a first-instance hospital if there was no hospital within the HSSC. The same applied to the specialized and ultra-specialized

	Care system based on the needs of service users	**Care system based on a population approach**
Responsibility	Individuals who use services	Population of the local territory, regardless of whether they use the services
Mission	Improve the health of the individuals who use the care, when they need it	Improve the health of the territory's population in the medium and long term
Service offer	Emphasis on diagnostic and curative services	Emphasis on a continuum of care, going from prevention to rehabilitation
Actors involved	Professionals and system managers, with their respective expertise	Care providers in the system and actors in the milieu, such as the population, the school and municipal environment, doctors with private practices, community organizations, all with their respective knowledge and perspectives

Chart continued	Care system based on the needs of service users	Care system based on a population approach
Practices	▲ Use of meaningful data and practice guides for the individuals using the services ▲ Process-based management	▲ Use of meaningful data in terms of effectiveness for the population. ▲ Making the population's health problems a priority, taking into account the effective interventions available and the consequences of resource allocation (efficiency) ▲ Defining target groups, showing a concern for inequalities (at-risk and special groups) ▲ Managing the use of services, including comprehensive, ongoing and personalized case management ▲ Integrating the various levels of care (primary care, specialized care, etc.) ▲ Health results-based management

	Care system based on the needs of service users	Care system based on a population approach
Main indicators	▲ Interest is focused on the numerator, in this case, those consulting ▲ Process indicators are preferred. For example, with regard to service production. The question is how many people a screening program reaches. ▲ Available resources and services are measured, as are waiting lists.	▲ Interest is focused on the relationship between the numerator and the denominator; ▲ In this case, the clientele and the population ▲ Result indicators are added to process indicators. For example, with regard to health production, interest is focused on decreasing the incidence of a given disease ▲ The state of health and well-being of the population is measured, as well as the determining factors of health and the gap between needs and the services provided

services that were made accessible to the population through the service corridors established between the HSSCs and institutions designated to offer those types of services. HSSCs were, therefore, the foundations for the new organization of services in their territories by ensuring accessibility, case management, follow-up and service coordination for the population. The CISSSs must now assume this role.

According to the hierarchical service-provision principle, the liaisons agreed upon between the HSSC and other service producers were two-way liaisons. On the one hand, they ensured access to secondary (specialized) and tertiary (ultra-specialized) services for the population in the territory; on the other hand, these liaisons guaranteed that territory residents had access to the front-line (general) services provided by the HSSC when they returned to their living environment following hospitalization.

To coordinate the hierarchical provision of services, the Ministry of Health created four Integrated University Service Networks (IUSNs) to oversee the distribution and production of specialized and ultra-specialized services throughout Quebec. Each network was based around one of the four faculties of medicine and the designated university teaching hospital to which it was attached. The other members of each network were the affiliated teaching hospitals and other specialized institutions, as well as the health institutes belonging to each faculty. The 93 HSSCs were divided between each of the four IUSNs, and each IUSN was responsible for developing the corridors of specialized services between the networks for which they were responsible and the designated specialized institution that provided them with the specialized care they needed. The development of the corridors of service meant that the HSSC physicians did not have to shop around for the specialized consults or services they needed and that there was an obligation for the specialized centres to provide those services in a rapid fashion to the HSSCs for which they were responsible. The CISSSs now have the coordinating role and the responsibility to ensure the corridors of service are developed.

The hierarchy of service provision assures the availability of services but it does so by moving away from a hospital-based service to a community-based primary-care model. Since this has not existed in the past, hospitals have filled the gap and developed many of the follow-up services. As a result of this situation, a large portion of the work done by specialists is primary care. If the system is to work effectively, we must transfer resources from our hospital system to a front-line primary-care system that needs those resources to build and maintain full access to diagnostic technology, specialist consultation, and access to the multidisciplinary teams needed to ensure follow-up care and chronic care, and management of the vulnerable population. This essential part of the reform is not yet happening and unless and until there is the political will to change our hospital-based culture, it will be difficult to achieve real progress in accessibility, better-managed illness, better quality of care, lower cost and a healthier population.

Health and Social Services Centres (HSSCs)
A Unique Mission

Because they combined the forces of the CLSCs (Local Community Service Centres), residential and long-term care centres (CHSLDs), rehabilitation centres (CHRs) and community hospitals in a given territory, HSSCs had a unique mission within that territory. The mission had three major aspects, each with its attendant management challenges:

▶ Evaluating the state of health and well-being of the population in its territory and taking the lead in actions aimed at improving that state (for example, programs to reduce tobacco consumption).

▶ Managing the use of the services placed at the disposal of its territory's population, and taking the appropriate measures to provide case management, assistance and support to users to ensure continuity from one required care episode to the next, within the health and social service network.

▶ Ensuring optimal management of the range of services provided, by ensuring that they are effective, efficient, relevant and meet users' expectations and the population's needs.

FUNDING BY PROGRAM

Programs for the population	Public health						
Service-programs	General services, clinical and assistance activities / Front-line medical services						
Programs designed to address specific problems	Loss of autonomy linked to aging	Physical impairment	Intellectual impairment and PDD	Troubled youth	Addiction	Mental health	Physical health
Support-programs	Administration and support for services						
	Building and equipment management						

Government of Quebec, Ministry of Health and Social Services.

In order to rise to these challenges, HSSCs had to equip themselves quickly with an organizational and clinical plan to mobilize their personnel and network of partners. In practical terms, this plan had to establish, for each territory, a local vision for provision of the broad range of services based on the state of the population's health and well-being. The plan had to consider any special characteristics of the population, and the services required to meet those particular health and social needs (for example, of aboriginal peoples). The plan also had to include agreements with various partners on the methods of collaboration and their contributions.

More precisely, the organizational and clinical plan or project had to specify how the HSSC would deliver the nine service programs and two support programs (See table on preceding page)), defined by the Ministry of Health, for which HSSCs received funding. Budget allocation methods will gradually move away from a trends approach toward a population approach, with a method based on indicators reflecting the needs of the population and the amounts of resources available. The CISSSs are now responsible for this planning function.

Health and Social Service Centres: A Central Role in Developing and Expediting Local Health and Social Service Networks

In order to be in a position to completely fulfill their mission, HSSCs had to set up and expedite a local service network and work in an increasingly integrated fashion to improve the health and well-being of the population and to ensure case management for users, particularly for persons with special and/or complex needs.

With this in mind, HSSCs were responsible for creating, with their partners, conditions that fostered the accessibility, continuity and the networking of general medical care. One of the first priorities was the creation of procedures that would enable general practitioners within the HSSC territory to easily access:

▸ technical support (equipment) for diagnostic services;

▸ clinical information, including the results of diagnostic tests;

▸ consultation with specialists.

HSSCs would be able to achieve this goal by developing contractual ties with partners in their territory, namely with the Family Medicine Groups (FMGs) and Network Clinics. This partnership would make it possible to provide medical services with or without an appointment, from 8:00 a.m. to 10:00 p.m., seven days a week. It would also ensure that the territory's general practitioners have access to the appropriate technical support (laboratories, imaging) for emergency tests. Finally, this association would guarantee the case management of at-risk clientele and liaison with the HSSCs' relevant programs. These tasks now fall to the CISSSs.

The Local Health Network
In addition to medical services, ties were needed with other sectors of activity that have an impact on health and social services, such as school boards, municipalities, housing environments, community pharmacies, social-economy enterprises, non-institutional resources and community organizations. By cooperating with these sectors of activity, the HSSCs would be able to develop a coherent vision and coordinate actions aimed at improving the health and well-being of the population. Each HSSC had the mandate to develop its local network and the authority to sign all the contracts that were needed to ensure the provision of care to its population. This is the path the CISSSs must now also take.

Implementing a Health Care Reform: Finding the Vision
Once the 12 HSSCs were set up, I participated with each of the board-selection committees to choose the CEOs to run the newly created centres. It was clear to me from the start that it would be essential to create a closely-knit team that could develop a unifying vision, one that each board could accept and work towards. I began by creating the Montreal Regional Management Committee (MRMC), which for the first years had the 12 network CEOs meeting for a half-day every two weeks to manage the implementation of the reform, share knowledge and experiences, and support one another in a learning exercise, since everyone was managing new organizations for the first time. After the first two years, the other CEOs of the non-integrated

institutions were invited to join the committee on a monthly basis.

Once the MRMC was up and meeting regularly, I suggested a planning exercise to develop a vision for Montreal that would guide the implementation of the reform. The exercise had two objectives: to develop a vision and to develop the team. To give the team unity of purpose, a common vision, a strategy of implementation and a culture of working together, it was important to create a sense of belonging to their region because I knew that after a few years their principal loyalty and concern would be to their institutions, their boards, their career advancement and the next, and larger, organization they could run. I had experienced these emotions many times and knew that the window of regional commitment was maybe four years, the length of a CEO's first mandate. To achieve these objectives, I set up a planning exercise that would look at some of the more advanced health care systems in the world, study them in detail and then organize study tours to look more closely at these systems. The Kaiser model in the United States has been recognized in the literature as one of the most successful in improving and managing the health of their rostered population. The reform in the National Health Service of England was based on the creation of primary-care trusts (PCTs) that commissioned services; this model showed some very positive results. The model of health care based on primary-care teams in the Catalan province of Spain had already been in place for 20 years. After studying these systems through a major literature review, study tours were planned to look at the Kaiser model in San Francisco, the PCT model in England, and the Catalan model in Barcelona. I organized the study tours, one a year, and had almost full participation of the 12 CEOs and some primary-care physicians. The trips not only allowed the MRMC to define a common vision but created the friendship and closeness that I was aiming to create in the regional team. This proved to be a powerful experience and allowed for far more collaboration among the CEOs and the centres than would have normally occurred.

The group was impressed with the Kaiser model of care, including its ability to improve the health of its population by reducing cardiac incidence to significantly better than the national average through chronic-care management; to reduce emergency room visits equivalent to 50 percent of the number of Montreal's emergency room visits for the same population; to lower the number of prescriptions; and to better control costs. Representatives from Kaiser were invited to Montreal to present their model of care to a much larger audience. Physicians, professionals and administrators were invited to the Montreal conference and subsequent reflection led to Montreal's vision for the implementation of the reform.

Montreal's Vision
The "Montreal Vision" that emerged from this exercise included the following elements:

▸ Develop a strong and completely reorganized primary-care model—a community-based rather than a hospital-based health care system;

▸ Introduce a managed-care model based on chronic-disease management;

▸ Engage the population in self-management of their own health status, and provide them with the necessary tools to do so;

▸ Develop performance measurements based on the development of an electronic health record (EHR), as well as on the interconnectivity of all medical data for the entire population of Quebec.

The boards of all the HSSCs as well as the regional council for family medicine approved these four elements. Each element was then elaborated into a strategy for implementation with an action plan that each centre was to put into place.

Primary Care: The Key Element for the Success of Quebec's Health Care Reform
Primary care has had a long history in Quebec and, were it not for the barriers that existed in the past, it would have one of the most advanced health care systems in the world. In 1966, the Government of

Quebec mandated Claude Castonguay and Gérard Nepveu to prepare a report for the implementation of a universal health care system. In 1969, the Castonguay-Nepveu Commission[1] recommended the creation of the Quebec Health Insurance Plan (Régie de l'assurance-maladie du Québec), referred to as RAMQ, and submitted, in 1970, a report that is the underpinning of the existing health care system in Quebec. The key recommendation of this report was the creation of three university networks (there were three faculties of medicine in Quebec at the time) with distinct levels of integrated health care services: primary (community), secondary (hospital) and tertiary (specialized services). The report recommended development of primary-care services within a number of CLSCs.[2] It was expected that the medical services in CLSCs would be offered by family physicians in collaboration with a group of health care professionals. The CLSC mandate included: managing the health care of the population living in their territory; the development of front-line social and medical programs to address the needs of the population (family planning, mental health, etc.); the development of social services; and a home-care program. The report recommended the creation of 256 CLSCs across the province of Quebec, each of which was to take responsibility for a population of 30,000 rostered persons. All the personnel working in the CLSCs would be employees of the Quebec Health and Social Services Ministry (Ministère de la Santé et des Services sociaux) and the physicians would be paid by fee-for-service or by salary.

The Medical Insurance Board was created by law in 1969, and the Quebec National Assembly approved the new law on health and social services in 1970.

The vision of our system developed by the Castonguay-Nepveu Commission faced serious opposition from physicians and, initially, even from the community sector. The physicians reacted negatively to state intervention in the medical profession by government regulation of their remuneration. From their perspective, it was a threat to their professional autonomy. This reaction took form in an almost unanimous decision among the general practitioners to boycott[3] the new CLSC structure when it was implemented. After more than 40 years, the CLSCs have still never achieved their objectives, and currently only 10 percent of primary-care physicians practice in the CLSCs.

Furthermore, we are far from achieving the full number of CLSCs envisioned for the whole Quebec network, due to the numerous reorganizations by successive Quebec governments. Quebec has only 156 of the 256 CLSCs originally proposed, barely 60 percent of the full complement.

The state paid physicians on a fee-for-service basis, and in the first years of the system physicians used the nurses with whom they had always worked to help them care for their patients, especially for patient follow-up. If a nurse gave an immunization inoculation to a baby, the doctor would bill the activity and, out of the proceeds, pay his nurse in the new fee-for-service model. Fearing out-of-control costs due to billing of increased activities, the government required that every patient be seen and treated by the physician directly; they refused payment for the activities done by a nurse and billed by the doctor. This meant that MDs were no longer able to pay for nurses or other professionals in their offices. This was probably the most significantly harmful policy decision made at that time; it resulted in preventing physicians from developing their clinics and, consequently, the reduction in physician accessibility did not allow adequate follow-up of patients. This led to the development of a very weak primary-care sector with no multidisciplinary teams and no capacity to manage patient care, especially for patients with a chronic illness.

The CSSSs (Centres de santé et de services sociaux)[4] were created 35 years later to address a number of health care issues: accessibility, continuity of care, chronic-care management, the difficulty of transferring a person from one level of care to another, and the management of services in an integrated manner. This reform and the creation of 95 CSSSs in a regionally-based structure, under the responsibility of the Health and Social Services Agencies (Agence de la santé et des services sociaux, or ASSS)[5], allowed a better integration of the services offered to the population, as well as a better follow-up of the population's health status. Meanwhile, the four university networks (there are now four faculties of medicine in Quebec), today known as the Integrated University Health Networks (Réseaux universitaires intégrés de santé or RUIS)[6], were created with the mandate to ensure medical coverage for third- and fourth-line services in all Quebec regions, and especially to ensure that there is no lack of specialized services in remote regions.

This structural reform brought a new vision of the health care system based on population responsibility and the development of a strong primary care system. To achieve the objectives of this reform, it is now necessary to make important cultural changes in our health system, and to go back to the original vision of Mr. Castonguay and Mr. Nepveu, but using a different approach to achieve the same objectives—an approach based on current realities.

The development of primary care is the key element if we are to successfully implement the objectives of the reform we have been implementing since 2004 and that we must continue with the new reform now being introduced. Primary care services are the first component of the common vision agreed upon by all the CEOs in the Montreal region. This development would allow the HSSCs to achieve a population-based approach and ensure the management of care and follow-up for their most vulnerable patients, or those with a chronic disease.

The development of strong primary-care services will allow for:

▶ Clearly defined levels of care that will provide the population with greater and more timely access to required services—the right patient in the right place at the right time.

▶ The cultural change in how services are accessed by the people who use the emergency room twice as often as the emergency utilization rates observed in systems with well-developed primary care.

▶ Better access to client tools that improve client self-management of health status, especially for those clients with chronic disease.

▶ Better utilization of general practitioners (GPs) resulting in greater accessibility for the population

▶ A major reduction in health care system costs due to improvements in patient management, utilization of medication, and utilization of diagnostic testing.

The most crucial component of this front-line vision concerns the development of GP offices capable of responding to the reform objectives. We must take a leadership position by supporting Quebec's general practitioners, encouraging them to reorganize their offer of services, to work in a multidisciplinary team, to reorganize their links with second- and third-line care by adding health and social-service professionals to their team, to assume the overall management of patient care, including the follow-up required by vulnerable clients with chronic illness and multiple pathologies. The concept of the medical assistant, fundamental to the Kaiser model, must be explored as a way to significantly increase the number of patients rostered by a family physician. The assistant has primary contact with the patient and does all the preparation and some of the intervention that the physician does, then passes the patient to the physician who focuses on the specific problem in a much shorter period of time. The assistant serves as the contact for patient follow-up and helps the interdisciplinary teams in chronic-care management of patients. The Kaiser model has allowed physicians to roster 2,200 to 2,600 patients, while in Quebec a physician is supposed to roster between 900 and 1,500 patients depending on the level of care needed for each patient. Even this lower level of rostering has not been reached in Quebec, and the current Minister of Health, Dr. Gaétan Barrette, is requiring general practitioners to roster a minimum of 1000 patients or see their fees for services cut up to 30%. Investment must also be made in the physical environment where physicians practice, to allow them to create the medical centres that can support multidisciplinary teams and the diagnostic and follow-up services needed by a comprehensive, fully developed family practice.

Family Medicine Groups (FMGs)

In 2000, the Quebec government planned for the introduction of 300 family-practice or family-medicine groups (FMGs), following the recommendations of the Clair Commission. The federal government, in their primary-care initiative in 2000, decided to provide funding to the provinces to develop family-practice teams as the bases for primary-care development. Montreal was beginning to develop FMGs, although much more slowly than in rural areas, the main reason being the difference in the nature of Montreal's clientele. In a rural area, most patients have a family physician they have been seeing for many years. In Montreal, over 30 percent of the population does not have a family physician. The population in rural areas is stable, whereas 50 percent of the population of Montreal moves every five years, either changing housing or moving off the island.

The idea that an FMG has to roster its patients and take on the responsibility for those patients is more difficult in an urban area where patients have much greater mobility. Most of the existing physician groups had large walk-in practices, thus allowing patients who needed to see a doctor rapidly to go to the walk-in clinic and avoid going to a hospital emergency room. In an FMG, patients have to be on the group roster and the FMG has to agree to be open for their rostered patients for extended hours. As part of the agreement, the FMG is paid a yearly sum for each patient on its roster and it receives two nurses from the CLSC, as well as technical and some support services. The annual value to the clinic is up to $350,000, depending upon the number of patients on the roster.

An FMG brings together eight to 12 "full-time equivalent" (FTE) physicians who commit to providing a full array of medical services to a clientele who have chosen to register with them. Each FMG is expected to have about 15,000 registered clients, or about 1,500 clients per FTE physician. The FMG provides services with or without an appointment, seven days a week. In practice, this means 12 hours of availability a day during the week, and four hours a day during weekends and holidays, with medical on-call services 24 hours a day, seven days a week for registered clientele when illness puts them at risk. The FMGs also feature extended nursing services[7], amounting to 70 hours of availability a week. The nursing staff is in a position to work with physicians to provide effective care from the time of screening all the way through systematic follow-up of at-risk clientele. The FMGs ensure medical case management of individuals, while the HSSCs and local networks are responsible for clinical case management by ensuring that health and social services are coordinated and continuous.

Network Clinics (NCs)

At the time of introduction of the FMG program, 60 percent of Montreal's family physicians worked in settings other than a family clinic and were reluctant to roster patients, since the responsibility for those patients was not yet clear and they felt that their autonomy was being threatened. I believed very strongly in the need to roster patients and I did not believe that the FMGs would threaten physician autonomy, but I had a serious problem. I needed to maintain and even increase the walk-in capacity of Montreal to avoid using the already overcrowded emergency rooms for patients who could be seen elsewhere. At the same time, I wanted to encourage the continuity of care that a rostered environment would provide. In discussion with the director of the Montreal regional department of family medicine (Département régional de la médecine générale or DRMG—a committee of the agence in each region elected by the GPS) a plan was suggested to create a network clinic in which physicians would not be required to roster patients but would be allowed to offer as many hours of walk-in services as services with appointments, and the clinic agreed to extend its hours to 12 hours a day, and eight hours on weekends. In return, the clinic would receive two nurses to help provide services, and some support and technical services. At full participation, the package would be about $250,000 per network. Montreal physicians were in favour of this proposal and it was presented to the ministry.

The ministry was not prepared to fund this model; they were more concerned with the importance of rostering patients and did not want to support two different models. I made a decision with the approval of my Board to fund the project out of regional funds and we moved forward with the program. It was so popular with the physicians, and was supported by their union, that the minister of health realized the benefit of adding this model to the ministry's approach. When I went to the ministry to get funding for the 19 clinics already set up in Montreal, however, I was told I would only receive funds for those set up after the minister's decision and that would amount to only $150,000, rather than the $250,000 that was the cost. This was yet another frustrating example of the resistance of civil servants to accept any proposal differing from what they had previously determined. In this case, their resistance punished a regional initiative because it was different from their defined policies or programs.

Integrated Network Clinics (INCs)

To fully meet the needs of the Montreal Vision, and using the Kaiser model as a template, the agency, working with the DRMG, developed a new model. The HSSCs and the Montreal physicians accepted the proposal to implement integrated network clinics, or INCs (Cliniques-réseau intégrées, or CRIs). [8]

This model contemplates the creation of about 60 INCs, each of which could register 30,000 persons, covering the 1.8 million inhabitants of the Island of Montreal. These clinics are to be open 12 hours a day, seven days a week, with an on-call capacity—organized by collaboration between INCs—to cover the remaining 12 hours of each day. They will have an average of 15 FTE physicians and 15 FTE professionals from different health-related professions (depending on their specific client population needs), and a support team that includes a radiology infrastructure. Three clinics were opened in Montreal during my mandate, and we can only hope that others will open soon.

One of the major obstacles to implementation is to actually group physicians in an environment that can support this new front-line reorganization. To date, the development of the FMGs and the INCs has not required major changes in the existing working environments (the buildings used by physicians). If we are to fully implement this system in Montreal, we must find a way to use incentives to stimulate the development of INCs. The original overall plan provided that at least 12 of the 60 INCs (one in each of the 12 CSSSs existing at that time) include the basic medical specialties, with diagnostic tools available, to ensure easier access for the clients in each territory. Medical leadership, initiative and creativity are essential to the success of a strong primary-care system such as this one. In order to work with the strong support of the health care community for this progressive model, we require government financial incentives for the creation of the infrastructure required to fully implement it.

To develop the INCs and to make progress with front-line services, it is necessary to ensure the conditions that allow for the cultural and environmental changes required in the practice of family physicians. The conditions required to effectively develop such a primary-care system are:

▸ An electronic health record (EHR) which gives access to all GPs, no matter what model they are working in, and the capacity to follow the medical history of their patients. In the Montreal agency's vision, all GP offices in the city would be integrated into a single platform.[9] The further interconnection between the EHR (in HSSCs, hospitals and physicians' offices) and the Quebec EHR, or QEHR (Dossier de santé du Québec, or DSQ[10]), would allow patient data to be accessible, wherever and whenever a patient receives health care in Quebec.

▸ Expansion of training of professionals, including physicians, to include courses and traineeships focused on patient-oriented teamwork. I believe we must move to a model of care that promotes managed care based on a multi/interdisciplinary team in our primary-care settings.

▸ Implementation of a sufficient number of FMGs, NCs and INCs to cover the entire population in Montreal.

▸ Creation of complete service corridors among FMGs, NCs, INCs and hospitals in order to simplify and accelerate access to the expertise and services required. Access to specialists for the urgent and semi-urgent needs of clients must be put into place through the use of protocols managed by nurses who can send prepared patients to a specialist for a consultation. For emergency room consultations, direct access is now well developed. For semi-urgent situations, we must implement clinical intake programs in all our hospitals with a goal to ensure a more direct and faster access to the specialist once the diagnostic tests are completed. In this type of program, a nurse coordinator initiates and coordinates the required diagnostic tests through the application of a set of collective protocols. The nurse can thus accelerate the procedure and facilitate access to the specialist. For the non-urgent clients, we must reorganize the appointment-making procedure for diagnostic examinations to make it more efficient and user-friendly.

▸ Development of management programs for chronic diseases[11]; these are necessary to give GPs and their teams access to more specialized teams for second-line services. These second-line teams take care of the patient for a short time period (six months) to do additional investigation, immediate treatment and education, after which they return the patient to the care of the family physician and his/her team for the follow-up. These projects are already being implemented in each CISSS on the Island of Montreal.

▸ Creation of a training plan to support practice change, including new curricula on interdisciplinary work in multi-disciplinary teams, for pre- and post-graduate education programs as well as for continuing education needs to be developed in our faculties of medicine.

The development of primary care is the most important change required in our health system. This new direction requires a change in the practices and working approaches of our health care professionals. Although this kind of change is widely considered to be the right approach, it is still difficult to implement. Consequently, we must be even more resolute in our efforts to make it happen. The development of strong front-line services will reduce accessibility problems to health care services for the population of Quebec and will put emphasis on the quality of care in our health system.

The Barriers to the Implementation of Primary Care

The Medical Care Act (1966), which defined our universal health care system, created a public system based principally around the hospital, where diagnosis, treatment and medication are covered under a public insurance program. In the hospital sector, operating expenses, infrastructure, equipment, and renovations are covered from the public purse, while in primary care only the physician fees are covered, with a negotiated additional fee for some office expenses. Outside the hospital, pediatric and adult primary care covers only physician remuneration for all medical acts that are administered on a fee-for-service basis. Over time, the hospital system was labelled "public" and the primary-care sector came to be labelled "private."

This false distinction between what is public and what is private goes a long way to explain the evolution of our hospital-centred health care system in which primary care has not received the necessary attention and resources. A move away from a hospital-centred system and the development of strong primary care will require a change in public policy. Discussion of primary care inevitably leads to the public versus private health care debate and, unfortunately, this debate is often based on a false premise. Private care refers to the agent who pays for the services, rather than the services being offered. If the payer is public, the services should be considered public; if the payer is the individual or a personal insurance program, the services should be considered private. Since primary care carried out by a physician is paid from the public purse, it is false to label this as part of the private sector. This artificial label for primary care has led to the undesirable outcome of creating some reluctance to fund it from the public purse since it is associated with private enterprise, even though it is an essential building block of an effective universal public health care system.

Expectations of the Population

The public is concerned with the following issues relating to their health care services:

Access to a family physician (this means not only being rostered to a family physician, but that the physician actually be available; this availability is ensured when the family physician is part of a larger group of physicians and a multidisciplinary team);

Access to technology (principally imaging technology) and laboratory services in order to obtain diagnostic tests and their results within a medically acceptable time frame;

Access to consultation with a specialist within an appropriate time frame;

Access to treatment that is guaranteed to be within a
medically required delay;

Access to a multidisciplinary team or program to help
manage chronic illness and support for the elderly;

Access to programs of prevention and promotion
related to the needs of individual patients, with the
appropriate support and education to enable patients to
practice self-care as much as possible.

The Difficulties of Developing Strong Primary Care

Policy-makers and analysts of our health care system understand
clearly that the development of a strong primary-care model is
essential. However, there are many barriers to this change from a
hospital-centred model to a primary-care model.

1. The primary-care physician's clinic is not considered to be
    part of the public system but rather a part of the physician's
    private office. Within the health care system, public financ-
    ing is provided for the hospital and long-term care system
    and is not intended for the private sector. There has long
    been reluctance to invest in what has unfortunately been
    misrepresented as the private sector, and consequently there
    has been little public investment in essential primary care.
    It is only recently that some financing has been made avail-
    able to fund certain professionals in family practice groups.
    This practice of paying physicians on a strictly fee-for-
    service basis, thus leaving the physician solely responsible
    for organizing an appropriate primary-care infrastructure
    in the community, has become one of the most significant
    obstacles to the development of primary care.

2. Investment in infrastructure, buildings and equipment, is
    principally for the hospital sector; support for primary-
    care activities do not benefit from such investments. In
    Montreal alone, over the past four years, $8 billion has
    been invested in hospital building and renovation, while

not a single dollar has been invested in the infrastructure for primary-care physicians.

3. There are no physician incentives to develop and expand primary-care activities. There is no support to develop clinics owned by family physicians because they are considered private enterprise rather than an essential part of the complex public health care system that provides essential primary care.

4. Primary care has not succeeded in developing a modern culture of functioning with a multidisciplinary team in which a broad range of professionals work in tandem to provide clients with interrelated services in a coordinated fashion. There is still a tendency for physicians to continue to function as individual medical-service providers, even within the newly developed family-practice groups.

5. Within hospitals there is a strong established culture of belonging to the organization, and physicians and other professionals are proud of working in their institution. This sentiment of belonging does not exist in the current primary-care environment. Primary-care physicians are often attracted to working in hospitals because of the working environment; in Montreal, family physicians spend almost 50 percent of their working time in the hospital rather than in the community.

6. There are no official structures to support primary care. A hospital (and now each CISS) has a council of physicians, dentists and pharmacists that is required by law to ensure quality care to patients. Primary care does not benefit from a similar official structure; the only representation of primary-care providers is from their union. Without a political lobby group, clinical primary-care providers have not had an effective voice to promote the development of primary care.

7. Primary care does not benefit from academic recognition for its role and importance in health care. Medical schools support and strongly encourage specialty services. Primary care and primary-care physicians have diminishing prestige and value, while specialty medicine and specialists are perceived as having increasing prestige. A hidden agenda in the medical schools encourages students to follow a career as a specialist rather than as a family physician. Specialists are also paid on a significantly higher scale then general practitioners. These are important constraints in the development of primary care.

8. The relationship between specialists and general practitioners is also a barrier to the development of the new efficient primary-care system. In Montreal, there are 3,700 specialists and only 1,700 general practitioners—50 percent of whom work in the hospital or long-term care sector. As a result of this imbalance, many specialists carry out primary-care activities, especially activities relating to follow-up of chronically ill patients. This means the specialists are less available for specialty evaluation and treatment of new patients. This is not the most effective way to use our physicians and it has led to long wait times for patients to see a specialist.

9. Currently, primary care does not offer incentives to follow up and manage vulnerable patients suffering from chronic illness. The multidisciplinary teams being set up are not yet adequate to respond to the needs of the chronically ill.

10. In the current Canadian system, prevention and promotion of health does not have adequate support or remuneration. It should be central to the work of a family physician.

11. Primary-care projects and funding don't offer politicians the same level of media coverage or visibility that result from large projects and investment in the hospital sector.

Primary-care activities are not considered "sexy."

12. Our hospitals—especially the academic institutions—have long experience of and high capacity for lobbying; this leaves little place for lobbying by the primary-care sector, which only has union representation and few resources.

13. The primary-care sector does not have an integrated universal information system for their medical records; hospitals have been using electronic records for many years. Only recently, as more family-practice groups are formed, have we seen the beginnings of the critical mass needed for the implementation of information systems that will help physicians outside the hospitals to manage their patients. The development of an information system in primary care is probably the most important factor in the establishment of a structured primary-care system.

We must work to break down these barriers and solve the problems in order to enable and facilitate the establishment of a health care system based on the development of a strong primary-care model grounded in managed care.

Our Achilles Heel: Managing Emergency Room Services
Improving the performance of emergency room services in our hospitals has been a priority in Montreal for many years, and though there have been periods of improvement we have yet to achieve sustained high performance. Since 1986, when Madame Thérèse Lavoie-Roux asked me to set up the Hospital in the Home program (see chapter three) to remove pressure on the Verdun emergency room by adding more beds to the system, the emergency room has played a prominent role in the media and been a major issue for every minister of health. Quebec has made significant investments so that the system can discharge patients more rapidly, especially those who need long-term and convalescent care. With these changes, we have achieved momentary improvement rather than sustained improvement. We must pursue a new approach that will ensure both appropriate and efficient use of our emergency

rooms. The core of the new approach is to refocus our health care system away from its current curative-based hospital orientation to a community-based primary-care system.

Emergency rooms have been managed institution by institution with local plans that focus on how the hospital manages patients who arrive on foot or by ambulance. This approach has not changed the way the population uses emergency room services or resulted in different approaches to how to offer health care. Until there is an alternative that offers timely access for the population to the health care services they need, the emergency room will continue to be the focal point of care. In order to change the system, in partnership with the CEOs of all the Montreal health care institutions, the Montreal agency developed a regional approach for an integrated management model to manage and coordinate all emergency room activity in Montreal. This approach established a set of six priorities, but, unfortunately, the change was not fully pursued because the barriers to implementation were not addressed, and this regional approach to integrated health management did not meet the need for an immediate response to headlines in the newspaper. These are the core priorities of this approach:

1. Implement an integrated regional-management model for emergency room services.

2. Reduce the number of visits to emergency rooms by 50 percent by offering the population 24-hour alternative access to care.

3. Ensure that primary-care physicians and the local health networks manage the care of vulnerable and chronically ill patients and improve their health in an organized, managed care model in order to reduce their episodes of crisis and utilization of emergency room services.

4. Free up hospital beds as quickly as possible by revising the processes and the utilization of resources related to patient discharge from hospitals and to admission to rehab and long-term centres.

5. Develop a program of care and follow-up for the elderly (before, during and after a hospital stay) to reduce their loss of autonomy.

6. Improve internal management of emergency rooms as well as services on the ward to streamline the process and remove unnecessary delays due to organizational issues and lack of prioritization of emergency room care.

This model was implemented in 2007 and it was clear immediately that the major system changes required to really put it into effect were not part of the political agenda. Quebec was proceeding with the construction of new, major teaching hospital buildings, all with private rooms and increased capacity. Major new facilities for the CHUM, the MUHC and Sainte-Justine were moving forward, and new plans were underway to expand the Jewish General Hospital, Maisonneuve-Rosemont and Sacré-Coeur. All the emergency rooms in each of Montreal's hospitals were also to be rebuilt. New investment in developing primary care was a fraction of what was being invested in our hospital facilities. It was clear there was no will to move away from a hospital-centred model to a community-based primary-care model.

I have spoken many times in other parts of this book about the zones of power and influence in Quebec. Over a long period of time, the various zones of power have remained focused on the growth and expansion of the existing hospital-centred system and they have maintained that focus despite the fact that other models of care, such as the Kaiser, the British and the Spanish models, have all been able to ensure more appropriate and less costly medical care and much better use of their emergency rooms by developing a strong primary-care model.

Managing at the Agency

Managing the Montreal agency was very different from managing in the hospital sector. Looking back over my 10-year tenure, we accomplished a great deal with the implementation of the new health reform in Quebec, which promoted the better integration of care.

In 2003-04, restructuring of Montreal was proposed to the minister of health, and in 2005 the CSSSs were established and the new

CEOs were chosen. The following years saw the successful implementation of 12 CSSSs in Montreal and the implementation of 48 primary-care groups. Network clinics were introduced in 2006, and in 2010, three integrated medical clinics were implemented.

The region approved and began implementing a city-wide information system (IS) platform in all health institutions so that everyone needing access to patient data, no matter where they are located, can be on the same platform

We reorganized post-hospital rehabilitation services by regrouping patients in specific centres (for example, placing stroke patients together) and in the merged rehab centres to facilitate greater synergies and increased volumes of care. We reorganized long-term services to increase the capacity and accessibility of services that are better matched to patient needs.

We began the process of restructuring laboratory services with the objective of regrouping them into high-volume centres and designating centres for specialized lab work. This restructuring has been attempted many times and was strongly resisted by the institutions through their pathologists and microbiologists who do not want to change their existing practices. The government has initiated a province-wide restructuring of lab services with a view to more specialization of these services in academic centres and to reducing the number of centres doing general lab work.

We realigned mental-health services through a program to take resources from the major psychiatric institutions and departments and transfer them to the front-line services of the CSSSs. This was slowly being implemented but was not yet fully operational. We had very good success in the implementation of chronic-care management programs in the different CSSSs and it is essential to continue to deploy this as quickly as possible. We achieved greater access to surgery by regrouping surgeries into larger volumes of the same surgery within selected hospitals, hence increasing their quantity and quality.

We fully funded and supported community organizations, and their concerns about being taken over by the new CSSSs have proven unfounded. We maintained prevention and promotion as part and parcel of the agency's major concerns, and this priority was transmitted to the ministry and all levels of the community, whenever and wherever possible.

We achieved all this while balancing the budget of the region for eight years, until the ministry stopped reimbursing the region for new activities that had been demanded by the ministry itself. This cutting of Montreal's regional budget led to the beginning of the deficit cycle in Montreal.

The agency was able to play an important role in improving the offering of services to the population. Unfortunately, however, without strong political leadership to fully implement a strong primary-care model, we were unable to follow through with the fundamental changes and appropriate investments required to move to this new culture of health care management.

Attitudes in the Ministry of Health changed and more and more of the system was run from the minister's office in a micro-management model, and the role of the agency slowly changed from a leadership role to a role of surveillance, control and execution of ministerial directives. This trend continued in fall 2014 with the introduction of Bill 10, which merged existing regional agencies with the autonomous institutions offering health and social services in the region.

Never Stay Too Long

As discussed throughout this book, the role of the CEO is leadership, which requires the passion, dedication, enthusiasm, and presence of the leader. More often than not, in the health care field or elsewhere, the hardest thing for a CEO to see is when it is time to leave, even though the signs may be all too clear: the work becomes too routine, one starts to look for other activities to keep one's interest, one stays on not knowing what else to do. When this happens, it's time to take a close, hard look at the situation and, if necessary, decide to move on.

Health care contracts are generally for terms of four years, and though one term is not enough to introduce change, in most cases, more than two terms is too much. Organizations need new blood and at some point it is time to leave. This is not an easy thing to do as one nears the classical age of retirement and one is not at all ready to retire. There is a tendency to hang on and I have seen this occur in many situations, to the eventual detriment of both the organization and the CEO.

After 10 years at the agency, I recognized that all the signs to move on were there. The nature of the work had altered and the conditions to introduce the changes I wanted to see happen were no longer present. A new minister interested in managing the system from his office in Quebec removed the autonomy that the agency had been given at the beginning of the reform by a previous minister. My team had been with me for most of the 10 years of my tenure and they were also preparing to move on to different stages in their lives.

I resigned from the agency on April 1, 2012, and within six months, many of my senior directors had also left and the new President and Executive Director appointed a new, younger team to carry out the mandate of the agency.

Lessons Learned During My Tenure at the Agency

Managing a region is different than managing an institution, and it is made more difficult than it already is when it is not clear whether the real authority in the region is the agency or the ministry. Using the agency as an office of the ministry adds no added value to the former as a distinct legal entity with its own powers and authority. It is better to make things clear. I believe that the agency as a regional leader plays an important role in development, organization and coordination that can greatly help improve regional health care delivery. This role will now be part of senior management's role in the newly created CISSSs.

Change takes courage and when the courage to change is lost, systems will revert to their natural state of resistance to change. Change must be encouraged, supported and explained. Resistance must be understood and discussed. You must provide adequate periods of transition to meet and counter the resistance to change. Change needs resources and if no resources are available, change will be very difficult.

A clear, agreed-upon vision allows the regional health players to work together, increases the chances of successfully moving forward, and leads to the efficient use of resources. The development of this consensus must include all the players, and once accepted, the vision must be presented in an ongoing manner to the health community.

Creating a strong regional team is very important and we accomplish this by building relationships among the CEOs, their boards, the medical community, professional groups and community organizations. It is the concerted actions of a team with a unified goal that will move things forward in a positive way. I recommend this approach to management in the newly created CISSSs as the best way to ensure their chances of success in the new model of our health and social service system.

CHAPTER NINE

Managing Health Care
in the Public Sector

THROUGHOUT MY CAREER, I have worked in the public and para-public sectors in Quebec and Ontario. I have discovered through experience that managing in the public sector is far more complex than managing in the private sector. This is due not to the complexity of the work, but to the presence of "capital P" Politics. Our system has particular management issues that are not present in the private sector because health care in Canada is managed by provincial governments through a minister of health. The direct management of services and the management of the system are both influenced by the concerns of government that go well beyond the issues of health care. It is important to understand this added dimension to managing our health care needs, and managers must adapt to this particular managerial environment.

I believe strongly in a publicly funded universal health care system in which health is considered a right rather than a privilege. Canadians are very lucky to have a publicly funded system that offers health care to all citizens through a single-payer model. The model is run and managed by governments that have partisan political concerns, and this environment influences decision-making at the macro- and even micro-level and can result in decisions that are not always the most efficient or effective for the running of a complex health care system.

I have tried many times and in many ways (even while I was junior minister of health) to change this model to a more arm's-length relationship between the managing of the system and the ministry. As a result of my experience over many years, I am convinced that the system will remain under the jurisdiction of our provincial governments. No government is prepared to delegate the spending of close to 50 percent of its budget into the hands of a third party, even if that third party is responsible directly to the minister. It would not be in the interests of politicians to remove the decision-making for health care operations, construction, new equipment and research from the political domain. All politicians, from premiers, ministers of health, ministers with regional responsibilities, to local deputies, are regularly solicited by health care institutions and community groups to support them, and politicians get a great deal of recognition from this. Given these constraints, my interest is to ensure that we nevertheless manage the system in the most efficient way possible, despite the political nature of health care.

Health care is a professional bureaucracy (as described by Mintzberg in *Structure in Fives*, 1983), in which all professionals gain their authority to practice from their own licensing corporations and in which the evaluation of their performance and discipline is performed by bodies outside their own organizations. This, combined with the added complexity of public-sector administration, turns health care management into a real challenge.

A Brief History of the Canadian Health Care System
The British North America Act (BNA) of 1867 defined the roles of the federal and provincial governments and this division of powers gave the provinces jurisdiction over health care. In 1957, the Hospital Insurance and Diagnostic Services Act proposed shared hospital costs between the federal and provincial governments (Turner, 1958). By 1958, five provinces had joined the program, with all provinces joining by 1961.

In 1960, Justice Emmett Hall was asked to look at the Canadian health care system and make recommendations for the development of health care in Canada. At that time, the leverage of the federal government was mainly financial. The Medical Care Act of 1966 offered the provinces 50 percent of hospital expenditures and 50 percent of physician expenditures under certain conditions. The provinces, wanting to take advantage of these new funding opportunities, set up their own commissions to put into place the requirements of the law. Quebec set up the Castonguay-Nepveu Commission and, in 1969, the Régie de l'assurance-maladie du Québec was created to pay physicians out of the public purse.

Physicians were very reluctant to give up their entrepreneurial activity of charging their patients what the market and patients could bear, and they opposed this redefinition of the health care system in Canada. Physicians were attached to their clinical and financial independence, and the belief that more recognized physicians could charge more than their colleagues was a symbolic reflection of that independence and of issues of physician recognition. After much public debate and a strike by physicians, agreements were reached in each province for a negotiated fee schedule. In return for this limit on entrepreneurial activity, physicians gained full professional discretion for clinical activity, control over clinical decisions, as well as overall decision-making for the location and organization of their practice. This fundamental agreement has had two main structuring impacts:

1. First, it placed physicians, through their unions, at the heart of decision-making at all levels in the health care system. The physician negotiating body became their union in each province and all improvements or changes to the system had to deal with the barrier of physician remuneration.

2. Second, it allowed the unions to become zones of power with the potential to influence the population and, hence, drive government policy. The medical unions across Canada focused more on protecting the interests of their members, and not necessarily on the most efficient or effective health care system.

In 1983, Monique Bégin, the federal minister of health, proposed legislation that was passed into law in 1985 as the Canada Health Act. The act established the five principles that are the basis of the present Canadian health care system. The act also contained two lesser requirements that are less well-known.

The first principle stated that health insurance plans must be administered and operated by a public authority, responsible to the government and accountable to the public. This requirement referred only to the administration of the health insurance part of the system; indeed, the act did not refer to public management of the services being offered. Provincial governments naturally decided that, since the provincial public purse was paying 50 percent of the costs, management of health services should be done in the public sector. Over time, the private provision of some health services, mainly radiology, has been allowed, even when it is entirely paid for by the public sector.

Each province also subsequently determined that some health services are not insured by the public and therefore remain the responsibility of each citizen. Today, Canada has about 70 percent funding of all health care services by the public sector, while 30 percent of funding is done privately through private insurance, direct payment for service by individuals, and certain other government agencies, such as the automobile insurance agency and workers' compensation. This figure for private funding is higher than that of many European countries, mainly due to government's decision not to publicly fund certain services, such as optometry and dentistry. It is interesting to note here that, according to the Canadian Institute for Health Information, or CIHI (2011), Canada is ranked as a high per capita spender on health care, but with some of the lowest performance results as measured by the commonly used indicators of health compared to all OECD (Organisation for Economic Co-operation and Development) countries.

The second principle of the act refers to a comprehensive system whereby all services offered in a hospital, and all fees for physician services inside or outside the hospital, are covered by a single public payer.

The third principle, of universality, ensures that the system covers all Canadians.

The fourth principle, portability, ensures that services are covered across all provinces and territories of Canada.

The fifth principle, accessibility, ensures that services are available without impediment: there can be no user fees or extra billing for insured services.

An important consequence of accessibility is that it gives leverage to the federal government to ensure that provincial health care systems do not gravitate toward a privatized or user-fee model. Indeed, federal funding is conditional on accessibility, thus limiting provincial leeway in making changes to the universal coverage model.

There are also the two other little-talked-about conditions in the Canada Health Act. The first requires the provinces to provide data to the federal government on health care, and the second requires that the provinces provide recognition for the federal funding they receive. The first condition led to the creation of the Canadian Institute for Health Information (CIHI), an arm's-length agency funded by the federal government and the provinces to collect data on the health of Canadians and the functioning of the health care system in each province. The provinces have never really implemented the second condition.

Public Management of Health Care

Managing in the public sector in Canada adds a level of complexity that health care leaders must take into consideration. Provinces have chosen to be directly involved in not only the management, but also the provision of health care services, and this has changed the playing field.

The Professional Bureaucracy: Who is in Charge?

Management expert Henry Mintzberg used the category "Professional Bureaucracy" to describe the management of a hospital or health care institution offering services, where the professionals offering the services receive their license to practice from a granting body of peers and are subject to the discipline of that body. For all clinical professionals excluding physicians, the organization in which the professional works can remove them for cause. For physicians—who are not paid by the organization but, rather, are paid directly by their provincial government—it is almost impossible to remove them once they have been given privileges in the institution. This gives the physicians' council in hospitals and other health care institutions a great deal of influence in the clinical organization of the hospital, the implementation of new programs, and the acquisition of equipment and new facilities.

It is useful to recall here that the professional bureaucracy within a hospital is typically divided into many zones of power and influence, both internal and external to the organization (Mintzberg, 1983). The physician group is by far the most powerful, followed by the nurses and then other professional groups. The unions, management, the charity foundation, the women's auxiliary, the users committee, and the board are some of the other internal zones of influence. The minister, the ministry, the regional authority, the mayor, the community (represented mainly by community groups), other sister organizations, the university, suppliers and especially the media are examples of external zones of power.

Running a hospital requires the classic components of managing any organization such as purchasing, recruitment (human resources), finance and infrastructure. The difference, however, is that in the Canadian universal system a hospital receives global funding and, by law, must not overspend its budget. Since they are autonomous, physicians in the hospital can—and do—demand different material from suppliers, determine the length of stay of a patient and use new and often experimental medicines without asking permission. Physicians work on fee-for-service and have an interest in increased volume. The administrator has to ensure that the institution remains within budget while being able to satisfy the clinical demands of the physicians who are responsible by law for the patients they admit. This last characteristic of the health care institution in the public sector is the real challenge for the CEO.

The Skills of a CEO in a Professional Bureaucracy

As described in an earlier chapter, there are three things CEOs of a professional bureaucracy must do well, according to Mintzberg, if they are to succeed and establish the credibility they need to run the organization. First, the CEO must be able to manage conflict between professionals (of the same or different groups), between departments, services, and even within the management team. The ability to negotiate and to seek out compromise is essential to obtaining the respect of the leadership in each zone of influence.

The second skill is the ability to obtain resources for the organization, to develop new projects, new equipment and new buildings. The recruitment of physicians, researchers, professors, nurses and other staff are examples of the ability to obtain resources.

The third component of a successful CEO is the ability to function well at the interface between the organization and the outside world; to be able to represent the institution well and defend its interests; to be able to communicate such that people are willing to listen and donate funds to the organization; and to be able to gain the respect of the media so the organization is invited to comment on issues of health care. The recognition of excellence of the organization and its staff through awards, praise from other associations and peer institutions, and recognition in the literature for an academic health-science centre also influence the CEO's credibility. In a professional bureaucracy, the authority of the CEO does not come from the board but from the credibility and respect that he or she can win from the professionals of the organization.

A good manager requires these skills whether they manage in the public or private sector; they are the same skills a manager needs in a university, or in an engineering or law office, where the autonomy of the professional defines the organization, though to different degrees.

The Idiosyncrasies of Public-Sector Management

Finally, the specific constraints of public-sector management come into play. Public administration is often criticized for being too slow, not innovative and buried in red tape (especially when compared to private-sector management); it evolves in a very different environment. Indeed, the good-governance imperatives, which include concerns such as transparency, accountability and equity, are, by definition, resource-intensive. This generates an image of inefficiency that is hard to explain to the public and the media. Furthermore, the highly political environment in which public management operates tends to highlight problems rather than successes:

> Public administration operates in a political environment that is always on the lookout for "errors" and that exhibits an extremely low tolerance for mistakes. The attention of the national media, Question Period and the Auditor General's annual report are sufficient to explain why public servants are cautious and why they strive to operate in an error-free environment. [...] The point is that in business it does not much matter if you get it wrong 10 percent of the time as long as you turn a profit at the end of the year. In government, it does not much matter if you get it right 90 percent of the time because the focus will be on the 10 percent of the time you get it wrong. (Savoie, 1995)

When taken together, the two concerns—the unavoidability of slow-but-democratic processes as well as the politicization of all decisions—generate a very peculiar environment in which public health care management must evolve. When contrasted with private-sector management, these concerns appear to be even more important and can serve, at the very least, as a basis for identifying contemporary issues in managing in the public sector.

Managerial Issues in Canadian and Quebec Health Administration

As stated previously, it is important to distinguish between private and public when referring to health care. The distinction is in the nature of payment of services, and whether care is universal (with the entire population being insured for the majority of their health needs by the state, or whether each individual is responsible to obtain his or her own health insurance).

Three categories of managerial issues can be identified: strategic management and institutional design; incentive issues in public management; and the political nature of public-sector management.

Strategic Management Concerns and Institutional Design
PUBLIC BOARDS

One of the differences in managing health care in the public sector is the governing structure of the public institutions whereby government defines board composition. In Canada each provincial jurisdiction decides its board composition. The management of the organization is very much influenced by these boards. In Quebec, for example, the government decided to include representatives elected by the population on the hospital boards. Elections are held every three years for two members of the 15 to 17 members. The elections in November, 2011, saw only a small fraction of one percent of the population participating. There are numerous cases where the unions have organized busloads of elderly people to vote at specific institutions to ensure their candidate would be elected. The law also provides for representatives of the hospital staff on the board. In certain situations, the public nature of the board causes multiple problems, such as information leaks to the media by board members who are in conflict with the administration. For the next three years the minister will name the boards of the newly created CISSSs.

Board education becomes a very important factor because many newly elected or appointed members are not aware of the board's role or responsibility. Public boards are often faced with the conflict between the demands they are presented with by staff for patients and the available resources. This is one of the reasons there are cycles of deficits, even though the law prohibits such deficits. Board accountability in the public sector is hard to define—and harder to implement—and much training, support and education are needed. Many boards are composed of highly committed people from the private and public sector; they volunteer their time and take great pleasure in helping to manage our public institutions. The level of implication of board members varies greatly and is often related to the culture of the organization and the experience and background of board members.

I have had the privilege of working with five different public boards in my career and the differences are striking. The CLSC Board was made up of community representatives and their concerns were the protection of services to their particular community and the capacity of the CLSC to take care of clientele in their mother tongue. The Verdun Hospital was dominated by local politicians interested in the economic impact of the Hospital in the community and by the union representatives seeking benefits for their members. Notre-Dame's Board was composed of people from business with strong academic representation and firm commitment to the reputation and excellence of the research, teaching, and quality of care. The Ottawa Hospital Board, charged with a complex merger, was composed of very strongly committed individuals with substantial experience in managing a large public organization. The government named the agency Board, and members fulfilled their fiduciary role, but this Board was largely at the mercy of the ministry and the directives to which the agency was subjected.

The variety in the quality of board members and their level of commitment, their knowledge of good governance, their knowledge of health care, and their vested interests greatly influence the role of the CEO and his or her ability to manage the organization. Board support and engagement is essential to the CEO's credibility and authority in the organization, and the CEO must spend the time and energy to ensure that the board is well educated, understands the issues, and maintains interest in the organization. Board retreats, strategic planning exercises, board working committees, social and foundation events are all important in maintaining board engagement.

The changes that have very recently been implemented in the Quebec health care system include the establishment of a mechanism to choose board members for specific competencies and vetting by a selection committee. Although the minister will appoint the board members for the initial three-year period, a different process will subsequently be established. This new process has not yet been defined.

PHYSICIAN REMUNERATION AND PLACEMENT

In the Canadian system, physicians are paid directly by provincial governments as required by the Canada Health Act. All physician fee schedules are negotiated between the provincial government and the unions that represent the physicians in each province. This negotiation influences the direction of the health care system and the degree of participation (or lack of it) that the medical profession is prepared to invest in system development. The most important consequence of this arrangement, where physicians are not employees of their institution, is the relations among the board, the CEO and the medical staff of the organization. Management in this environment requires special skills because most situations that arise are not specific clinical issues where the physician has full authority, but more organizational and behavioural issues that affect the smooth running of the institution.

Government also determines the placement of physicians through regional quotas, which is a major constraint on the development of organizations. It is especially problematic in academic health-science centres, as the staffing needs of those organizations are not necessarily linked to patient demand but rather to the volume of research being conducted. These regional quotas, often determined on a yearly basis, make long-term planning more complicated. Yet, they are necessary to ensure appropriate distribution of physicians to bring care as close to the patient as possible, especially in outlying regions.

In the public sector, the government also determines the number of residency places available, and hence the number of new physicians produced each year. As a strategy to control cost in the public sector fee-for-service system, government has at times reduced the number of places available. This has led to major errors in manpower management and planning, and has led to physician shortages that lasted many years due to the time it takes to train new physicians.

The difference in physician remuneration between general practitioners and specialists has greatly influenced the choices students make in career planning and has contributed in large part to the difficulty in developing a robust primary-care system. For example, when my own daughter decided to go into medicine, given my interest and concern about primary care and how I am convinced that an efficient health care system is based on a strong primary-care sector, I tried to convince her of the importance and value of becoming a primary-care physician. In the middle of her second year in medicine, we had a conversation about health care and she outlined her thinking on what type of physician she would like to become. She said that for her a general practitioner in the present system knows a little about many health issues, has difficult access to diagnostic technology and specialty consultation, and has little or no professional support. As a result, she felt she would always be anxious as to whether she had made the right diagnosis. She would be working principally alone with no team support, yet she would have complete responsibility for her patients. On top of it all, she would earn $100,000 less per year than her colleague specialists who would know everything about their specialty, work with a team, and have full access to diagnostic technology and consults from colleagues in the hospital where she would be working. She asked why I still wanted her to become a family physician. I said I believed the remuneration would change with time, as it has in England, and the leadership of the system would come from the general-practitioner group practice. She would have better access to the technology with corridors of service for specialized exams and treatment in the hospital. She smiled at me and said something about wishful thinking. This conversation clearly demonstrates the problem.

Recently my daughter told me my words had some effect on her and she is now thinking of going into family medicine.

In the Quebec health care system, the government defines the mission of each organization. This constraint of mission exclusivity does not permit certain institutions to offer services that would be more effectively provided within their organization (for example, certain rehabilitation or home-care services that could be more efficiently provided by an acute hospital). The Ministry of Health defines program areas, and funding is provided by program. This has produced silos of care in an environment where the continuity of care is sometimes more difficult to achieve. The transition from one silo to another has been difficult and led to the Quebec reforms of 2004, where health care networks were created combining different health missions into a single organization. Although structural integration has now been achieved, clinical integration is still a challenge, given the historical silos of care.

It is hoped that the creation of integrated networks will permit physicians in the hospitals and the CLSCs to work more closely together. An example of this silo effect of distinct missions influencing the delivery of services is the Hospital in the Home program discussed in chapter three, that I introduced while I was at the Verdun General Hospital. The minister of health Thérèse Lavoie-Roux had asked me to develop this program, which I had been recommending as a way of increasing beds for emergency room patients without any new construction and at a lower cost per bed. The physicians at the Hospital, especially the general practitioners who were looking for more beds for their patients, were very enthusiastic about the program and fully supported the idea. We were able to secure very rapid funding because the minister was being questioned on the emergency room crisis in the National Assembly and wanted to be able to announce a government action that would demonstrate a response to the situation.

The program was developed in three different hospitals and they were working very well, with strong medical participation and enough clients to fill 20 beds in each hospital. As the success of the program was being demonstrated, the CLSCs, which had the mission to deliver home-care services, became increasingly concerned and began to lobby the government that the program should be under the jurisdiction of the CLSC. It does not matter who administers the program, as long as the doctors of the hospital are in charge and remain involved and committed. I was very concerned that this would not be the case and felt that this program should remain at the hospital. As a result of the lobbying, the government decided to transfer the program and in a short period of time the physicians were no longer participating. Home care took on a more intensive role but it was no longer a "hospital in the home." Unfortunately, since there was no longer a treating physician responsible for patient care, the accepted degree of illness of patients in the home decreased, and hospital beds were not freed up. The strict defining of missions in the public sector does create silos. We hope that with the integrated networks this will diminish and allow for more continuous, harmonious care to patients.

The Impacts of Managing Health Care in the Public Sector
Dealing with Individual Initiative

As with most large and complex organizations, public administration does not deal well with individual initiatives, creativity, entrepreneurship or original thinking. It does not adjust rapidly to new situations. This makes it more difficult to adjust quickly to regional differences in policy application. An example of this is the introduction of family-practice groups in Quebec. In 2000, the government decided on a strategy to develop family-practice groups by offering physicians funding if they grouped together and agreed to roster their patients. They would be paid a fee annually for each rostered patient and would, in turn, have to ensure access for extended hours during weeknights and on weekends. They would also be provided funds for an information system as well as the services of two nurses.

In Montreal, the family physicians were less interested in rostering their patients, as they already see many patients in their walk-in clinics. Walk-in availability of care is also an important factor in reducing the utilization of emergency room services, which is a very expensive way to see a family physician and creates long wait times. In recognition of the particular situation in Montreal, a new model was worked out with the physicians and presented to the ministry. This model was called "network clinics": physicians would agree to provide extended hours, 12 hours on weekdays and eight hours both Saturday and Sunday, and would stay open 365 days a year.

They would agree to provide as many hours of care to patients with appointments as with walk-ins, so as to ensure continuity of care. They would also accept new, vulnerable patients who had no family physician. There would be no rostering, so the walk-in would be open to the entire population.

The ministry refused to pay for this model, as it did not follow the defined program, but the Montreal agency chose to go ahead with the project anyway, and provided the funds out of the regional budget. It became so successful and the demand for this model so widespread that the ministry had to accept the new model provincially and provide funding. When I asked for the amount we had been funding out of the regional budget, an amount less than the family-practice groups were receiving, I was only given partial funding and told to find the rest, even though the program had been accepted. This highlights the problems that may arise from centralized ministerial management of health care.

Time-Consuming Processes

The public sector tends to be very short-sighted in its investment decisions, favoring short-term solutions over longer-term changes. Making decisions in the public sector is a political exercise and it takes time to ensure that all the players are on board and that the appropriate compromises have been made before moving forward. Managing in the public sector is managing the time and the process to get things done. There are many more stages of approval, more players to involve, more lobbying to be done, and the manager in the public sector requires a more complex strategy to move organizational projects forward.

As there is no financial imperative to investing and the notion of return on investment is not a consideration in the public sector, delay often has no penalty, and even the impact of inflation on the cost of a major project is not enough of a threat to move things forward more rapidly. The most recent example is the time lapse between mergers of both the MUHC and the CHUM, and the beginning of construction of each of their new combined facilities. It was 15 years for the CHUM and 17 years for the MUHC. The cost went from the estimated $800 million when the mega-hospitals project was first presented, to more than $2.5 billion for each hospital, with a large portion of the increase related to inflation.

The implementation of an information-system strategy for health care in Quebec is another good example of the delays involved in moving forward. As soon as there is political criticism, justified or not, the government, ministers and their civil servants become very nervous and their first reflex is to stop ongoing activity. This occurred following criticism of the Quebec program for introducing information-system integration. Following a scandal in Ontario in which certain contracts were awarded in an improper manner, there were also allegations that there were no tangible results for all the money that had been invested in Quebec in the provincially led information-system program. The government called for a moratorium on all pro-projects and passed a law creating a new governance model to manage information-system implementation. A hospital that wanted software to upgrade their maintenance program had to wait until the moratorium ended more than a year later; after the moratorium ended, projects were required to go through a new approval before they could go forward.

PUBLIC TENDERS

The public sector uses public funds: as such, there is consensus that those funds must be used in a fair and open competition. To ensure efficiency and economy, two contractual tools can be used: public tendering or ad hoc negotiations. The public tender has been developed as the tool to ensure that the awarding of public contracts is done in a fair and equitable manner. As the lack of trust grows between the public and their elected officials, the scrutiny over public contracts by the media grows as well. Although empirical evidence shows that ad hoc negotiation often yields better results (Bajari, McMillan, & Tadelis, 2008), it is discouraged and sometimes disallowed. This highlights the tensions between efficiency and due process that exist in public management.

For example, at the beginning of 2000, the two major teaching hospitals in Montreal merged their information technology (IT) efforts under one director for both hospitals and decided to go to public tender for a new IT system. The regional authority had to approve the IT plan and then seek government approval. It was decided at the regional level to add a clause to the tender which stated that if other institutions wanted to use the same system, they could do so as an extension of the contract the companies were bidding on. It was also included in the tender that the Montreal agency would act as a broker for other regions if they were interested in piggybacking onto the original contract. Many firms bid on the contract and it was awarded according to public-tender rules.

Two years later, the agency was able to convince the other CEOs in Montreal to join together to implement the same system that the two teaching hospitals had adopted. There was an agreement to pay collectively and it was clear that there would be some economies of scale, even though the two university hospitals managed close to 35 percent of all the acute-care beds.

The agency began negotiations for the licenses, implementation and the ongoing maintenance costs of the city-wide project, and was able to reduce the overall cost significantly for a city-wide implementation. The company saw such large organizational benefits from a type of implementation that had never before been done in any other jurisdiction that they were open to some very aggressive negotiation. I had my team do the initial negotiations and they were able to get some significant reductions in the cost of licenses. When I was presented with the results of their talks, I was still convinced there was a way to go before we arrived at a price I was willing to pay. Once I had negotiated a new price for unlimited licenses for all institutions in Montreal, it was time to negotiate implementation cost, implementation strategy, the timeline and a payment model. The overall savings to the hospitals and the HSSCs was substantial and allowed Montreal to move forward with this beneficial city-wide implementation project. This was all done without seeking government approval, as it was done using the regional funds that were available to the institutions in the region. The ministry was well informed and followed all the negotiations. A number of years later, with a new minister and deputy minister in place, I was asked who gave me permission to do the city-wide project even if it used regional funds. I answered that the law gave me the authority. Today, no projects can be carried out without permission.

This example demonstrates clearly that when there is a possibility of negotiations, beneficial agreements can be reached on all sides. Public tenders would gain from being more flexible, although due process must always remain a concern. The scandal in the awarding of contracts in the construction industry in Quebec and the level of fraud that has been uncovered demands even more vigilance in awarding contracts. The challenge is how to do this while still maintaining some flexibility and capacity to negotiate.

Public Sector Management is Risk-Adverse

The public sector is continually scrutinized by the media and it is very easily criticized by the public or the Opposition in Parliament and it is consequently very reluctant to take risks. When an error is made, a scapegoat is often found and this leads to a very conservative, rule-abiding civil service that values accountability more than efficiency. As a result, risk, innovation and creativity needs are not encouraged and sup-ported. The following example illustrates this situation very well. A long-term care institution decided to change its food-production method by deciding to prepare all food centrally and distribute the food to each floor. This optimized food production and generated cost savings and more uniform quality. However, the elderly had been used to having their toast in the morning prepared on the unit and residents missed the odour of the bread being toasted, as well as the crispness of fresh toast. A family member complained to the media and the headline of an article in the paper criticized the management of the organization for not respecting the elderly. The criticism was also clearly aimed at the minister of health responsible for geriatric care in the province, as a tool of the media to increase readership through attention-seeking headlines. In this context, it is difficult for managers to initiate new ways of operating even if the benefits clearly outweigh certain inconveniences. Managers need to feel they are being supported in the public sector to allow them to take certain risks required to improve care and the overall operation of the system.

Lack of Incentives

Management in the public sector is viewed differently in different provinces and attitudes toward senior management are also very different. Management texts talk at great length about the importance of incentives as a driver in striving for excellence. Most organizations use some form of incentives, such as performance bonuses, to encourage staff to meet targets and achieve goals. In Quebec, an attempt was made to provide bonuses: CEOs, by decree, were allowed to earn up to 10 percent of their salary if their performance was judged appropriate according to certain criteria; for example, a balanced budget. The boards in Quebec almost always awarded the 10 percent to their CEOs because salaries in Quebec were considered, both by their boards and the CEOs, to be very low for their level of responsibility. In 2010, the media decided to look at bonuses in the civil service, not only health care, and TVA (a privately-owned French language television network) published both salaries and bonuses. In the opinion of the public, civil servants were already overpaid, working in very cushy, secure jobs with big pensions; public criticism was so strong at the idea that they would receive bonuses when the government was indicating a deficit that the government decided to remove all bonuses. This highlights the tensions between the public and political nature of public administration and the search for efficiency using incentives-based management.

The Political Nature of Public-Sector Management
The fact that the public sector is under the jurisdiction of elected officials defines the nature of its management. Since governments are elected for relatively short periods of time, obtaining power and maintaining it become the driving forces of most political parties. The party in power always takes into account the impact of their decisions on the next election. Responding to the wishes of major party donors is sometimes also a factor in decisions taken by government.

An example of the influence of politics in the implementation of public policy is the Government of Quebec's decision to pay for in-vitro fertilization out of the public purse (Lacoursière, 2010). After having a successful in-vitro fertilization procedure (which was paid privately, since the procedure had never been covered in the public sector), a television personality and some colleagues decided to mount a campaign to have the procedure paid for by the government. In-vitro fertilization has allowed many women who were having difficulty getting pregnant to have children; however, it also yields much higher rates of low-weight babies, multiple births and other health problems. The question of priorities therefore arose and there was much controversy around the issue. Many health care providers and managers felt that this should not be the priority area of investment if new funds became available. Financing the health care system is an ongoing struggle and there are many unmet needs of the population. However, for political reasons, the government introduced this controversial program, which according to a recent declaration of the minister of health has cost $120 million. The new Liberal Govern-ment has decided to change the program and greatly reduce the public offering through the introduction of a co-payment model.

It is the role and responsibility of government to determine policy and the programs it wants to implement. There are many different reasons for certain government decisions and the role of the administrator is to put these decisions into action. Managing health care in the public sector includes a much closer and more direct relation between policy and its execution. It is the direct in-volvement in the execution of policy of the democratically elected (and thus legitimate) government that distinguishes the public-sector management of health care from private-sector management. Nevertheless, this ability of politics to influence public policy (even in ways that can seem undesirable from a priority point of view) must be interpreted as the necessary consequence of democratic decision-making and accountability.

Impact of the Media

Since health care is a major concern of the public, the media will gain attention from almost any related issue they publish. The media's power and influence, the competition for readership and the ability to influence public opinion are all drivers that make health care an easy target for media criticism. The headlines in the morning paper fuel the questions of the Opposition during Question Period in Parliament. Administrators in the health care system receive calls early in the morning to provide briefings to the minister's cabinet on the issues the media has brought forward. For example, at the agency in Montreal, a part of the communications team monitors the media every morning and prepares briefings for cabinet as required.

In particular, the media will closely monitor information regard-ing management salaries, expense accounts, bonuses, and travel agendas. Requests for information are continually submitted and this data is regularly published, often under a very critical headline.

Public-sector scrutiny by the media is a constant concern for managers in health care. This often critical monitoring of the system for political reasons greatly influences the perceptions of the public. For example, recently, the care given to the elderly was criticized heavily by the media and has led to a great deal of worry and stress to the elderly that the health care system will not be able to provide them with the care they need.

As with all other public policy issues, the media has a role to play in bringing forward legitimate problems and abuses in the health care system. At times, this role can be overplayed and this can certainly lead to a very risk-averse approach to management on the part of both political policy-makers and front-line administrators seeking to provide effective management with limited resources.

Impact of Local, Provincial and Federal Members of Parliament

In the Canadian system, local members of Parliament represent their ridings; they also support and lobby for those issues beneficial to their ridings. Since health care is an issue that touches everyone, all health care organizations in a riding seek the support of their local deputies to obtain resources, new facilities, new programs, or simply additional funding. Depending on whether or not the local representative has greater or lesser influence within the government, the local institutions will or will not succeed in their requests. This dynamic is thus important for health care managers to understand, as influential representatives can help them gain access to resources.

Most provinces are divided into regions, and ministers with specific portfolios are also given responsibility for regional development. These ministers are very important in influencing the decisions of the minister of health and they work hard to obtain resources for their region. Once again, the CEO, the board, and the foundation must be involved in the political activity of their riding.

The dynamic between the local deputies, regional ministers, the minister in charge of the ministry, and the health organization is an enduring one for all elected officials. Being solicited is important for political power brokers and it is one of the reasons that government is not interested in an arm's-length agency managing health care in a less political environment.

Impact of Elections and Their Timing

Another example of the influence of politics on public-sector management is the timing of elections. At the beginning of a mandate, a newly elected government is ready to introduce fresh reforms, programs and policy; at the end of a mandate—close to an elec-tion—the dynamic changes.

For example, in 2000 the Parti Québécois had been working on a health care reform that would better integrate health care and develop a stronger primary-care system. The merging of several institutions into a population-based health care centre was the core of the reform. The community-care and primary-care organizations were opposed to the reform, as they were afraid that merging with hospitals would reduce their influence and authority. They were also worried that they might end up coming under the domination of the acute-care sector. Since the Parti Québécois drew support from community-based organizations and since an election was looming, the government made a decision to not introduce the reform. The PQ lost the following election and the newly elected government decided in the first year of its mandate to bring in the reform to integrate health care organizations into population-based health care centres. The reform has since been recognized as an important step in providing better health care through a population-based, integrated health care model.

Impact of the Personal Vision of the Minister of Health and Impact of the Management of the Ministry

Managing in the public sector is also greatly influenced by the minister in charge. Depending on the personality, style, level of knowledge of the sector, personal interest in the particular ministry, and ambition, the impact of the minister will be different on those managing the system. A minister most often manages through his or her ministry, which then manages the system through a deputy minister and his or her assistant deputy ministers. Health care managers are more or less autonomous in managing their institutions or regions, depending on the degree of intervention the minister or deputy minister exercises. Given the constraints of managing in the public sector, the level of trust is low and this is reflected in the degree of autonomy. A minister who chooses to try to manage the system by him or herself risks short-circuiting traditional lines of authority, thus making it more difficult for administrators to manage the system. It's a delicate balance.

During my time as minister, this was the lesson that my deputy minister offered me when it was clear I was looking at the job as though I were still the CEO of an organization. A minister is present, involved, encouraging, and makes the decisions for the direction of the system and the policies that are needed. He or she does not, however, try to manage the system him or herself as its CEO.

Impact of the Provincial Medical Associations, Unions and Professional Corporations

In a public health care system, the influence of the medical associations, unions and professional corporations is very important, and managers must always take this into consideration. It is important to develop close relationships with the leadership of these organizations, the major teaching hospitals, and the larger, more influential regions. Not only do these organizations have a strong influence on government, they have influence and often intervene at the local and regional level when their members are not satisfied with a particular direction taken. An example is the pressure the federation of specialists put on the Ministry of Health to maintain on contract a private clinic doing day surgery, even after a decision had been made to return this type of activity to the public hospital sector. Medical associations, unions and professional corporations have a greatly increased presence in the media, and, therefore, have a greater political influence and impact due to the public nature of health care.

A Strategy for Regional Management in a Public Health Care System

I have discussed the governance model of two-tier and three-tier systems that have developed across the country. In a two-tier system, the ministry defines the mandates, budget and policy and evaluates performance, while the region manages and coordinates all services in their territory through a multitude of different organizations. In a two-tier system, there is only one CEO of the regional authority and he or she names the director of each institution. Depending on the size of the region the CEO can be a very present, hands-on manager in a smaller region, or a much more removed manager in a larger region, leaving the functioning of the individual organizations in the hands of the directors. As I look back at my management of the Montreal region, I realize how the situation would have changed if I had been the CEO of all of the institutions on the Island that named a director responsible for each organization. I was able to find directors with tremendous commitment, interest, passion and enthusiasm because they were the CEO of their own institution with their own committed board of directors. Until the changes introduced by Bill 10 in 2014 and implemented in April 2015, Quebec has had a three-tier management model, with a regional authority coordinating the CEOs of the region who ran their own legal entities, each with its separate board. The new model merges all institutions in a region with the regional agency, resulting in a two-tier model with 33 institutions in Quebec with regional coordination and service delivery mandates.

Until the recent changes there were 43 CEOs in the Montreal region for 12 health networks, eight non-integrated hospitals and 23 specialty institutions that range from youth protection, psychiatric hospitals, physical and mental rehabilitation centres, to culturally specific long-term-care hospitals. Each CEO had a board to observe and evaluate his or her performance on a monthly basis, to listen to the organization, and monitor its growth, development, and well-being. If I had been CEO of the whole region I would not have been able to do this and, furthermore, my directors would not have had the level of engagement they had as the CEO of their own organization. My role was one of coordination and stimulation, focused on regional development and each organization's contribution to that development.

This has now changed to a two-tier model where the activities of the regional authority are combined with the direct offering of services and where all the institutions in a region are being integrated into a single new organization. In Montreal there are five new integrated regional centres (CISSSs) merging the 43 existing institutions that will now manage the offering of all services on their territory and also assume the role of regional coordination for their territory.

In Quebec, before the recent changes there were 93 health and social-service networks making up a total of 182 independent institutions. Effective April 1, 2015, the mergers created 33 new networks that will offer and coordinate care in their territory. This reduced number of institutions could play a role of real regional coordination and development, providing government the data they need to evaluate and measure the performance of the system, while ensuring a dynamic offering of services led by a CEO who hopefully will be more clinically than bureaucratically focused. Unfortunately, since the present reform is based on cost cutting with no clear vision for the way health care should be delivered, there is a very high risk that the result will be the implementation of a very bureaucratic model of management characterized by strong control by the ministry. There are 17 health regions in Quebec; in 2010, the regional CEOs and the Ministry of Health considered reducing this number to eight in order to create economies of scale and better coordination. When this recommendation came to the elected deputies of each region, there was great resistance to such a change as each deputy did not want to lose their regional status and autonomy as a distinct region. The ministry maintained the status quo as a result of political resistance and there are still 17 health regions of very different sizes in Quebec. After the April 2014 election the new government in Quebec, facing a large provincial budget deficit, decided to bring in a new reform to merge institutions within the regions into integrated regional groupings while keeping the same overall number of regions. This maintains a regional entity that local deputies wanted while at the same time it allows for much more direct control of the health system by the ministry.

The organizational model of care to be managed greatly affects the nature of management and the management skills that are required. Managing a hospital, no matter how large, is managing the production of services, teaching and research. I have described the skills required to manage in this professional bureaucracy. Managing a region adds another layer of complexity but is fundamentally the same, depending upon the size of the region. If the region is too large, the CEO's role is less clinical and more bureaucratic; if the region is too small, it is difficult to ensure continuity of care. In a very large region it is better to have CEOs who manage their own institution, with the region coordinating care and supporting development initiatives. In both these models, government can play a greater or lesser role in the direct management of the system. A lesser role is always preferable. The new reform creates very large integrated institutions, CISSSs (Centres integrés de santé et de services sociaux) that will manage regional care; this brings with it the very real danger of senior management becoming more bureaucratic and less clinical. I see this as the greatest danger of the reform. It is important that the public monitor the changes very closely to ensure there is no deterioration of quality of care.

Managing at the Agency: Part of the Public Sector

At the agency, I developed a strategy that focused on defining a clear common vision, developing a strong leadership team, ensuring innovation and creativity, ensuring the transfer of knowledge, and using and supporting all actions with data.

Defining a Clear Vision

Defining a clear vision is the first priority for any organization. In the public sector, the strategic plan of the ministry outlines the direction in which the health care system should be moving. However, each region can define its vision, as long as it follows the current government orientation. In defining Montreal's vision it was important to me that all the CEOs were involved and made a strong commitment to the realization of the vision. Montreal was in a very fortunate situation, as new integrated health and social-service centres were just being created. This meant that a new board was to be put into place and a new CEO was to be chosen by the board and the agency. Once the new centres were in place and the new CEOs chosen, it was very important to create a common health care vision that would guide each organization's development and become part of each organization's strategic plan.

We organized a series of trips with all the CEOs to study existing health care systems and to look at population-based hierarchical systems of care. With the Kaiser Foundation we designed and organized a one-week study session so the whole group could better understand a managed-care model based on primary care. We arranged a visit with the London Strategic Health Authority to study the reform being introduced in Britain. We also looked at Barcelona, in the Catalan region of Spain, as it had a population-based model of primary care that had been established for more than 20 years. Travelling together had the added benefit of allowing the CEOs to develop close relationships early on, at a time when no one in the group had experience managing an integrated network. This exchange among the newly appointed CEOs and the discussions around a common vision for the health system in Montreal also meant that the CEOs did not feel so isolated at the beginning of their new mandate.

The danger of the three-tier model was that the agency would simply be considered an extension of government, a regional office, in which case the leadership role would be very weak and the main role would become one of evaluation and analysis of projects that would then be transmitted to the ministry for approval. The ability to play a real leadership role for an agency in a three-tier model is completely dependent on the credibility and respect the CEO of the agency can build in the region. With the new two-tier model the CEO of the CISSS is named to his or her position by the minister rather than by the board of the institution. The CEO must directly manage the offering of services as well as manage and provide leadership for the regional needs. With these new merged responsibilities, the CEO must now combine the skills of a great hospital or health care administrator with the skills of a regional manager directly responsible to the ministry. It will be important to ensure that the CEOs succeed in balancing the regional and clinical needs without turning to a wholly bureaucratic management model.

Create Trust and Develop Relationships

It was clear from the beginning that the agency was caught between individual organizations that wanted to develop their own entities, and the government, which wanted to control cost, implement policy, and respond to the media and the demands of the population. To be able to execute the regional mandate, it was essential to develop a very close relationship with the CEOs of each of the institutions in the region. The introduction of the reform provided the opportunity to create the Montreal Regional Management Committee (MRMC). This committee was initially composed of the 12 newly appointed CEOs of the health centres; it met once every two weeks for a half-day to discuss the management of the region, the development of the organizations it comprised and the implementation of the vision. Eventually the other CEOs joined the group, which had formed many subcommittees to look at specific issues of care. Another key concern was that the regional strategy must ensure the involvement of the key decision-makers. Creating trust, building a strong team of regional leaders, taking into account the local community organizations, professional corporations, unions and the media, and managing the region should all be considered key success factors.

Ensuring Creativity and Innovation
It was very important from the beginning of the reform to position the agency as a leader in innovation. This was done to gain the attention of the CEOs and their boards so that the agency could be expected to present and support new initiatives, but also to demonstrate that the agency was an important partner with the institutions.

The agency spearheaded initiatives such as "Network Clinics," chronic-care programs, city-wide information systems, study programs outside Quebec, and performance evaluation models. From a regional perspective, the agency had to be an added value to the institutions, rather than just a control mechanism executing the ministry's instructions. The authority of the agency came from the same qualities that Mintzberg (1983) described for CEOs: the ability to manage conflict; to obtain resources; and to work on the interface between the region, the government, the media, and the population to give the agency the credibility needed to manage the region effectively.

Ensuring the Transfer of Knowledge
The regional agency is in the ideal position to be the information broker and the clearinghouse of knowledge for the institutions in the region, as well as for the government and the other regions of Quebec. This transfer of knowledge enables the distribution of information about pilot projects to other organizations, the comparison of performance among institutions, the recommendation and support of new programs, and ensures that the best practices are in place. The role of knowledge broker falls clearly within the mandate of the regional agency and the extent to which it succeeds in this role will greatly influence its ability to manage the region. This is the most important argument for ensuring that a region in a three-tier model has the critical mass to develop a very strong planning team, a performance evaluation capacity, and a biomedical and construction service that

can help plan and support the individual networks and hospitals in their development. Clinical expertise in program management and implementation is also very important. The region's role in knowledge transfer—and consequently its credibility—will be greatly reduced if it does not have the critical mass to develop this expertise. Under the new two-tier model the critical mass will exist in each region and will allow the new CEO and the management teams to execute both roles that are essential for the success of the new organization.

Using and Supporting Data and Data Collection

One of the early strategies I adopted for the agency was the need to use data to support the development and adoption of best practices. To this end, we supported the Montreal institutions in the development of a fully integrated information system for the region in order to ensure we had timely and reliable data.

The use of data in infection control has played a major role in reducing the infection rates by allowing the concentration of resources and by convincing the professionals that changes were required. Health professionals respond well to data and when confronted with comparisons that demonstrate best practices they are quite willing to change.

Emergency room management, bed management in the hospital, admissions and discharges from long-term and rehab centres, diagnostic test scheduling—these all require real-time data, and the first priority must be to ensure that the administrative information systems are in place to collect and compile the data. The clinical information systems based on the electronic medical record that is shared between systems is then essential to the success of the system.

Managing a Public System is Different

My experience managing the Montreal region showed me how different managing a system is from managing the delivery of services in a health care organization. The CEOs of Quebec's new integrated centres will be required to do both. Managing in the public sector adds challenges to the role, but the leadership skills that I have discussed are essential to manage well in this complex environment. None of the issues I have described pose problems that cannot be surmounted and I am convinced that by being aware of and taking into consideration the issues intrinsic to managing in the public sector, we can develop an efficient, effective, well-run health system in Quebec and in Canada.

CHAPTER TEN

The Importance of Leadership

MANAGING HEALTH CARE is considered to be one of the most complex types of management. Working in a professional bureaucracy adds some special characteristics to this complexity. Managing health care in the public sector, as is the case in Canada's universal health care system, adds a challenging dimension to an already complex managerial environment. To navigate these turbulent waters requires a leader who can simultaneously manage the offering of services to the population, the system of care and the politics of care.

Such a leader requires a set of skills that must be learned and practiced. The essential tasks required of a great leader include: build a collective vision, build relationships, build trust, and build knowledge. A great leader must have ambition, knowledge and integrity and be able to gain credibility within his or her organization by being able to manage conflict, obtain resources and represent the organization on the interface with government, the media, other health care institutions and the population. Such a leader will be able to focus his or her organization on quality patient care that is effective and efficient. He or she will be able to guide the system to provide integrated care that sees the person and not the disease.

Leadership is Not Management

Leadership encompasses management, but it is much more. An organization can be managed well and yet stagnate, can be cost-effective, yet still lose market share. It is important to understand the difference between leadership and management since health care in a public universal system tends to be more managed than led. For our health care system to succeed, we must encourage, not discourage, leadership. We must support and honour innovation and creativity, rather than settle for the one-size-fits-all approach. This is a challenge in the public system where the objective is to minimize risk, especially political risk.

Leadership in health care presents a vision of the future, of a healthy population and how to get there, a clear and focused picture of what we want to achieve. Managers, on the other hand, want a work plan to follow. Leaders speak to the whole organization, while managers speak to the next managerial level. Leaders look to develop, improve and innovate, while managers look to maintain the status quo. Leaders support and provide energy to those around them, managers tell employees what needs to be done. The leader will focus on people and how to inspire, motivate and encourage, while the manager focuses mainly on structure and process.

At the beginning of my tenure at the Ottawa Hospital, I found a work force of 13,000 people who were worried about the mergers they were being subjected to and concerned about the reorganization that was coming as three hospitals closed and activities were divided among the remaining sites. I knew that I had to be very present and visible in supporting staff, but I also had to find something solid and concrete that staff could rally around and that touched their everyday experience, some activity that would focus staff energy and develop pride and commitment in their organization and the work they were being asked to do.

I had noticed that each of the hospitals had deteriorated in their level of cleanliness during the two-year period of turmoil that led up to the recommendations for merger. They were certainly not as clean as they could and should be. I noticed that if there was a piece of paper on the floor, staff would pass right by without picking it up and putting it in the trash. The employees had lost the sense of ownership in their hospital during the restructuring and merger exercise; they felt their institution was being taken away from them, that things were out of their control. I met with senior staff and explained that I wanted to develop a cleanliness campaign for all the sites and put pride and ownership back into the hospitals and the new organization we were building. This seemed a very minor issue to my VPs, considering the daunting task they were facing in the merger of the different sites and clinical programs.

I asked them to hear me out and I worked hard to get them to go along with the idea. I said our people were more important than our structures and we had to connect if we wanted to get their support and participation in our new adventure. I indicated I was willing to spend money on new cleaning equipment, any new technology that would help, and any painting or minor repairs that would be required to make the hospital shine. I wanted the cleanliness program to focus on quality of care mainly through control of infectious disease, especially as hospital-acquired infections were beginning to be a very serious threat, with bacteria becoming more and more resistant to antibiotic drugs. Wendy Nicklin, director of nursing, was very enthusiastic about the program, since quality care was her major focus. (She later became, and still is, CEO of Accreditation Canada, where she develops quality standards and quality measurement for all hospitals in Canada.)

This program was discussed as one of my strategies at the Ottawa hospital and as the spokesperson for the program I demonstrated to staff the level of priority I assigned to it. This simple leadership move not only succeeded in cleaning the Hospital, improving quality of care and reducing infection, it also gave pride to staff at a delicate moment in their lives and it allowed a relationship to develop between myself and the staff of the Hospital that also demonstrated some of my passion and commitment to quality care.

The Professional Bureaucracy

I have described how working in health care is not like working in a professional bureaucracy where there is traditional top-down control, or the many more innovative versions of this approach, because in health care the relationships among the actors are fundamentally different. This is accentuated in a universal health care system managed in the public sector.

It is a challenge to be a leader responsible for an organization in which many others are each leaders in their own specialty area of the organization. The head of nursing leads a team of professionals, as does the head of psychology, occupational therapy, social work, biomedical engineering, and the heads of each medical department. To manage these leaders takes a leader with excellent knowledge of the working environment. I have discussed what it takes for a leader to gain credibility in the hospital: resolve conflict among the different professionals, obtain resources for the organization, and be present and credible in the interface between the organization and multiple stakeholders. What are the leadership traits that a director needs to gain this all-important credibility?

Ambition, Competence Integrity

A good leader does not get people to do what needs to be done; he or she gets people to want to do what needs to be done. There are three characteristics that I believe are the backbone of good leadership: ambition, competence and integrity. When applied appropriately, these characteristics build credibility, the essential ingredient for leadership.

Ambition

When we hear the word ambition, we almost always have a negative reaction. I believe there are many different sides to ambition and that a leader emerges when ambition is combined and balanced with competence and integrity. Ambition is the driving force that keeps the adrenalin flowing and the mind stimulated to produce a constant flow of new ideas and fresh approaches. It is the desire to succeed and be proud of our achievements. Great leaders have ambition mixed with idealism and it is their sense of endless possibilities that is transmitted to others. It is ambition that allows you to be rejected at numerous job interviews and still keep trying because you believe in yourself and your capacity to get things done. When I look back over the last 40 years, I realize that it was not always smooth sailing.

I was not chosen at my first job interview and that was easy to justify since I was just beginning my career and I had no practical managerial experience. I succeeded my second time around and began my career as CEO of a CLSC. My next job interview was for the position of CEO at Verdun. That was a real challenge but I was fortunate to be selected. I then applied to my first teaching hospital, the Royal Victoria Hospital in Montreal, one of the largest English teaching hospitals in Quebec, and was rejected. Next was Hôpital Sacré-Coeur de Montréal, a francophone teaching hospital run by the Sisters of Providence where, again, I was also not hired. A year later, when the position became available again, I reapplied and was still not chosen. I kept trying and was finally hired as CEO of Notre-Dame, Quebec's most prestigious teaching hospital. When Notre-Dame merged into the CHUM, I was not chosen to head the new hospital although it was a position I really desired—it was a challenge for which I was ready. The message here is not to give up; if we believe in ourselves and feel we can do the work, we must keep on looking for what we want to do.

228

Being ambitious also means you know yourself well and you understand your strengths and weaknesses. Know what you don't know and then find out where to go to get the knowledge or skills you are missing. Being ambitious is also about being passionate and the ability to communicate one's passion to others. An ambitious person is willing to take risks, to think outside the box, to innovate and try out new ideas. He or she is proud of his or her organization and has a vision, often idealistic, of where it should go and what it should achieve. An ambitious person inspires and motivates others and is able to get others to reach their full potential.

Competence

A good leader must be competent. To be competent requires knowledge, expertise and experience. A competent person is someone who is curious by nature, is always asking questions, remains open to new ideas and learning, and is willing to share his or her knowledge with others. This capacity to teach others is an important characteristic because a leader needs followers, and followers only follow when they have someone to respect. A good leader knows how to work with people, is able to understand their needs, and is able to communicate their passion and commitment.

A good leader understands about being relevant and how being relevant leads to credibility and trust. M.R. Covey, in discussions about capabilities in his book *The Speed of Trust*, argues that a combination of talent, attitude, skills, knowledge and style are the foundation of competence.

Talents are the particular abilities each individual has developed or enhanced over time. Some have photographic memories, some have a rich, deep voice that is easy to listen to, others have an artistic talent. But everyone has talents, and a leader is able to understand his or her strengths and weaknesses and continually seeks to improve and develop new talents.

Attitude is how we see the world around us, how we see life and how we confront each day and the challenges we encounter. Some see their cup as half empty while others see the same cup half full. Attitude is written in our body language and is easily read by others. Leaders examine, evaluate and work hard at changing their attitude to support and encourage those they are working with and the people they meet in life.

Skills are the abilities we learn and develop. We might be talented or gifted to very different degrees but with hard work and commitment we can improve those talents and learn new skills. Some people are not great public speakers. They are uncomfortable in front of groups of people or the media, but they realize that communication skills are important to good leadership. They work hard at learning the skill, and though they may never become great speakers, they become competent enough to respond to the needs of their organization.

Knowledge is one's current state of awareness, understanding of an issue or problem, and the ability to find solutions. Training, learning, acquiring new skills, deeper understanding of issues, relations and oneself are all part of gaining new knowledge, and leaders are always looking for ways to increase knowledge for them-selves and their organization.

Style is the way we approach people, issues, problems and everyday happenings. We all have different styles, but a leader can adapt his or her style to better respond to the needs of the organization at a particular moment in time. A leader is aware how style affects those he or she is working with and that not everybody is the same or responds in the same way.

Competence, then, is a mix of these attributes and is essential in establishing credibility and trust in an organization. In a professional bureaucracy with a highly professional and very specialized staff, the need to establish credibility and trust is even more important if leadership is to succeed in getting everyone moving in the same direction towards a common set of goals.

In earlier chapters the importance of developing a common vision was discussed, and this becomes a cornerstone of building credibility and demonstrating competence.

Integrity

The third characteristic of leadership is integrity, and it guides and uses the other two qualities, ambition and competence. It can change the outcome of a leader's actions, leading to positive or negative consequences. Integrity grows out of a moral code, a set of standards used to guide our actions. It is a framework with which we can judge what is right and wrong both for ourselves and for others. It is a mark of integrity to be open and transparent with no hidden agenda. A leader with integrity lays his or her cards on the table and is prepared to listen to criticism. Sharing information demonstrates integrity since information is power and the sharing of power is essential to strong leadership

Integrity means holding and acting upon, a set of values that are respectful of others, and that includes honesty, fairness and good judgement. A leader with integrity champions inclusion of others and a sharing of leadership. Great leaders show humility, and their values and integrity help ensure the success of their organization when they are no longer there.

A leader with integrity and competence but no ambition will be a good manager but a poor leader. A leader with ambition and integrity but little competence will not be credible or well respected. With ambition and competency but little integrity a leader can become dangerous to his or her organization or even to the world at large. Good or great leaders possess all three characteristics.

Building Relations

I cannot stress enough how important it is to successful leadership in health care to build positive relationships. Health care is about people dedicated to helping, curing disease, relieving pain, and supporting people as they live with different long-term illnesses. There is an expectation that managing in this environment must show the same caring that health professionals show their patients. This sentiment comes through the building of relationships.

The basis for building good relationships is building trust, which I will discuss in detail in the next section. The CEO, senior management and administrators throughout the system should be aware that building relationships begins with an interest in the other person. You must take into account their profession and the work they are doing, their concerns, needs, hopes and fears, and how you can support their professional mission. It is not essential to have a personal relationship, although a genuine interest in the personal life of the people we work with is important.

A CEO must at times be close and yet keep a certain distance from the managers and staff with whom he or she works. I often found it easier to have a more personal relationship with the medical staff, who saw themselves as colleagues working in the same organization rather than as part of a hierarchical relationship. Often, being CEO or the leader of an organization requires not getting too close to staff. The expression we have all heard about it being lonely at the top has its origins in the real world of management.

Know the Person

When you enter a new organization, no matter at what level, building relationships is one of the most important components of success. You need to know the people you are working with. Today's online social networks provide easy access to information that did not exist until recently. It is now possible, even before meeting your directors or co-workers, to get their profile, and this can then become a basis for getting to know each person. In meeting your colleagues, get to know their history, family, and work experience, as well as their accomplishments, ambitions, values, concerns, strengths and weaknesses. When you meet with people, listen actively. Listening actively means listening accurately, hearing the various meanings in what is being said. It is important to respond appropriately, even repeating if necessary some of the same words or phrases you have just heard. As a leader, it is important to show concern, indicate what you are planning to do about what you have heard, and make sure there is timely feedback.

Build Networks

The school network, a sports-team network, your social network—these are all groupings of people who have a set of common interests, who interact, and can support one another and learn from one another. Building networks is important for a CEO or any director in an organization and it is a way of keeping up to date about what is happening in your area of interest. Information is influence and there is no better way to get information than through a network. I like to refer to a spider web of interest that allows us to catch what is new as soon as possible.

Find Partners

A leader will look for partners who are ready to share risk. These relationships are important for growth and support, often through parallel interests that complement each other. There are always associations of CEOs, hospitals, or professional groups that are fertile ground for the development of partnerships. Sharing risk can demonstrate leadership skills and gain great credibility in the organization. A good example of this is a hospital partnering with the regional health authority to implement a pilot project, with the hope of extending the project to other institutions. As CEO of the Montreal Health Authority, I was continually looking for partnerships with the health care institutions in Montreal and with the major suppliers of health care products and services. We established pilot projects in chronic-care management in partnership with Montreal CSSSs, and once the pilot proved its sustainability, the program was implemented in the other CSSSs. A partnership with a major IS (information system) company to install a city-wide information system was a great advantage for the agency, Montreal health care institutions, and the IS company, and it led to significantly reduced costs. Each of these partnerships built relationships and increased trust.

Communicate Well

I cannot stress too much the importance of communication. Effective personal communication requires self-confidence and practice. We are not born great speakers. A good example is King George VI of Great Britain during the Second World War. He stuttered and as a result had no self-confidence. It took a great deal of training and determination for the King to become an important voice for the people of England during the war. It is important to have a clear and precise message, to be open and transparent, to communicate often, to be consistent and always to the point.

Organizational communication means listening as well as speaking. A good leader knows how to listen to the organization as he or she works to develop buy-in to the collective vision. It is also important to set up a feedback mechanism that will allow you to understand and address the things that are not helping the organization and are creating resistance to change and improvement. Communication is a very important tool for gaining the credibility a leader needs in his or her organization. Following Mintzberg's three principles for gaining credibility in a professional bureaucracy, a credible leader manages conflict, obtains new resources for the organization, and works well in the interface between the hospital and the outside world; and none of this is possible without effective communication.

At Notre-Dame I was able to hire a director of communications, Jacques Wilkins who was such a personable character that he became close to the physicians and staff. He was able to communicate their concerns, help them in writing their proposals, and was always ready to listen. He became a barometer of what was happening in the Hospital and was helpful in counselling me in many of my decisions. He became an extension of me in the Hospital, since everyone knew we were close, and he could be counted on to present their concerns in a clear and honest manner. He was sometimes called The Confessor as people were willing to tell him things that they would rarely mention to others. He later went on to be the director of communications for the premier of Quebec.

Communications tools are the means we use to get our messages out, and to collect comments and ideas from others. The Hospital journal was a very important way to communicate with staff and I was involved in every issue. I held weekly CEO breakfasts for staff who expressed an interest in speaking with me by sending an email to my office. I toured the Hospital on the day, evening and night shifts to be in contact with staff, and spent time having ad hoc conversations about the Hospital or other issues of interest to them. I was available to any department that wanted to meet with me. I organized cooking classes with the physicians who were interested and arranged learning trips at home and abroad. I used participative meetings outside the Hospital at my country house, where directors had to cook and clean together while we planned the yearly strategy of the Hospital.

Communication also means being seen in public as the representative of your organization in the media, at health care events, at conferences, foundation activities and social events. It is also important to realize that wherever you go, you always represent the hospital, and your actions and comments reflect upon and affect your staff. If one of your staff members is home on a Saturday night having dinner and you are being interviewed on television, and the staff member says to his or her family, "Hey! That's my CEO, let's hear what he/she is saying," and is proud to work at the institution, then you know you are succeeding as the leader.

234

Building Trust

Relationships are built on trust. In the absence or presence of trust, in different degrees, the relationship will change. In an organization with little or no trust, you may find an environment that is very dysfunctional, with open sabotage, intense micro-management, and a redundant hierarchy with a punishing philosophy. An organization with low trust might exhibit unhappy, dissatisfied employees and stakeholders, hidden agendas, a political atmosphere with polarized camps and bureaucracy, and redundant structures with slow approval of projects. In an environment where trust is not an issue, neither present nor absent, the workplace is a healthy one, there is good communication, good alignment with objectives and structure, and little politics. As trust increases, there is a much stronger focus on work and results, effective collaboration and partnering, strong creativity with support for innovation, acceptance of errors, high levels of transparency and individual autonomy.

The impact of trust or the lack of trust on personal relationships is dramatic and can move the climate of an organization from dysfunctional, hostile, and energy-draining to a cooperative, supportive, uplifting, joyful and transparent atmosphere that gives energy and strength, along with a sense that anything can be accomplished and that you are never alone.

In *The Speed of Trust*, Covey discusses the importance of trust in relationships and how trust is an essential component of leadership. Trust is having confidence, and lack of trust is suspicion. Trust is based on character/integrity and on competence; both of these components are necessary in building trust. Character refers to the morals and ethics of a person and the values he or she holds, while competence refers to the ability to get results and achieve one's objectives. Good or great leaders build trust with and among the people they work with and this allows them to succeed.

Covey describes 13 behaviors that capture very well what I have learned about building trust over my career. These behaviours work and enable us to build the trust we need in a healthy organization. These 13 behaviours may seem obvious but it is important that they be repeated so that they become part of a leader's automatic responses.

▸ It is important to talk straight, which means being honest and telling the truth at all times.

▸ You build trust by showing respect and caring for others.

▸ Let others see what you are really doing so there is no perception of a hidden agenda.

▸ If you make mistakes, correct them, and always apologize to those who may have been affected.

▸ Build trust by being loyal to your staff and those you work with, and asking for their loyalty in return.

▸ Give credit to others, praise work that is well done. Encourage working to a higher standard that you yourself clearly strive to achieve.

▸ Be a winner by demonstrating that you can achieve the objectives you have set for yourself. Expect others to do the same.

▸ Continuous quality improvement is a strong value and trust will grow when others see this is your approach.

▸ Always be present in your organization and when difficult issues arise, internally or externally, ensure your organization sees you confronting them head on.

▸ Ensure that both organizational and personal objectives are clear and make your staff aware of your expectations for them.

▸ Develop a culture of taking responsibility. Make it clear that you take responsibility for your decisions and actions and expect others to take responsibility for theirs.

▸ Listening well is an art. It is a real skill that can be learned and one that is vital if you are to gain the respect, trust, and confidence of those you work with.

▸ If you say you will do something, make sure you do it. If it is not possible, be open and transparent with your explanations.
(Covey, 2008)

To garner trust you must extend trust to others and be recongized as a trusting person. Following the behaviours that Covey describes in more detail in *The Speed of Trust,* has helped me build trust in the organizations where I have had the privilege to work.

Acting according to the following principles helps create a trusting organization; one where trust is present is different than one where trust has not yet been achieved or has been lost. A trusting organization is one where information is available to everyone and secrets are not part of the culture. Mistakes are allowed and are considered part of the learning experience. It is best not to worry about mistakes if they are made when trying to do something better. It is important, however, to avoid making the same mistake twice.

A trusting organization is one that supports creativity and creates an environment that supports innovation. All parts of an organization benefit from the positive affects of trust. (Covey, 2008)

Building Knowledge

This component of leadership complements all the others since knowledge is key in ambition, competence and integrity. The leader of an enterprise has the responsibility to implement a culture of knowledge in the organization. Knowledge acquisition and knowledge transmission are part of this. A culture of knowledge goes hand in hand with a culture of quality and of continuous improvement. The human resources of any organization are its richest assets and they must be continually stimulated to learn and to try new experiences.

Physicians and most other professionals are required to complete a certain number of hours of accredited education every year to maintain their licences to practice. In the hospital, however, there are no requirements for ongoing learning and it is important for the CEO to ensure that a learning culture develops. There are always students in a teaching hospital or affiliated university setting and this helps to promote a learning culture. This applies to management, as students also do their internships in hospital management in a hospital. But it is not necessary to have an academic teaching environment to develop and maintain a learning culture. A CEO who supports this culture will encourage and support staff going to conferences and then will have them present what they have learned in hospital forums. It's important to encourage and support innovation and experimentation monetarily. Honour successes both inside and outside the institution and provide grants and time off for those who want to further their studies.

While learning and experimenting with new ideas, errors can occur, but a good leader knows how to support errors and encourage people to try again. In a learning organization no one is afraid to make a mistake. It is very seldom that the same mistake is made twice because the first one was the learning experience.

The CEO's learning organization approach must also have the buy-in of senior management. It is the leader's responsibility to ensure that the senior leadership values learning as much as he or she does, and if this is not the case then the CEO must work to change this attitude by demonstrating the importance of learning.

Building Leadership: A Lifelong, Continual Process

Throughout this book I have examined issues surrounding managing in the public health care sector, from a primary-care environment in a CLSC, to major teaching hospitals, through mergers, and on to regional management. Each situation was a learning experience and through trial and error I was able to apply most of the principles I have discussed in this chapter. Ultimately, the examples I have provided demonstrate the application of the principles of building leadership. Although I did not know it at the time, throughout my career, thanks to learning and good mentorship, I have been able to avoid making too many major errors while achieving most of the ojectives that each organization developed in its collective vision. Changing the system is, however, a different and much more challenging task and one that I only began to influence. It will take many leaders working together with a common vision to influence the forces of politics that dominate the decision-making process in a universal public system. The ability of politicians to impose the changes needed is influenced and determined by many opposing and conflicting forces. The public system still remains the most equitable, and it is clearly what the public wants and expects. It is our collective responsibility to break down the barriers that hinder putting into place the solutions to our health care needs. These solutions are well known and understood, yet vested interests and politics keep us from their implementation.

CHAPTER ELEVEN

A New Reform of the Quebec Health Care System

Bill 10

IN THE FALL OF 2014, Quebec's recently elected Liberal government introduced a new bill (Bill 10, *An Act to modify the organization and governance of the health and social services network, in particular by abolishing the regional agencies*) thereby reforming the structure of health care in Quebec. With some amendments, it was passed into law in February 2015, ushering in the most drastic changes to the Quebec health care system in the last 40 years. I believe this reform has great potential to change the delivery of care in a positive way but I also believe that it presents far more risks than benefits to health care in Quebec if the dangers in the reform of the health care system are not avoided—only time will tell in which direction Quebec will go.

The law begins with a set of objectives that are the same as those presented in the 2003 reform introduced by then minister of health Dr. Philippe Couillard, now the premier of Quebec: improve access to services for the population, improve the quality and the safety of services provided, and improve the efficiency and the efficacy of the health care system. These same objectives have been the motivation of all the reforms introduced in Quebec over the last 40 years but the lack of response of the health care system to many of the needs of Quebeckers remains a major problem, as I have discussed throughout this book.

When the Liberal Party, under the leadership of Dr. Couillard, won the election in Quebec in the spring of 2014, they were confronted with a provincial deficit that forced them to introduce many cost-cutting measures, including a revision of all government programs. A committee was established to examine Quebec's programs and to evaluate what could be changed. Their first evaluation indicated that government spending for health and education was in line with the other provinces but that the social and welfare programs offered to Quebeckers were much more generous than what was available in the rest of Canada. The government, however, required all ministries to cut back, and the Ministry of Health was no exception.

As discussed in Chapter nine, there is a common belief in Quebec government circles, and especially in the office of the minister of health, that the only way to control the cost of the health care system is through direct management of the system by the Ministry. This belief was reinforced when the CEO of the MUHC (Arthur Porter) was accused of fraud and the Hospital was running a deficit of over $60 million. After the CEO was removed, a supervisor was sent in to run the Hospital. The move to even greater direct control of health care by the ministry was evident when the minister removed the CEO of the Université de Montréal teaching hospital—this time not for deficit reasons, but due to an unresolved conflict with the physicians. A supervisor from the ministry was appointed to run the Hospital, and before a new CEO was chosen he revised its organization chart and appointed new directors to the executive positions. When the new CEO arrived, he was not authorized to change the organization chart or the newly appointed directors for a period of at least three years. This level of control or prescription had never before been seen in the Quebec health care system, and it was the precursor of things to come.

With the arrival of the new government in 2014, the supervisor of the CHUM was named deputy minister and six months later Bill 10 was introduced—a new law that basically centralized all decision-making authority directly in the hands of the minister and the ministry.

The New Reform

The reform to the health care system introduced into law at the end of 2003 and implemented in 2004 was the result of recommendations from both the Rochon and Clair Commissions in Quebec, with the objective to integrate services and ensure a better continuum of care. Each region was asked to carry out a consultation process to suggest which health care establishments should merge to form a new organization with responsibility for the health of the population of a given geographical area. I discussed in detail in chapter eight the objectives and implementation of this reform and the steps taken to establish the new CSSSs (Centres de santé et de services sociaux) in the Montreal region. The CSSSs were set up in a three-tier system wherein the minister provided direction and policy, regional authorities provided regional coordination, and the CSSS itself provided the management of services adapted to the needs of its population. The CSSSs also had the mandate to develop local networks, RLSs (Réseaux locaux de service) that would combine the energy, initiative and programs of multiple actors in a given region to work together to improve the health of its population.

This reform included the creation of a population-based model of care integrating hospitals, CLSCs and nursing homes into new health and social-service networks. There were 93 networks created, covering the 17 health regions of Quebec. This model of care had been in place for 10 years and was beginning to show real benefits to the health care system. It had taken five years to consolidate the mergers before the focus could turn to the continuum of care, clinical issues and managing chronic illness. Relationships were being cemented among the different actors in the network, and trust and confidence were finally beginning to emerge.

From the beginning of the implementation of this model, there was frustration on the part of the minister of health, his cabinet and the civil servants in the ministry that the system, with its many distinct boards, was difficult to control, even though this had always been accepted as the price to pay for a more democratic, participative health care system.

The 2014 priority of the newly-elected government to reduce public expenditure set the stage for introducing a new reform of the structures and functioning of the health care system in Quebec. But this time there was no consultation and the regions were not involved in a planning process; the new reform was driven by a small group whose main objective was to control costs.

The new system reduced the number of institutions from 182 to 33 new institutions with the creation of Integrated Health and Social Service Centres (Centres intégrés de santé et de services sociaux, or CISSSs). Under the supervision of the Ministry of Health, these centres will play the role of a regional agency and will also manage the delivery of all health care services in their region. For the first time in the history of Quebec health care, a single organization has in its mandate the different missions of acute care, long-term care, chronic rehabilitation services for physically and intellectually handicapped persons, youth protection and psychiatric institutions. The government argues that this will allow for better integration of services, better continuity of care, better management of information, less bureaucracy and easier control, all with a savings of $220 million.

Moving to a two-tier system where regional agencies (CISSSs) are in direct control of the delivery of services is in itself not a bad way to deliver care; this makes it easier to implement regional programs and better assume the continuity of care. The real danger is centralized management of the system and the bureaucratization of care as the ministry and the minister of health try to control and manage costs. The organizations become so large that their leaders grow disconnected from the professionals who deliver the care. The people who work there and deliver the care lose their sense of ownership of their institution and the pride they have in the work their organization is doing. Unless these dangers are avoided the reform could do much more harm than good.

Health care is a person-to-person affair and when we are ill or suffering we want health care delivered by people who enjoy their work because they are supported and encouraged by their organization. It is hard enough for a CEO to create this environment in a single institution for which he or she is responsible; to do this with 10 to 15 different establishments with many different missions and 8,000 to 15,000 employees is a huge challenge. The way this has been done in other two-tier systems in Canada has been to develop a bureaucracy that is mainly focused on control. Layers of control are established and management loses flexibility and innovation. Projects take longer to be approved and leadership becomes more and more removed from front-line professionals offering services. Middle management becomes frustrated because they have no say in decision-making and are expected to simply execute directives.

The new reform centralizes all decision-making in the hands of the minister. He or she now has the power to name all board members, as well as the CEO of the organization. The minister determines the internal management structure of the new organization and all the programs to be offered, and also names the second-in-command who replaces the CEO when he or she is absent. The board, which has always had as its main role the choosing of the CEO, will no longer be the employer of the chief executive officer. The minister even appoints the board's chairperson.

This puts into question the role, responsibilities and the degree of authority of the boards, who are reduced to monitoring the performance of the organization, the performance of the CEO, and reporting to the minister. The new law also provides for financial remuneration for board members, whereas in the past these have always been volunteer positions whereby members of the community give their time and expertise to the institutions most important to them.

This new dynamic in Quebec's health care system fundamentally changes the role of the CEO to the point where I question whether the title is still applicable. Since the government appoints the CEO, his or her status is that of a deputy minister, with the legal obligations that this entails, and as such the CEO can no longer criticize or question government actions or policies. He or she can no longer publicly present ideas and innovations without obtaining government approval to do so, since a CEO named by the government always speaks in the name of the government. I believe the way in which each CEO manages this new status in the regions will determine the new dynamic of health care in Quebec since they can provide the sole barrier to complete centralization

This new dynamic changes the nature of management in the health care system, making the issues I discussed in chapter nine on managing health care in the public sector all the more relevant. Every CEO becomes an extension of the minister in his or her region and as such is politically responsible for all issues that arise in the region. The CEO will be monitoring the media each morning and a team will be required to collect the data needed to prepare the response he or she will have to make in the local media and to provide the information the minister will need to answer questions in the National Assembly. This activity will be in parallel to that in the minister's office.

The CEO's shift of focus from the offering of services and the quality of services to a more political role will change the position of the CEO in such a way as to force the implementation of a more rigid controlling mechanism. I believe this process of bureaucratization will slowly dominate all of the health care system; a media attack on a CEO will be a direct attack on the minister and it can be used by the opposition in the National Assembly to criticize the government.

Understanding a Professional Bureaucracy

In earlier chapters I have often referred to Henry Mintzberg's work in which he makes the clear distinction between a mechanistic bureaucracy and a professional bureaucracy. He clearly demonstrates that health care institutions are professional bureaucracies and that management must take this into account. The professors in the Department of Health Administration in the School of Public Health at the Université de Montréal describe this issue in their November 2014 brief to the Parliamentary Commission studying Bill 10. (Please note that many of the ideas that appear in this chapter were first presented in this brief, which provides more details.)

In a mechanistic bureaucracy, resources are used to provide goods and services based on the relation between the resources available, the production of the goods and services, and the achievement of specified goals and objectives internal to the organization. There is a best practice to produce those goods and services and achieve those objectives. The person in charge knows the best practice and, in a clearly top-down approach, implements the management model that will succeed.

In a professional bureaucracy, the objectives are external to the organization; for example, making patients well. The production of the goods and services is carried out by professionals who have the right to practice their profession by authority of an autonomous professional body outside the organization. There is no best way to provide all the goods and services all the time and the professionals are expected to use their skills and expertise to seek the best outcomes using available scientific data.

The minister and the Ministry of Health see health care institutions and the system in which they function as a mechanistic bureaucracy and it is this vision that has led to the reform in Quebec. But a professional bureaucracy cannot be centrally run and therein lies the error in the vision of Bill 10 and the present reform.

As discussed in chapter nine on managing in the public sector, the challenge is now even greater as the public sector has been introduced into the direct management of services, with the government-appointed CEO not only responsible for regional coordination of health care, but also for the delivery of care across multiple missions. The type of management required to succeed in this new environment will rely on good leadership skills.

The tension between the mechanistic and professional vision of the health care system will direct energy away from clinical care, new technology, new treatments, innovation, and a focus on quality toward administrative issues of cost and funding. Unless this tension between the professionals in the organization and the management team responding to the needs of the minister is addressed through a strong partnership between the professional and administrative components of the organization, there is a real danger to the success of the reform.

More, Not Less, Bureaucracy

A major argument used by the government to justify the current reform is that it will reduce bureaucracy. The premises are clear: Moving from a three-tier model to a two-tier model will reduce the levels of decision-making and flatten the structure. Removing 1,400 management personnel from the system will save money by reducing what the government wants the population to believe are non-essential staff. These assertions have not proven true in other jurisdictions that introduced the same type of health reform. The November 2014 Université de Montréal brief to the Parliamentary Commission stated clearly that the model centralizes decision-making and increases bureaucracy.

As health care institutions merge and become much larger, the way they are managed changes. Managers now manage a large health care system and, as I have discussed, managing a health system is very different than managing an institution. In the new structure, the CEO, named by the minister, is first and foremost responsible to the minister rather than to the board, the organization, or the community, as was the case in the past. This change of allegiance allows for much more centralized management of the health care system and much more control over the decisions being made in the system.

As President and CEO of the Montreal Health Region, I was witness to this change in direction to a more centralized management model during the 10 years I was responsible for the organization of care in Montreal. I have discussed in an earlier chapter the implementation of an IS/IT system throughout Montreal for an electronic medical record. This was done by developing consensus among the Montreal institutions, that this was the best way to modernize their patient electronic medical records at the best price, and they all accepted to pay the cost with their regional funds. I had informed the ministry of Montreal's direction and proceeded with the project. Four years later, I was asked by the ministry: "Who gave you permission to do this?" I replied that the law gave me the authority since, with my Board, I was responsible by law for the management of regional resources and coordination of care on the Island of Montreal. With the changes in the law, the level of autonomy I enjoyed in managing care no longer exists in a two-tier model that is being promoted as less bureaucratic.

There are examples of increased bureaucracy in other Canadian provinces that have followed the route Quebec is now taking. Alberta moved from multiple individual institutions to a regional model—from 17 regions to nine—and finally to a single corporation, Alberta Health Services (AHS), which is in charge of all health care in the province. This has been studied in depth and, in her 2013 report (*Review of the Alberta Health Services Organization and Structure, and Next Steps*), Janet Davidson, Official Administrator of Alberta Health Services, describes clearly the consequences of centralization and the ensuing bureaucratization.

The CEO and his or her staff are under the direct control of the minister and the deputy minister. As the political party in power changes, so too does the board chair and CEO, both of whom are named by the minister. The management team is no longer part of the delivery of care and finds itself both physically and psychologically removed from the day-to-day contact with patients and their concerns. The clinical dimensions of the organization are left to the local management teams who have little authority to initiate, change or develop new programs, while upper management concentrates on the political and corporate concerns of the organization and the Ministry of Health.

Management concentrates on crises, the media, preparing internal documents, responding to ministerial requests and controlling expenditure, thereby avoiding the real problems of care delivery. The traditional zones of power in the health care organizations shift from the internal clinical groupings of physicians, department heads, nurses and other professionals to the external zones of power: the media and the Ministry of Health. This distancing of management from clinical concerns has serious results for clinical staff, reducing motivation and leading to demoralization and a sense of abandonment. Meanwhile, management looks for new ways to collect administrative data and implement controls.

In Quebec, the concentration of decision-making in the central authority not only changes the dynamic between the professionals in the institutions and the central authority, it also changes the relationships among the different communities and their local leadership. The focus of attention of local officials is now shifted towards the central authority and further removed from local issues. All the existing union accreditations in Quebec will be reorganized into four large accreditations in each CISSS; the unions will move their offices to the central authority's location and will be further removed from the local issues and concerns of their members. The Council of Physicians, Dentists and Pharmacists, which each institution is legally required to have to oversee the quality of medical practice in the institution, becomes a much larger body combining all the medical and dental staff throughout the whole region. Aside from the infighting for the control of this political body among physicians, the Council itself becomes much more bureaucratic and removed from the more clinical concerns of its members.

Davidson goes on to report that the tools, abilities, knowledge and learning needed for innovative management and the development of clinical services have been redirected to demonstrating results (often through volume of activity), and the control mechanisms that serve the central administration are of little or no use to the individual health institutions and the delivery of services.

I have discussed throughout the book how important it is for the CEO to be in contact with the leaders of the different zones of power and influence in the organization and to be available to listen and respond to their issues. The heads of departments at Notre-Dame

Hospital could simply knock on the door of my office and, if I was there, sit down for a few minutes to discuss their concerns. With the new CISSS organization, the CEO will now be so far removed from day-to-day operations that this type of timely communication and collaborative problem-solving will be next to impossible.

Mergers Do Not Save Money

One of the driving imperatives of the mergers into regional entities is to save money through reduction in the number of management personnel and through economies of scale. The brief presented by the professors of the Department of Health Administration in the School of Public Health at the Université de Montréal demonstrates that neither the three-tier model of health care management nor the two-tier model have any significant impact on the administrative cost of the system. Administrative costs include all costs of running the organization and the system other than direct patient care and the management of that care. Between 1975 and 2014, the general administrative cost of health care in Quebec went from about four percent to 1.6 percent, compared to an almost five percent increase in the overall cost of the system per year, mainly due to salaries, increased use of medication, and inflation. The portion of administrative costs is a very small part of overall expenditure. The real cost savings come from a fundamental change in the way health care is delivered. The new reform in Quebec does not address this issue. At first glance, it seems that merging institutions will save money, but in practice the complexity of the new organizations necessitates added management to apply the controls that are required.

Regionalization in Quebec over the last 40 years has not had any effect on increasing or decreasing administrative expenses. The mergers in Alberta that led to the creation of Alberta Health Services have increased administrative costs due to the complexity of managing large organizations. In Quebec, the creation of the CSSSs led to increases in management and staff due to clinical issues, while at the same time staff in regional authorities had been decreasing over the past five years as a result of budget cuts.

Mergers have been demonstrated to work best in those areas where there is a complementary technology that allows each party to the merger to benefit from the other. But the mergers brought about by the recent legislation integrate missions that are not in the traditional continuum of health care. The creation of the CSSSs led to the merger of primary care, acute care, acute rehab care and long-term care—services that follow the patient through life and intervene when necessary. The logic for this merger was the increased continuity of care offered to the population. The new regional institutions will also merge youth protection, psychiatric care, and rehab service for the intellectually and physically handicapped.

Mergers work best with a homogenous population and this is not the case with the integration of institutions with such different missions. The increased complexity of the services offered by the CISSSs reduces efficiency, and bureaucracy will increase as management of the different professionals becomes more difficult.

The cost savings, which are being presented as the rationale for this reform, have not proven true in other jurisdictions. After the reduction of some administrative costs in the back office, the addition of management staff to oversee more complex administrative issues increases costs. In real-world situations, the cost of merging and combining administrative and financial services, IS/IT, data collection and required control mechanisms leads to increased rather than decreased cost.

Mergers in health care can be both structural, such as in Bill 10 wherein multiple missions and organizations are under one CEO, or virtual wherein the integration of care is done through contractual agreements between organizations complementing each other. As has been mentioned, mergers cause management to concentrate less on clinical issues and more on merger issues and it has been shown to take a minimum of 18 months before already approved programs can begin to be implemented. Virtual integration has demonstrated better outcomes and savings, better performance, better satisfaction of staff, better adaptability to changing environments and to the needs of patients. It is service integration, not structural integration, which has demonstrated greater success in achieving clinical objectives.

The Loss of Identity

Health care institutions were initially developed to respond to the needs of particular groups. Before the 1950s, the Catholic Church in Quebec and the different ethnic communities in Quebec initiated most hospitals, rehab centres, mental-health institutions and nursing homes. The Jewish, Italian, Irish, Polish, and Chinese communities all developed institutions to serve the needs of their growing constituencies. After the introduction of universal health care, these institutions maintained their ethno-cultural identity though they served all Quebeckers equally. Employees became attached to their organizations, regardless of their own personal origins, and a sense of pride and belonging grew stronger as institutions continued to develop. Foundations became more important and communities contributed to the building, expansion and new equipment for their institutions. The boards of these institutions reflected the community's attachment and were an important part of the life of the organization.

Bill 10 removes all the existing boards and merges all the institutions in a given geographical area into one new organization with one new board whose members are appointed by the minister. One of the real challenges in this new organization is for the CISSSs to be able to maintain the links and connections to the communities that the diverse institutions had in the past. Existing foundations supporting a particular institution will maintain their specific relationship but the decision-making body for the use of foundation funds will now be centralized with the CISSS, which has concerns very different from those of particular institutions and their foundations.

For example, the Polish long-term care centre (Canadian-Polish Welfare Institute) has been serving the Polish and Slavic communities for decades, and the majority of staff and the CEO speak Polish. Board members are from the community and the institution serves as a focal point for the Quebec Polish community. It will be important to maintain those connections because the role that the institutions play in their communities is a contributing factor in maintaining the health of the community. It is essential to maintain strong consultative boards that will provide recommendations to the main CISSS board on specific issues relating to their communities, and that the recommendations from these boards will be received with appropriate consideration by the CISSS boards.

Pressure from the Anglophone community, mainly in the West Island municipalities of the Island of Montreal, led to an amendment that ensured bilingual status to certain new institutions and even removed a predominantly francophone CSSS from an anglophone regrouping and placed it with a francophone CISSS in the centre of Montreal.

The Danger to the Social Services Now Being Offered

There is a particular concern that has been raised about the social services that Bill 10 has fully integrated into the new CISSS structure. These social services include the social integration of mental-health patients, the physically and mentally challenged patient, public health, prevention and promotion programs, social services in social housing programs, social services to the itinerant population, and inner-city problems. These concerns stem from the nature of the new regional organizations and the focus of senior management.

In the new configuration of health care, with the emphasis on cost-cutting, there will be added pressure on organizations to balance budgets. As the acute-care hospital institutions generate almost all of the deficit, and as the new CEO and his or her team are responsible to the minister, if one wants to keep one's job there is a great incentive to do everything possible to balance the regional budget. The tendency will be to take money from the different missions where the offering of services can be more easily reduced than with the cutting of acute-care services. Unless there is a fundamental shift from acute hospital care to a robust primary-care and community-care model, the pressure will be to balance budgets at the expense of social services. These services should be protected by law—which has not been done in the new reform.

Does the Reform Help Answer the Pressing Needs of the Quebec's Health Care System?

Unfortunately, the current reforms do not address these issues and do not provide any new direction to changing the way health care is delivered. The system remains a hospital-focused acute-care system and until we shift to a community-based patient-centred system there will be little change in the results. The changes brought about by Bill 10 will not improve access to family physicians, there will be no increase in evening or night-time coverage, emergency room overcrowding will not diminish, wait times for specialists will not be reduced, home care and chronic care will not be improved, errors in medication will not decrease and the system will not be more financially sustainable. We can only hope that these issues will not be aggravated.

The real challenge to the new CEO and his or her management team will be to move forward, as much as possible within the current framework, with the real changes that are required to improve health care services to the population. It will be up to them to realign care in their region and hope for as little interference as possible from the ministry. Hopefully, the ministry will allow experimentation and encourage replication of those changes that demonstrate the best results. The real changes needed to shift to a community-based patient-centred delivery of health care will not be easy and the criticism from the vested interest groups, mainly the acute-care hospital sector, will pressure government to resist.

Managing the CISSS

This book has been about managing in health care: managing a professional bureaucracy, managing a regional authority, managing in the public sector. I have discussed the issues of leadership and how one goes about managing in a newly appointed position. The new CEOs of the CISSSs will all be beginning their adventure at the same time and under the same conditions. The principles of good health care management will be important in getting things off to a positive start, and these are my thoughts on how they may proceed.

Getting to Know the Organization

First and foremost, the new CEOs must establish the new management team needed to run the organization. To do this, it will be crucial to get to know the organization and the people who are in place. A small team made up of the existing CEOs should be set up as an advisory body to help plan the first stages of the integration. It will be important to meet individually with each of these CEOs of the institutions being merged and have a meeting with each of the previous boards to get a good idea of the concerns and issues that are already on the table.

During the initial meetings, it is important to see if there are serious financial issues, personnel issues, quality issues, organizational issues, program issues or patient-care issues that must be dealt with immediately. What were the concerns of past boards for the future and what was the strategic plan of each organization? How well has the organization done in respecting the management contract signed with the regional authority?

Once this is accomplished, it will be important to obtain each CEO's portrait of the management teams they had been working with in the past. Within each of the merged institutions, it will be crucial to meet with the CMDP, as well as the different professional groups and the union executives, to hear their concerns about the merger. It will be important to meet with the user groups in each organization to look at their concerns and fears about the mergers. This series of meetings should be done very quickly, with written feedback to each group to clearly show that their concerns have been registered. It is not advisable to make promises during this period as the inability to keep a promise will hurt future credibility.

Communication and information-sharing is essential and should be an early priority. There should be information coming directly from the CEO's office, sent out almost daily, informing staff of the steps being taken to effect the transition and of the different activities of management and the board. A feedback mechanism is also important in order that comments and concerns can be regularly collected and responded to as quickly as possible. A transparent, well-informed organization goes a long way to building the trust that will be required for the mergers to succeed.

The first order of business will be to meet with the newly named board and the board chair so everybody can get to know each other and share their concerns The CEO, named by the minister rather than the board, has to show the board that he or she is capable and competent to run the new organization, and must stress how important the new board is to achieving the mission of the newly created CISSS.

The CEO will have to establish his or her credibility in the organization, and the first months are crucial. The moment a CEO first arrives in a new organization is the ideal time to put into practice the steps to building leadership. As discussed in detail in chapter 10, the ingredients to building one's leadership in an organization include: building a common vision, building relationships, building trust and building organizational trust.

Building a Common Vision and Building Trust

I believe that this stage should begin as soon as the CISSSs are formed and while the transition period to a merged organization is underway. Thus it will be necessary to move forward with administrative consolidation while building a common vision. Administrative consolidation is likely to take at least a year and will include things like new payroll, human-resource and financial systems that will have to go to tender to find new suppliers. Simultaneously, a visioning exercise should be undertaken, making sure to involve all the players in each institution. A steering committee should be set up, with subcommittees carrying out different parts of the overall mandate. Careful attention should be paid to the past academic activities of each of the merging institutions, as well their individual reputations locally, nationally and internationally, so the merged institution can include these characteristics in the vision. The focus should be on rallying the diverse professional staff around patient care and the notion of the organization's responsibility for the health and social well-being of the population which they serve.

These first steps will lay the foundation for trust in the organization and greater ownership of each of the merging institutions. Looking at Mintzberg's formula for success in a professional bureaucracy, managing conflict, obtaining resources and functioning well on the interface between the organization and the external environment still remain the key ingredients for success of the leadership team. If the board and the senior management can keep their focus on clinical issues while still responding to the ministerial requirements, and can remain present for the clinical staff and mission of the organization, there is a good chance to achieve the overall objective of integrating care and developing a sustainable health care system. Special attention must be placed on the management of the social services offered, as the board will be easily distracted by the acute-care issues of the new institution.

The CEO and Politics

There will be 33 CEOs in the Quebec health care system. Each one will be chosen by the Minister of Health and named by an order in council. Each will have the status of a deputy minister with all the restrictions this imposes regarding confidentiality and adherence to ministerial policy. The independence of the CEO is severely constrained in this model. This poses an important contradiction and dilemma for the CEO. As Mintzberg has clearly stated, a CEO needs credibility in a professional bureaucracy to manage and one gains credibility on the interface between the organization and the community. The CEO must be present in the community, participate in community activities, help in fund raising and publicly show support for the issues and concerns of his or her region. To do so puts the CEO in direct conflict with his or her deputy minister status and the fear of being removed by the minister if the minister or government is not pleased with his or her actions.

The CEO becomes a political figure simply by running a health care organization that directly serves the population. He or she cannot be seen as always toeing the party line if that is not the direction of his or her region and the CEO wants to establish credibility with the community. Bill 10 has made health care in Quebec much less democratic, but if the CEO is able to establish his or her own political base in the region through contact with the local deputies, mayors, community groups, chambers of commerce, local merchants and industry, it will be possible to put some pressure on government and allow for at least some political dialogue in health care. Here lies the real challenge for the CEO in the new health care world in Quebec.

The manner in which the new organizations are managed will determine whether or not the reform being put into place will be successful. There is potential for real improvement in our health care system if the objectives of patient care are clear and senior management can work closely with the professional staff and maintain focus on clinical issues. The new administrative demands are daunting and the dangers of the bureaucratization of management will be unrelenting, but if the concerns of the board and the CEO can remain on patient care, then I believe we can improve our health system and ensure its sustainability.

CHAPTER TWELVE

Answering the Questions and Finding the Solutions

I BEGAN THIS BOOK with a series of questions, and while describing my journey through our health care system I have attempted to view them from different perspectives. We can now go back to these questions, examine the available solutions to the problems presented, and discuss why these solutions have not been implemented.

▸ Why is it so hard to find a family physician?

▸ Is our health care system financially sustainable?

▸ Why is there so little health care coverage on evenings, nights and weekends?

▸ Why do we wait so long for care in Emergency?

▸ Why do we wait so long to see a specialist who our general practitioner (GP) says we need to see?

▸ Why do we wait so long for surgery in a universal public health care system?

▸ Why is so difficult to find home care for elderly and chronically ill patients?

▸ Why are there so many medication errors?

▸ Why is it so difficult to get the vulnerable and the chronically ill to comply with their care plans and participate in their own health care?

▸ Why is the prevention of illness and the promotion of health of so little interest?

But the Big Question remains: When we know the solutions to these problems, why is it so difficult to implement them?

Why is it so hard to find a family physician?

The number of GPs in Quebec with licenses to practice is sufficient to cover all the primary-care needs of the population and to provide access in a medically appropriate lapse of time, which can be the same day for more urgent needs and within 48 hours for less urgent concerns. The FMOQ (Fédération des médecins omnipraticiens du Québec) is not arguing for more family physicians; the increase in university places has responded to the aging of the medical profession and the government buyout of physicians in the 1990s. This buyout was done to reduce costs to the health care system by reducing the medical services available.

The real issue is where family physicians work and how many patients they are able to see in their offices in the community. If we look at the situation in Montreal, with a population of 2.5 million to serve, we notice that 50 percent of the working hours of general practitioners is spent in our hospitals and other health care institutions, while only 50 percent of their available time is spent seeing patients in the community. The second issue is that whether general practitioners are in a group or in solo practice, they work alone with very little assistance in seeing their registered patients. Registered or rostered patients are those patients who sign up with a general practitioner and then become part of that physician's responsibility. In Quebec, physicians are paid a yearly fee for registering patients, and a patient can only be registered to one general practitioner at a time. Because of the lack of assistance with seeing their patients, a full-time equivalent physician in Quebec (36 hours/week) registers 1,000 patients at best, while in the Kaiser model in California or the primary-care teams in Barcelona, physicians will maintain anywhere from 2,000 to 2,600 rostered patients. It is clear we could significantly increase access to physicians by increasing the support available to them. Dr. Barrette introduced Bill 20 in December, 2014 in an attempt to address this issue.

As primary-care teams are being built up, multidisciplinary professionals are being added to the patient-care teams to better manage chronic care, yet physicians are indicating that this additional offer of service—which greatly improves the quality of care and management of a patient's utilization of the system—does not result in the physician being able to register or see more patients. The two most important solutions to improve access to a family physician and rostering the population are: returning physicians to the community, and providing them with the support that will allow them to see more patients in their workday.

Family physicians work in the hospital environment because they have support from hospital staff, access to diagnostic technology, access to specialist consultations, and follow-up for their patients leaving the hospital. Working in a hospital is attractive to the family physician because working with a team, and having access to the technology physicians need to better treat their patients, is very satisfying. In addition, the fee structure in the hospital is more attractive.

When a patient is admitted to a hospital there is an assigned treating physician responsible for that patient's care until discharge. Normally, it is a specialist working in a specific department who takes on this responsibility. When there are GPs working in the hospital, they become the treating physicians for many patients while the specialists become the consultants. Each then gets a fee-for-service for taking care of the patient, which often means paying double since there is the fee for the family physician as treating physician and a fee for the specialist consult. When there are no specialists, or only visiting specialists, it is necessary to have GPs admitting patients and covering the hospital.

To ensure physician coverage in specific areas of care, Quebec introduced AMP (alternative medical practice). AMP requires general practitioners with fewer than 20 years of practice to provide 12 hours a week of their time in a prioritized list of designated areas if they wish to be paid for their services. Emergency room service is first on the list, which also includes care in other institutional positions. This obligation means that these general practitioners will work that many hours less in the community.

To ensure general practitioners spend a much greater per-centage of their time in the community seeing their registered patients, we must:

▸ Reduce hospital fees, compared to the community fee schedule, to provide the incentive for family physicians to move back to the community.

▶ Revise the AMP policy.

▶ Provide physicians in the community with easy access to imaging technology and other diagnostic services.

▶ Ensure that multidisciplinary teams are available to support the continuing care of chronically ill patients.

▶ Provide physicians with assistants, which will enable them to see more patients.

▶ Improve the working environment of community physicians.

▶ Introduce best-practice protocols to ensure the pertinence of the diagnostic tests requested, the treatment plan provided, and the medication prescribed.

▶ Develop hospital protocols that will enable access to diagnostic testing without having to go through a specialist.

▶ Ensure that the medical record in the community physician's office and the patient's hospital medical record are connected and accessible from wherever the physician is, and that both of these are kept up to date.

If these measures are put into place, I believe that there will be a major increase in the capacity of each physician to register and follow many more patients, and that the number of general practitioners providing community care will also increase.

There are reasons, however, why each of these changes has not already taken place, and it is important to understand these reasons to be able to overcome them.

1. Changing the fee schedule by which physicians are paid is a complex negotiation between the government and the medical unions or federations. The FMOQ negotiates for the GPs (general practitioners/family physicians) and the FMSQ (Fédération des médecins spécialistes du Quebec) represents the specialists. These unions, which began

with the introduction of the RAMQ (Régie d'assurance maladie du Québec) in 1969, have become so powerful that it is difficult for any provincial government to introduce significant changes without the threat of a very public battle with the physicians that would damage the government politically. Under the guise of professional autonomy, physicians have remained independent entrepreneurs and it is very difficult for a government to influence medical practice, even if these fundamental policy choices would be beneficial to physicians, patients and the health care system as a whole.

To move GPs back to the community it is necessary to make community practice more rewarding, both financially and professionally. As I have stated throughout this book, our health care system has been hospital-centred since its inception and there is strong resistance by the professionals in our hospitals to change this. Specialist physicians in the hospitals are very happy to have GPs, interns and residents in the hospital to reduce their workload and their on-call availability. GPs do not see a policy shift away from a hospital-centred system as in their interests since there has been no investment in the community infrastructure that would make them more effective there. The government has instead invested massively in hospital renewal throughout the province in the past few years, with the creation of two mega-hospitals in Montreal and massive, expansive and expensive renovations in many other hospitals.

If we are to begin a transfer from a curative-based and hospital-centred system, we must develop a clear vision and policy statement of change. One of the most significant barriers to this policy change is the notion that the community is the private sector, while the hospital is the public sector. The confusion this has generated in the public/private debate has led governments to not support community development for fear of criticism from the Opposition in the National Assembly.

Physicians in the community are considered private entrepreneurs, and though their fees are paid on a fee-for-service basis from the public purse, their activity is considered to be in the private sector. Any reference to the private sector brings up a threat to the universal health care system through the possible introduction of user fees or co-payment. It brings up the image of two parallel systems, one public and one private. Any support to the infrastructure of the GP's office is considered as support for the private sector. This misunderstanding, which is prevalent in the public/private debate in health care, should be clarified so that support to family physicians in the community is clearly perceived as acceptable and not seen as a first step towards the privatization of health care and the introduction of the American model of care.

2. AMP (alternative medical practice) was introduced in Quebec after a crisis in the emergency room of a rural hospital when there was no medical coverage available and the emergency room had to shut down. The government at the time was criticized for not being able to manage health care and was held responsible for the threat posed to the population by the closing of an emergency room. In response, general practitioners were required to fulfill certain obligations to practice in designated areas of the system, and community practice was not one of them. These requirements mean that family physicians must spend 12 hours a week outside community practice, in areas commonly referred to as AMPs. If we wish to ensure appropriate primary-care access to the population, we must revise this restriction. This, in turn, would limit the inappropriate use of emergency rooms since it would be easier for more patients to be seen in the community. Yet government is hesitant to make this necessary change in its hospital-centred system.

3. A general practitioner needs certain diagnostic tools to be able to diagnose the patient in a timely fashion. In a hospital-centred system, the tests required are offered in hospitals, at no charge to patients, while very few tests are offered free of charge in the community. Lab services and most of the more specialized radiology services are available only in the hospital. If you are an outpatient with a prescription from your family physician, the wait time for these services is very long as a result of rationing of services in a universal system with limited operating funds. Inpatients have priority while outpatients do not have a dedicated service to respond to their needs in a timely fashion.

A good example of this is the use of ultrasound technology, a diagnostic tool used to investigate many medical conditions. The test is provided without charge in the hospital but not in the many radiology clinics outside the hospital where only traditional radiology is covered under the universal system. As a result, it can take many months to schedule an appointment—to the frustration of the patient and the family physician. Patients who can pay for the ultrasound out of pocket can purchase the test themselves. It is unacceptable that such an important tool of medicine is not available in all radiology clinics free of charge, yet this is the case. Until these types of problems change, general practitioners will have less interest in working in the community.

The barrier to this change is the fear of major increases in utilization, and hence cost, to the public purse. This can easily be avoided by developing protocols for the use of the technology. There should be enough incentive to introduce this change because of the advantage to the patient in reducing anxiety, more rapid diagnosis, and more rapid treatment, as well as for the satisfaction of the physicians; yet, though this has been discussed for the past 10 years, it has still not been introduced.

4. We require multidisciplinary teams working with general practitioners to effectively manage the long-term care of chronically ill patients. The chronically ill include patients with cancer or HIV, or with cardiac, musculoskeletal or pulmonary illnesses, etc. Multidisciplinary teams are essential to properly manage care in these cases; they relieve physicians of much of the follow-up care of patients once the diagnosis is made and treatment has begun. Governments are realizing this and are slowly building up teams in the general practitioner's office.

A major issue for many clinics in Montreal, however, is whether these teams should be made up of public employees, or whether funds should be provided to the physicians to build up their own teams. This stems once again from the public/private debate, and from the mistrust of government over how the physicians would manage and use the funds if they were given control of their use. This poorly resolved issue has led to a much slower introduction of teams and, in many cases, poor use of their services. The trend is growing, however, for greater acceptance of public employees working with physicians on these teams, and as training is introduced to improve their functioning and use in medical care, their value and efficiency will continue to increase. Funds for the new teams must come from the existing system by redefining the services actually provided, eliminating services of less value and moving this type of service from the hospital to the community. But we must move more quickly and definitively to implement these changes.

5. Physicians must be able to see more patients in a day; using physician assistants as part of a medical practice is one of the most effective ways of accomplishing this. A physician assistant is a support person, for example, a nurse assistant, who can work with one or two physicians and help manage their patients by preparing the visit with the doctor, taking histories, updating medical records and maintaining contact with the patient. This practice allows physicians to significantly increase the number of patients they are prepared to register, and its widespread use would go a long way to solving the problem of accessibility.

Once again, there are funding issues, union issues and cultural issues that create barriers to this important change.

6. As has already been mentioned in looking at primary-care issues, the environment in which physicians work in the community must change, and government support is required to create these new environments. Billions of dollars have been spent renewing the hospital structure, while no expenditure has been made to develop a community-based infrastructure for physicians. Again, this is due to the entrenched notion that physicians are private entrepreneurs and governments should not support the private sector in health care.

7. Medical protocols facilitate and assist general practitioners to follow best-practice guidelines, ensure quality of care, and the pertinence of the testing and treatment provided. If community physicians follow carefully established protocols, they should then be able to access tests in the hospital without the delays stemming from the current requirement for a specialist's prescription before the test can be carried out. Quebec-wide protocols for this type of activity would ensure uniformity of care and allow for testing once certain requirements of the protocol have been met. This would enable easier, more fluid, and more timely medical practice in the community. It would eliminate unnecessary duplication, increase efficiency, and eliminate some of the frustration felt by physicians

working in the community. There is strong resistance to provincial protocols, even as guidelines, because this is perceived by some physicians as an attack on their autonomy, even though physician-approved protocols for many different situations are an established part of medical practice.

8. The patient electronic medical record is now an essential tool to facilitate patient care. Electronic medical records not only follow the patients no matter where they are treated, they are instantly updated for all users, and they are also connected to data-collection tools that can provide useful, system-wide information. This makes it easier for the physicians, the physicians' assistants, and the members of the multidisciplinary teams to work with a larger number of patients.

The need for the development of the patient interconnected electronic medical record was established in 2000 when federal funding for this purpose was made available to the provinces. Fifteen years later this has not been fully achieved. Each province went about the implementation in different ways. Fear of mismanagement of funds has slowed progress to a snail's pace. This is one area where the return on investment is very high in terms of quality of care: fewer errors (especially in drug utilization), avoidance of duplication of testing, more rapid diagnosis and treatment, and reduction in emergency room utilization and hospital admissions. The savings and benefits for full implementation of this are enormous yet the investment is far less than what has been invested in the construction of new hospitals.

Is our health care system financially sustainable?

The sustainability of our universal health care system is questioned at every financial crisis. The rate of increase of expenditure is greater than the growth of our GDP. Our population is aging and baby boomers, the largest age group of the population, are now between 55 and 69 and will be putting additional pressures on the system as they age. New technology and new medication will continue to increase costs, especially in the area of personalized or precision medicine. The question of whether or not our system is sustainable is very legitimate.

The consensus is that the system is sustainable but we must make some major changes.

1. We must introduce a new financial model if we are to ensure sustainable financing of health care. "The funding should follow the patient" is the focus of this model, which has been adopted in many advanced health care systems with much better results and lower costs than we have been able to achieve in Quebec or other parts of Canada. The objectives of this model are:

- ▸ Increase accessibility
- ▸ Control costs
- ▸ Improve quality and
- ▸ Ensure equity.

The underlying principle of this model is that each episode of care provided to a patient is financed separately on a predetermined scale and institutions no longer have a global budget.

The February 2014 report "Pour que l'argent suive le patient" prepared by an expert group for the Government of Quebec makes an excellent argument for the sustainability of the system if we follow this principle. The change to this new model of funding is a real challenge because of the complexity of our system. To put this model into place, we would have to determine the average cost of a category of care and establish the measures of quality of care and expected outcomes. The complexity of our system and the number of vested interest groups mean it will take firm government leadership and some initial investment to put this model into place.

2. We must implement the data-collection tools to collect and analyze the data from the electronic medical record and the information systems that can help manage the quality, pertinence and cost of the system.

3. Medical leadership must look at not only the clinical role physicians play, but also their responsibility for the sustainability of the system through best-practice protocols, safe practices and the most efficient use of health care personnel and health data. The medical community can no longer be responsible only for the offering of services, but must also take responsibility for the results and cost of care.

4. We must implement new ways of offering care in less expensive environments. There is broad consensus that a substantial part of existing hospital-centred care should move into the community.

5. A very large portion of health care costs is incurred during the last months of life. This often includes interventions to maintain life at all costs as opposed to a palliative-care approach to help patients cope with end-of-life issues. We must actively engage in a public debate so the population is aware of the costs and consequences of excessive end-of-life care.

6. We must establish system-wide, physician-approved, best-practice protocols that help determine the pertinence of tests requested and medication prescribed. This will probably be the factor that reduces cost the most and makes health care in our system much safer.

Why is there so little health care coverage on evenings, nights and weekends?

The answer to this question is simple, but the solution is complex. The only available medical service in the evening, at night or on weekends in the Quebec health care system is in an emergency room that is open 24/7 and where there is access to both a physician and to the necessary medical diagnostic technology. This is very expensive care because emergency room protocols require a complete evaluation to eliminate all possibilities and far more detailed investigations than would normally be done in a physician's office, whether or not they may be required.

Physicians have historically been in solo practice in the community and haven't worked evenings, nights and weekends. All their patients needing care were referred to the emergency rooms during these periods. As group practices are developing with walk-in capacity, many clinics are open 12 hours a day and eight hours on weekends. This still does not cover the other hours. If clinics were open 7:00 a.m. to 11:00 p.m., seven days a week, the population would be much better served at a lower cost. It is not necessary for clinics to be open 24/7 but expanded hours would make a major difference. This change requires more physicians working in the community to ensure the medical coverage; the introduction of the medical assistant is also an essential part of this model, to enable physicians to see more patients. Multidisciplinary teams that follow patients—especially chronically ill patients—would also reduce the need for many costly emergency room visits. The introduction of the health coach for chronically ill and very vulnerable patients has been shown to reduce emergency room visits by supporting and educating the patient in self care. Health coaches should be part of primary care teams and have responsibility for patient support and follow-up.

Why do we wait so long for care in Emergency?
And once seen, why do we remain there so long ??

Real emergencies do not wait and for trauma, major accidents and ambulance arrivals there is no waiting time as all energy is concentrated on these patients. However, this leads to wait times for all other clients who are of lower priority. Most nights, only one physician is available in the emergency room and in many cases—except for larger teaching hospitals—even on most evenings and weekends, there is only one physician present. Any serious case will take the physician's time and waits become longer for other patients. If there were greater accessibility in the community, the majority of cases that were not immediately urgent could be seen and evaluated outside the hospital. Unfortunately, this capacity is not yet available in our system.

Once a patient is seen in the emergency room and if tests were required, the patient then waits there for the results; this waiting should be done in a different environment. Emergency rooms should get patients out within four hours, sending them to more appropriate areas for diagnosis and treatment. Once diagnosed, if a patient must be admitted there can be a wait for a hospital bed and this can be quite long for certain specialities where beds are limited. We need continuous monitoring of the patient's length of stay in a hospital bed, and very well-organized discharge planning to free up beds as quickly as possible so urgent cases can be admitted from the emergency room in a timely way. A stronger home-care model with a "hospital in the home" approach would also free up beds more quickly.

Why do we have to wait so long to see a specialist?

In Quebec, wait times to see a specialist are among the longest, even though the number of specialists per capita in Quebec is one of the highest in Canada. The main problem here is that a large part of the work done by the specialist is primary and secondary care, and primary-care follow-up of their patients. This practice is lucrative and less stressful than seeing mainly new acute cases. Much of this activity should be provided by the family physicians and their teams in the community, thus freeing up the specialist to see more patients in a more timely fashion. In our most academic tertiary hospital, only 15 to 18 percent of care is tertiary while the rest is secondary and primary care. Outpatient clinics in the hospital take up a substantial amount of the time of our specialists; general practitioners or specialists doing this work in the community would be a much more effective use of the time of our specialists. If more specialists had an office in the general practitioner's clinic where they could offer consulting time a few hours a week, this would greatly reduce wait times for seeing specialists.

Why do we wait so long for surgery?
Wait times for surgery are not due to the availability of the surgeons. They are ready to operate day and night. The limiting factors are operating funds in the system and wait times are a means of controlling cost. It required almost tripling the number of surgeries per year and significant investment in this area in order to reduce hip and knee replacement wait times to less than six months. Wait times are also related to a prioritization of the gravity of the case, and as more serious cases arise, less serious cases wait longer. Elective surgeries are often cancelled and rescheduled due to emergency cases or a lack of bed availability due to increased hospitalization. Patient choice for a specific surgeon will often increase their wait times since some surgeons will be busier than others. Busier physicians will not be allotted more operating-room time, as OR availability must be shared equitably among the surgeons.

Process management has made the functioning of the operating room more efficient, has improved the organization of patient transport, and greatly ameliorated scheduling. These measures have reduced the wait times, but the real issue is the operating budget allocated to surgery. Even in a model of funding where the money follows the patient and hospitals are paid for each case they do, there is a fixed budgetary envelope that is determined at the beginning of each year and that must be respected. The only way to respect the budget is to control the number of surgeries by having people wait longer for less urgent surgeries.

Why is it so difficult to find home care for the elderly and the chronically ill?

Home care has developed over the past 25 years as an integral part of the health care system. The costs of this care are covered to the extent that funds are available. Even though this is an insured service available without charge, the public can purchase additional home care from the private sector. Home care has three main components:

▸ Acute care following an acute episode.

▸ Long-term or chronic care for patients who need continuing care for one or more chronic illnesses.

▸ Care for the elderly to maintain their autonomy as long as possible in their own home environment.

Until recently this care was been offered and coordinated through the 93 CSSSs, and it is now the responsibility of the CISSSs. Home care includes an evaluation component, a nursing component and a support or maintenance component. The amount of care awarded is limited by the funds available. Once the service is the most efficient it can be and the travel routes are organized to take the least amount of time possible, the only avenue to increase services is through more funding of new technology and added hours of care in the budget.

New technology in home care introduces monitoring to collect biometric data on patients, and monitoring of patient activity. This latter application has not yet been introduced in Quebec, while biometric monitoring is slowly being implemented. This monitoring allows the patient to self-care by collecting data such as weight, blood pressure, blood-sugar levels, heart monitoring, and device monitoring, and sends that data to a nursing station for follow-up. If a problem is noticed the nurse will contact the patient to ensure the appropriate follow-up. This support for home care has proven to be very successful where it has been introduced and has increased the number of patients that can be followed by the home-care team.

The difficulty with home-care service is not with the acute-care component, but with the longer-term care needed, especially care for the elderly. The problem is one of accessibility, including the time it takes to do an evaluation once a request is received from an elderly person, and the quantity of services that can be offered. It is in the interest of the health care system to keep elderly patients autonomous in their own home as long as possible, but the funding is limited. Public employees currently provide most of the home care but we are asking the question of whether funds should be provided directly to the user who can then seek services from accredited organizations offering care. We must also examine if there is a way to better support family caregivers financially so they would be interested in providing more care. We must engage in public discussion of these issues since it will be difficult to continue to add additional funds for the needed home care.

Why are there so many errors in medication?

Medication poses some of the biggest safety issues in the system. Medication errors, dangerous interaction between different medications, and side effects of medication all cause serious consequences to patients and add a very significant cost to the system.

The causes for these problems are many, including:

▸ Poor or no information about the drugs that patients are already taking.

▸ Lack of information about patient allergic reactions.

▸ Poor compliance by patients who simply forget to take their medication, or who skip their medication, then take too much.

▸ Patients who do not renew their medication and this information is not in their medical record

- Hospital errors that occur due to
  - Poor labelling
  - Inappropriate dosage
  - Nurse distractions during administration
  - Giving the wrong drug or the wrong dosage to the patient
  - Lack of timely updating of the patient's medical and pharmaceutical records

We must better document patient allergies and ensure the patient's pharmacist has timely access to this information in the patient's medical record. Drug information must be easily available in language the layperson and the elderly can understand, and a care manager should be accessible to explain the role, importance and side effects of medications.

The elderly, who often take many different drugs, can become confused, and sound management of these patients is essential to reduce problems associated with medication. This can be done effectively through home monitoring and follow-up by a care manager, if one is available. As the patient's medical record develops and is combined with their pharmaceutical record, there will be less error and much better follow-up of patients. The introduction of personalized or precision medicine using genomic evaluation will also reduce the errors and side effects of medication by ensuring the right medication for the right patient, as determined by their biological makeup.

To prevent the majority of in-hospital errors, we must introduce strict protocols and processes for medication in all our hospitals.

Why is it so difficult to get the vulnerable and the chronically ill to comply with their care plans and participate in their own health care?

Health is complex and each individual deals with his or her own health in different ways. Some people refuse to see a doctor when they are in pain; others are so worried that they run to the emergency room at the slightest symptom of any illness. There are patients who follow their physician's instructions to the letter and those who forget them after they leave the doctor's office. Sometimes, medication prescriptions are filled but not renewed. Some patients believe that as soon as their symptoms are gone, no further treatment or follow-up is necessary. It is estimated that there is up to 30 percent noncompliance in the proper use of prescribed medication.

The lack of what is called "self care" is one of the most costly components of the health care system. It is a cause of poor health for many and often eventually leads to multiple visits to seek health care services that could have been avoided. Minor illnesses become serious and the quality of life for many patients is diminished.

Self care includes the following elements:

▸ The patient or individual should be aware of his or her health status.

▸ There should be regular checkups, more or less frequently, depending on the disposition for certain illnesses or an existing condition.

▸ Seek care when needed.

▸ Follow the care plan prescribed by the physician.

▸ Individuals monitor their health through self-monitoring devices and observation and make the appropriate contact with the health care system, as required.

Unfortunately, often this does not happen and the consequences to the health of both the individual and the health care system are enormous. As a result, there is poor management of chronic illness by both the system and the patients themselves, with resulting deterioration in the health status of the chronically ill and poor utilization of health care resources.

The "patient as partner" is a new field that is being studied extensively; it has two main directions.

The first direction in the patient as partner is the development of programs, their evaluation and revision, their implementation and the way they are accepted or not by the patient. The patient participates in improving the quality, performance, pertinence and cost of the services being offered. This input can help ensure that the care programs offered are as patient-friendly as possible and are easy to follow and understand.

To this end, there are training programs for patients interested in becoming good partners. There are courses for professionals on how to work with patients, how to integrate patients into the multidisciplinary team, and how to support and encourage patient self care. There are also courses for patients or users of the system who are interested in participating in the planning of programs and services, or participating in the governance of health care institutions.

The other direction for patient engagement, or the patient as partner, is self care. This refers to how the patient participates in his or her own care. Whether this is managing a loss of autonomy as we grow older, managing a chronic illness or managing an acute illness, the ability to self-manage is important and is recognized in the literature as a vital component to the health and well-being of the person, as well as a way to more efficiently use the heath care system.

Patients Canada, a group dedicated to the role of the patient in health care, has developed educational tools to support patient self care. The use of new technology, new tools and new apps make self care much easier. There are ways to self-diagnose and send images to your physician about health issues ranging from skin problems to heart concerns. One interesting example is dealing with inner-ear problems by taking a photo of your inner ear with a special tool and sending the photo to your doctor.

Patients will be more prepared to self care if they meet the following criteria:

- ▸ They are encouraged by health care professionals to self care.

- ▸ They are provided with an easy-to-follow care plan.

- ▸ They are provided with easy-to-use biometric monitoring tools.

- ▸ They are connected to a health care provider acting as their care manager.

- They are supported by family members.

- They have easy access to follow-up.

- They are in contact with a support group.

These measures support self care, which will in turn improve the quality of life of the chronically ill and reduce utilization of the health care system.

New biometric data-collection applications now become available on a regular basis and are becoming more and more sophisticated. The introduction of these devices, and especially their interface with the patient and the professionals, will continue to grow. It will be important to manage the data highway to allow for easy accumulation of the biometric data, rapid transmission, rapid evaluation by the professional, and then feedback to the patient for follow-up and change of treatment, if necessary.

Patients can use certain devices to help them monitor their state of health and interact with the health care system when necessary. Self-monitoring also supports a patient's self-management of chronic illness not only through biometric data, but through the evaluation protocols that provide the ongoing measures to be undertaken in the management of their illness, and also gives feedback directly to the patient. This system calls for the active involvement of both those who are well but are worried, and those who are ill.

The patient's medical record is intimately tied to biometric data collection and evaluation and it is very important that the data be entered in the patient's electronic medical record in a timely way, and that it be accessible to him or her and all caregivers, at all times.

An excellent example of this is a product offered to patients at their pharmacy; they can have their own pharmaceutical record, allowing them to better manage and renew their prescriptions. The client can also have online access to information on the nature of the medication they are using and can also participate in a program offered by the manufacturers of the medication to help them with the management of their chronic illness through a better understanding of the medication, its uses, and any other activities they should be following in their care plan.

There is an important loss of revenue to the pharmaceutical companies due to noncompliance of patients in the proper use of their medication. Pharmaceutical companies are thus interested in ensuring better compliance from patients in following their prescriptions, and are supporting patient self-management to achieve this.

Why is the prevention of illness and the promotion of health of so little interest?

I have not discussed at any length the role and the importance of public health in the health care system. This is not in any way to diminish the role public health plays in protecting the population, as was highlighted during the H1N1 flu virus danger, or its role in evaluating the overall health and well-being of a population.

Prevention of illness and promotion of health are the first and most value-added components of a population's health, yet health systems have invested only a very small portion of their budgets in this area. The impact of seat belts, better and safer cars, reduction in tobacco consumption, better sanitary conditions with increased inspections, and better control of nosocomial (hospital-acquired) infections are all examples of the importance of the role of public health. The impact of the environment, housing, job safety and security, what we eat and how active we are: these are all public-health concerns that affect our state of health and our need for health care.

It is well known that one's socio-economic situation and level of education affect one's health, and especially one's interest in, and ability to, self care. Public health looks at the issues of poverty, homelessness, scholastic maturity of children entering grade one, drug use and abuse, the social conditions that lead to prostitution, and the spread of infections and sex-related diseases. We recognize the importance of public health yet there is not the same level of engagement in our public system as there is for acute care.

The reason stems once again from the origins of our universal public system where only acute care in hospitals was funded by the federal government on a 50-50 basis with the provinces. Our system became an acute-care, hospital-centred system with the concentration of funds, buildings, equipment, personnel and physicians allotted to our hospitals. The competition for funds within the health care system is fierce and given the strength of the acute-care system, politicians have been very slow to invest in public health over the claims of acute care. We fund a new cancer drug before we support a new suicide-prevention program.

Despite the lack of a strong public profile, prevention and promotion have proven to provide the biggest bang for our buck. For example, obesity and poor nutrition lead to enormous avoidable health care costs and government must be much more aggressive in this area to stem the tide of future demand for care.

We are slowly moving in the direction of better tools and methods for prevention and promotion. Screening programs are being introduced for specific diseases and this helps improve early discovery of these illnesses. These screening programs can be expensive measures and cost/value assessments must be done before they are widely implemented. The mapping of the human genome has led to the field of personalized or precision medicine that will open the door to new predictive tools of illness and new measures of prevention.

I believe that every health care program must have a prevention and promotion component that must include the training of professionals and education for patients.

What Should We DO?

I have attempted to describe the different problems in our health care system and propose solutions. So why has it been so difficult to implement the solutions that in many cases have proven to be successful in other countries?

1. The first reason is that the acute-care nature of our system is based on hospital care. This hospital-centred system has grown stronger with time and is still growing. Until there is a new vision of health care by society and our governments, this is not likely to change.

2. Physicians as autonomous entrepreneurs paid by the public purse have become so powerful that their influence on public policy is more often focused on their own concerns rather than the drive to have the most efficient health care system possible.

3. The fact that specialists are paid more for their time than family physicians has led to a two-class system that supports hospital care as opposed to community care, and encourages episodic as opposed to continuous care. The result is that most specialists do far too much primary and secondary care, and hence are not available to see and diagnose new patients.

4. Fee-for-service remuneration has led to a volume-driven system that provides neither the holistic health care the population needs, nor appropriate follow-up of vulnerable and chronically ill patients.

5. Lack of government support for multidisciplinary teams in the community has held back needed reform and progress in the system.

6. Lack of government support for the development of the community sector has resulted in inappropriate use of emergency rooms, restricted use of diagnostic tools and increased wait times.

7. The management of health care from within the civil service and through a political filter has neither permitted the development of a strong health care managerial culture, a culture of innovation, a culture of efficiency, nor the flexibility large organizations need to be able to respond to new situations.

These are some of the barriers to change, and only by acknowledging and better understanding them will it be possible to reduce their impact so we can move forward with the implementation of the solutions needed to improve our system.

CHAPTER THIRTEEN

Conclusion

CANADIANS HAVE A HEALTH care system that should be the envy of every country in the world. It is a universal system that provides services to patients without financial barriers. The limits to access to care are related to the availability of funding from the province. Health care is a right, not a privilege, and Canadians understand that it is a collective responsibility.

Our acute-care system is second to none, but access to primary care, diagnostic testing, and specialist consultations are not as readily available as they should be.

All of Canada's provinces have the same basic health care model, with greater or lesser differences in the management of the offering of services and how services are organized. Throughout Canada, we have a single-payer system that is financed from taxes and government revenue, and since this revenue is tied to economic growth, the level of funding is not unlimited and rationing of care is necessary to control costs. Our system meets acute-care needs rapidly and efficiently. Rationing of care is mainly in the primary-care sector, for both diagnosis and follow-up care.

Since we are limited by available resources, if we hope to have a sustainable system that takes advantage of new technology and new medication, we must change the way health care is provided to the population. Our needs have changed over time, evolving from a need for acute care to cure infections and intervene surgically, to increasing needs to manage chronic and long-term illness. Cardiovascular disease, diabetes, obstructive pulmonary disease, Alzheimer's, AIDS and cancer, to mention only a few, are the new diseases that health care must now manage. If we do not manage our needs well, we will not be able to sustain our system.

I do not advocate abandoning acute-care services—of course, they will always be needed—but I am convinced that we must move away from a hospital-based acute-care system to a community-care system. To meet our current realities, we must have a holistic health care system in which the nexus of care is in the community, with the family physicians and their teams at the centre. The family physician must become the orchestra leader managing the care their patients need.

If we do not make this move, maintaining our present system will lead to greater rationing of services and increased wait times. It will also result in an increasing demand for privatization from those who are able to purchase additional care privately. This is already happening, and the very real danger here is the further weakening of the quality of the public sector because qualified staff will move into the private sector, and the voice of the population will be diminished as the more well-off are able to satisfy their needs outside the public system.

I believe the key to a sustainable Canadian health care system is the development of a robust, dynamic primary-care system that has the capacity to take charge of every citizen and be responsible for his or her health care from birth to death. In order to do this, I believe our hospital-centred system must evolve into a community-centred model that can enroll each citizen with a multidisciplinary team of caregivers who create and maintain a complete medical record throughout the life of the individual. This model has proven to provide better, safer, more effective care at lower cost than our existing hospital-centred acute-care model. This is the model that will be both sustainable and effective over the long term.

We are entering a new era of medical discovery and we can either perpetuate the existing model of care or use these new discoveries to accelerate change. The decoding of the human genome and the new technology that has reduced the cost of genome sequencing has opened the door to many new discoveries in both the causes of illness and the treatments that work and don't work. We are beginning to understand which medications will work and which will not benefit the individual, based on his or her genetic makeup and particular chemistry. We can also predict with greater certainty the possibility of acquiring one illness or another.

With this more precise information, we can focus more of our energy and resources on the prevention of illness and the promotion of health. We have never been so close to unlocking the mystery of our bodies. To benefit from these discoveries, we must ensure a sustainable health care system—and we can only do that if we implement the changes we have been discussing in this book. The challenge is great because we are confronting a 45-year-old system that has provided wonderful acute care, yet now costs too much because prevention, promotion and the managing of chronic illness and geriatric care have not been developed to the extent needed to efficiently manage the health of our population.

We owe it to each and every person in our community to find the courage to make the necessary changes to move forward with the development of an excellent community health care system that will sustain all our needs into the future.

Sources

CHAPTER 4
Gestion (volume 21, number 4, December, 1996), published by the École des Hautes Études Commerciales de Montréal (HEC).

CHAPTER 6
Marlin, Randall (1998). *The David Levine Affair: Separatist Betrayal or McCarthyism North?* Winnipeg, MB: Fernwood Publishing.

CHAPTER 8
[1]Source: Guide pour l'implantation du projet clinique, MSSS, consultation document.

[2]Castonguay-Nepveu Report, Report of the Commission of Inquiry on Health and Social Welfare, Volume IV (Health), Government of Quebec, Volume VII: 1970.

[3]Blain, Gilbert, « La réforme doit prendre un second souffle », *L'Union Médicale du Canada*, tome 104, January 1975, p. 45

[4]*Le Devoir*, November 12, 1970, p. 1,6.

[5]CSSS « Centre de santé et de services sociaux », Loi sur les sevices de santé et les services sociaux, L.R.Q., c. S-4.2, article 99,4, Éditeur officiel du Québec, 2005.

[6]ASSS « Agences de santé et de services sociaux », Loi modifiant la Loi sur les services de santé et les services sociaux et d'autres dispositions législatives, L.R.Q., c. S-4.2, art 339-342.1, Éditeur officiel du Québec, 2005.

[7]RUIS « Réseaux universitaires intégrés de santé », Loi modifiant la Loi sur les services de santé et les services sociaux et d'autres dispositions législatives, L.R.Q., c. S-4.2, chapitre 1.1, art 436.1, Éditeur officiel du Québec, 2005.

[8]The Clair Commission recommended nurse clinicians or nurse practitioners provide these services.

[9]CRI « Clinique-réseau intégrée », Orientations for the Development of Integrated Family Medical Groups and Network Clinics, Montreal Health and Social Services Agency, Department of Planning and Strategic Development, Regional Department of General Medicine, p. 8.

[10]Plan stratégique régional 2006-2010 des ressources information-

nelles, Région de Montréal, Version 1.0, 2006, p. 44.

[11]Conditions governing the implementation of the second phase of the experimental Quebec Health Record project, June 17, 2006.

[12]The management-of-population care models that have been proven to be the most beneficial are based on a rigorous chronic-disease management and a follow-up for clients with risk of complications, using clinical, multidisciplinary and hierarchized protocols.

CHAPTER 9

Bajari, P., McMillan, R., & Tadelis, S. (2008). Auctions Versus Negotiations in Procurement: An Empirical Analysis. *Journal of Law, Economics, and Organization*, 1–28.

Blanchet, J.-N. (2012, January 8). « Québec sera incapable de faire face à la musique » — Lise Denis. *Le Journal de Québec*.

Canada. (1867). British North America Act, 1867 – Enactment no. 1. Retrieved November 14, 2012, from http://canada.justice.gc.ca/eng/pi/const/lawreg-loireg/p1t11.html

Canada. (1985). Canada Health Act. Retrieved November 17, 2012, from http://laws-lois.justice.gc.ca/eng/acts/C-6/

Canada Health Infoway: Unlocking the value of health information systems- Corporate Business plan 2010-2011. (https://www. Infoway-inforoute.ca)

Canada. (2005). Royal Commission on Health Services (Hall Commission). backgrounder. Retrieved November 17, 2012, from http://www.hc-sc.gc.ca/hcs-sss/com/fed/hall-eng.php

Canadian Institute for Health Information. (2011). Health Indicators 2011. Retrieved November 16, 2011, from https://secure.cihi.ca/free_products/health_indicators_2011_en.pdf

Eisenhardt, K. M. (1989). Agency Theory: An Assessment and Review. *The Academy of Management Review*, *14*(1), 57–74.

Hutchison B, Abelson J, Lavis J, Primary care in Canada: So much innovation so little change, *Health Affairs* 2001 20(3): 116-3

Jensen, M. C., & Meckling, W. H. (1976). Theory of the firm: Managerial behavior, agency costs and ownership structure. *Journal of Financial Economics*, *3*(4), 305–360.

Lacoursière, A. (2010, July 13). Procréation assistée: les traitements payés dès le 5 août. *La Presse*.

Larmour, J. (n.d.). Grève des médecins de la Saskatchewan. Retrieved

November 17, 2012, from http://www.thecanadianencyclopedia.com/ articles/fr/greve-des-medecins-de-la-saskatchewan

Miller, R. A. (1975). Economy, Efficiency and Effectiveness in Government Procurement. *Brooklyn Law Review, 42*, 208.

Mintzberg, H. (1983). *Structure in Fives: Designing Effective Organizations*. Upper Saddle River, NJ: Prentice-Hall.

Observatoire de l'administration publique. (2012). Le réseau de la santé et des services sociaux. Retrieved November 16, 2012, from http:// netedit.enap.ca/etatquebecois/docs/ste/organisation/a-sss.pdf

Ontario. (n.d.). Local Health Integration Network. Retrieved November 17, 2012, from http://www.lhins.on.ca/home.aspx

Québec. (2005). Loi modifiant la Loi sur les services de santé et les services sociaux et d'autres dispositions législatives. Retrieved November 17, 2012, from http://www2.publicationsduquebec.gouv. qc.ca/dynamicSearch/telecharge.php?type=2&file=/S_4_2/S4_2.html

Portail Santé Montreal (http:/ www.santemontreal.qc.ca)

Québec. (n.d.). Groupe de médecine de famille. Retrieved November 17, 2012, from http://www.msss.gouv.qc.ca/sujets/organisation/gmf/ index.php?a-propos-fr

Radio-Canada. (1989). La commission Castonguay-Nepveu. Retrieved November 17, 2012, from http://archives.radio-canada.ca/ sante/sante-publique/clips/1083/

Savoie, D. J. (1995). What is wrong with the new public management? *Canadian Public Administration, 38*(1), 115.

Savoie, D. J. (1995). What is wrong with the new public management? *Canadian Public Administration, 38*(1), 112–121.

Turner, J. G. (1958). The Hospital Insurance and Diagnostic Services Act: Its Impact on Hospital Administration. *Canadian Medical Association Journal, 78*(10), 768–770.

TVA Nouvelles. (2010, March 24). Chère, l'Agence de la santé.

Vedel, I; Monette, M.; Béland, F.; Monette, J.; Bergman, H.; Ten years of Integrated Care: Backward and Forward. The Case of the Province of Quebec; *International Journal of Integrated Care*, 2011, Jan-Dec.

CHAPTER 10

Covey, Stephen M.R. (2008). *The Speed of Trust: The One Thing that Changes Everything*. New York, N.Y.: Free Press. pp. 143-229, 236.

CHAPTER 11

Département d'Administration de la santé, Le. École de santé. (2014). Mémoire à la Commission de la santé et des services sociaux sur le projet de loi 10. Montreal, Quebec: Université de Montréal.

Mintzberg, H. (1983). *Structure in Fives: Designing Effective Organizations.* Upper Saddle River, NJ: Prentice-Hall.

Quebec. (2014) Loi n°10 : Loi modifiant l'organisation et la gouvernance du réseau de la santé et des services sociaux notamment par l'abolition des agences régionales.

Quebec. (2014) Projet de loi n°20 : Loi édictant la Loi favorisant l'accès aux services de médecine de famille et de médecine spécialisée et modifiant diverses dispositions législatives en matière de procréation assistée

CHAPTER 12

Quebec. *Pour que l'argent suive le patient.* (2014) Report of the Expert Panel for Patient-Based Funding.

List of Abbreviations

AMP	Alternative Medical Practice
ASS	Agence de la santé et des services sociaux
CEGEP	Collège d'enseignement général et professionnel
CIHI	Canadian Institute for Health Information
CHAU	Centre hospitalier affiliée universitaire
CHU	Centre hospitalier universitaire (a University Health Centre or teaching hospital)
CHUM	Centre Hospitalier de l'Université de Montréal
CISSS	Centre integré de santé et de services sociaux (Integrated Health and Social Service Centre)
CIUSSS	A university-affiliated CISSS
CLSC	Centre local de services communautaires
CSN	Centrale des syndicats nationaux
CSST	Commission of Occupational Health and Safety
CSSS	Centre de santé et de services sociaux
CUSM	Centre universitaire de santé de McGill, also known as the MUHC
EHR	Electronic Health Record
FMG	Family Medicine Group
FMOQ	Fédération des médecins omnipraticiens du Québec
FMSQ	Fédération des médecins specialistes du Québec
FTE	Full-time equivalent
GP	General Practitioner
HSSC	Health and Social Service Centre
INC	Integrated Network Clinic
IUSN	Integrated University Service Network

LINS	Local Integrated Health networks (Ontario)
MAC	Medical Advisory Council
MRMC	Montreal Regional Management Committee
MUHC	McGill University Health Centre
NC	Network Clinic
PCT	Primary-Care Trusts
PDD	Problems of Development Difficulties (Troubles d'envahissement du développement - TED)
PDG	Président-Directeur général (President and Executive Director)
RAMQ	Régie de l'assurance-maladie du Québec (Quebec Health Insurance Plan)
RUIS	Réseau universitaire intégrés de santé (Integrated University Health Network)

Index